The Poetics of Fear

The Poetics of Fear

A Human Response to Human Security

By
Chris Erickson

continuum

NEW YORK • LONDON

2010

The Continuum International Publishing Group Inc
80 Maiden Lane, New York, NY 10038

The Continuum International Publishing Group Ltd
The Tower Building, 11 York Road, London SE1 7NX

www.continuumbooks.com

ISBN: HB: 978-1-4411-0102-0

Library of Congress Cataloging-in-Publication Data
Erickson, Chris.
  The poetics of fear : a human response to human security / by Chris Erickson.
    p. cm.
  Includes bibliographical references.
  ISBN-13: 978-1-4411-0102-0 (hardcover : alk. paper)
  ISBN-10: 1-4411-0102-0 (hardcover : alk. paper)
  1. Fear–Political aspects. 2. Political psychology. 3. Political violence. 4. Achilles
  (Greek mythology) 5. Political science–Philosophy. I. Title.
  JA74.5.E75 2010
  320.01´9–dc22

                                                          2009036244

Typeset by Newgen Imaging Systems Pvt Ltd, Chennai, India
Printed in the United States of America

For Kieren and Aidan,
May you live fearlessly and therefore powerfully.

Contents

Acknowledgments

"Beware, for I am fearless, and therefore powerful."

These words, spoken to Dr. Frankenstein by his spurned creation, are a reminder that to master one's own fears is to claim the right to choose one's own way. They once adorned a hand-made poster on my dorm room wall as an undergraduate, and they have stayed with me since. In the process of completing this project they have come to me more than once. As is the case with most first books in academia, this one comes out of my doctoral dissertation. As a dissertation it never quite fit the mold. It was not a review of the literature, followed by a collection of data summarized and commented upon. I did not make use of charts, graphs or statistical regressions. I have been told that it did not look like a work of Political Science so much as Philosophy, Classical Studies, or perhaps Communications. And yet I persisted. I would not take no for an answer. Perhaps it did not fit the usual patterns, but the ideas it contained worked. They allowed alternatives to be seen that might otherwise remain occluded. Given the abstract nature of the writing, it was useful in a surprisingly practical way. It was, at least, original.

No project of this size is ever completed in isolation. This one is no exception. I have benefitted greatly from the input, challenges and guidance offered by a variety of people. First among those are James Der Derian, Briankle Chang, and Roberto Alejandro. Each of them have at times set me straight when I was adrift, offered criticism where it was warranted, and encouragement when it was needed. I am grateful to Sandra Maclean and David Laycock of Simon Fraser University for giving me the opportunity to present these ideas from the front of a classroom. Thanks go to Genevieve Fuji Johnson for a most fruitful seminar on Plato, and for her wonderful hospitality. At the University of British Columbia, Allan Tupper and Barbara Arneil have provided both institutional and moral support.

I have learned much from my exchanges with Jenny Peterson. Thanks also go to Marie-Claire Antonie my editor, for her input and guidance.

Portions of this book have been presented at a number of conferences, including the ISA-NE, WPSA, ECPR, and the Terrorism and Empire conference held in Ottawa. I am grateful for the discussion and the feedback provided by the respective audience members at those conferences. I have also used variations this material as the core of a course entitled "Political Philosophy and the Politics of Fear" which has been offered at both Simon Fraser University and the University of British Columbia. The feedback from the students in that course has helped to shape and refine this book. Moreover, I have learned from them just how far afield the tools developed in this book can be applied.

On a more personal level, I would be remiss if I did not give thanks to Lloyd and Joan Erickson for their support, their kindness and their love when I needed it most. I am thankful to Noreen Wedman and Kim Wise for life-changing conversations that really kicked things into high gear for me. I also want to recognize the unconditional support given to me over the past two years by Natasha Hugessen. Most of all, I want to acknowledge the perspective and the joy brought to my life by my two sons, Kieren and Aidan Erickson.

1

Introduction: The Politics of Fear

These are frightening times. The threat of imminent doom by nuclear holocaust has subsided, mostly, only to be replaced by a host of more insidious, but no less deadly threats. Terrorism, disease, rogue states, religious extremism, environmental catastrophe, crime, economic meltdown, natural disaster, all vie for our attention as the most frightening prospect. The collective weight of these tales of dread and woe, spread non-stop via 24-hour news stations and other mass media outlets, render their audience politically paralyzed, unable to act. Action is left to the politicians. Reaction is all that is left to the rest. This is the rule of the politics of fear.

What is the politics of fear? How does it work? How might it be resisted? I aim to answer these questions. I will narrow the scope of my inquiry by focusing on a specific and yet highly significant manner in which fear is used for political purposes. In particular I will focus on those instances that are stated using a simple binary logic, following the formula "this is the way things are, and there is nothing (else) you can do about it." This is precisely the logic that underlies the realist tradition of thought in international relations theory and security studies, although that tradition does not hold anything near a monopoly on its use.

At the outbreak of the Second World War President Franklin D. Roosevelt called for the realization of four freedoms:

Freedom of speech.
Freedom of worship.
Freedom from want.
Freedom from fear.[1]

President Roosevelt's words place fear at the forefront of the security agenda. There is no small irony that the diverse range of concerns that have come to the fore as security matters all push forward their respective agendas utilizing the same logic of fear that was so prevalent during the Cold War. Indeed this is the same logic that has been so readily deployed for at least three millennia. In retaining the use of this logic of fear, we are not fixing the problem, but perpetuating it.

As the decades have unfolded since President Roosevelt articulated his four freedoms, the scholarly emphasis has been squarely placed on the role of political institutions in bringing them about. This tends to hold true even of the critical approaches to the subject. The present argument departs from those approaches on exactly this point. Rather than concentrating on the variety of institutional responses to new "human security" threats, or suggesting how a revised institutional response might be structured, the aim of this book will be to provide a *personal* response to the logic of fear. After all it is the individual who is subjected to the incessant bombardment of media images and reports through which the fear spreads. No doubt there is a need for a better understanding of how various institutions might or should respond, but there is also a need for *a human response to human security matters*.

Retracting the "Intractable"

We live in a time of pervasive fear. There is a sense that events on the local and world stage are moving too fast, that things are falling apart, that they no longer make any sense. Amidst rumblings of "globalization," there are the beginnings of an awareness that all of the ways and means for understanding, classifying and living in the world either have failed or are beginning to fail us. The situation will not be remedied by relying on the usual approaches or the standard ways of thinking employed more efficiently. This will only bring us more efficiently to the same conclusions. It is for this reason that this book argues for a different approach. The argument here bears similarities to the various schools of security studies, but also departs from them. Nor are the insights presented here limited to the field of international relations, or even political science as a discipline.

It may be said that this project looks a lot more like classical philosophy or political theory than security studies. One might also add to that list literary criticism, communications, media and cultural studies. This is deliberate. Each of these categories demarcates a specific field of study, but there is a sense that these categories are themselves suspect. In circumstances such as these, it is not the case that a wholesale abandonment of the existing categories is required, although the transgression of them is.

There is an economy to this approach. It would be foolhardy to suggest that all of the work that has brought us to this moment and that makes it possible should be tossed out. It would be foolhardy because we rely too much on it. We owe to that tradition, and to those traditions, all of the perspectives that they make possible, even the critical ones. Rather than advocating a wholesale rejection of tradition, I suggest instead that we already have all the parts and pieces that we need to make something new. All that is required is that we look at the parts and pieces in new ways. This is the way that I understand Nietzsche's comment that "if a shrine is to be set up, a *shrine has to be destroyed*."[2] Thus the argument here may best be considered an extended immanent critique. It offers an alternative based in the same canon of thought explicitly to demonstrate the feasibility of that alternative. It is an unorthodox interpretation of what we have already been working with rather than a rejection of it. With that in mind, each of the chapters to follow addresses one or more of some of the central figures in the canon of Western political thought.

There are multiple avenues by which one can come to the conclusion that something is amiss, not least of which is in the arena of international politics. I am using international relations in general, and security studies in particular, as a gateway to the topic of the political use of fear not because it is restricted to that area, but because it presents a grand stage on which the discussion might take place. In this respect I follow in the tradition of Plato's *Republic*. In that text, the question of the just individual is projected onto the screen of the state, so that its contours might be enlarged and made easier to see.

> The investigation we are undertaking is not an easy one, in my view, but requires keen eyesight. So, since we are not clever people, I think we should adopt the method of investigation that we would use if, lacking keen eyesight, we were told to identify small letters from a distance, and then noticed that the same letters existed elsewhere in a larger size and on a larger surface. We would consider it a godsend, I think, to be allowed to identify the larger ones first, and then to examine the smaller ones to see whether they are really the same.[3]

The operating assumption here is that identities and institutions tend to shape each other such that to discern the parameters of one is to suggest the parameters of the other. This is not to say that these provide insights into any ontologically necessary, pre-existing mapping of one onto the other. The argument presented here operates on the basis of an understanding of language that is, in the words of Lene Hansen, "ontologically significant: it is only through the construction of language that 'things'—objects, subjects, states, living beings, and material structures—are given meaning and endowed with a particular identity."[4]

The situation in which we as a globalizing population find ourselves is the result of a long history of thinking about, speaking about, and acting in the world, rather than a stage in a predetermined unfolding of the world. These traditions of thought make possible certain ways of living and being in the world. They make possible all of the technological, intellectual, and emancipatory progress that has been made. But no tradition is complete. Each has its limits where the very advances it makes possible outrun its ability to comprehend them. This has happened before and it is happening now. Such times call for the re-thinking of assumptions. Such times call for what Nietzsche dubs a "re-valuation of all values."[5]

That we are living in such a time began to occur to me during the breakup of the former Yugoslavia. News reports were rife with stories of "ancient hatreds" that were intended to explain the outbreak of "barbarity" in Europe itself. I began to notice how easy a thing it was to accept the "intractability" line and to unburden ourselves of any kind of responsibility. "That is just the way the world is." "Nothing you or I can do about it." Or so the story goes.

After seeing this same sort of thinking crop up again and again over many years, and in a variety of circumstances, it struck me that this kind of thinking was not just an excuse for all kinds of horrific behavior, but it was also instrumental in the perpetuation of that behavior. Clearly something had to be done, not just about whatever event happened to be subject to this kind of understanding, but about the understanding itself.

We can only come to the world from within some given framework. The parameters of this framework appear, from inside them, to be fixed and permanent. Moving beyond them is not possible, or at least so it would seem. Most introductory psychology textbooks have a photograph somewhere in them that looks almost incomprehensible until someone points out what it is. Once you see it, it is obvious and you are hard-pressed to not see it right away from then on. Perhaps these "intractable problems" were like that? Any student of Western thought, (using this as a short hand rather than as an unquestioned acceptance of a "unified" tradition), will notice that a major component of that tradition is the claim to be breaking with it. There is hope in this observation.

Certainly there can be and are different frameworks in place and in operation at the same time. An illustrative example of this is the Copernican Revolution. On the empirical level, *nothing changed*. The available data remained the same, but the framework for comprehending the data altered radically. More accurately, it altered in a subtle way that had radical implications. One could still stand in an open field and watch the sun pass overhead. And yet doing so no longer provided definitive proof that the sun circled the earth. It was no longer possible to be secure in one's position as the very centre and pinnacle of God's creation, even if this was no hindrance to people continuing to do just that for some time afterwards.

If we want to address the recurrent or "intractable" problems then it seems to me that it would be advisable to examine them from multiple frameworks rather than just from multiple cases within the same framework. It may very well be that what appears irresolvable within the parameters of one framework may seem obviously simple to resolve in another. Take for example the claim "parallel lines always intersect." At first glance this is obviously false. However the very same claim becomes obviously true once one adopts the framework of a non-Euclidean geometry. While it is true that parallel lines drawn in a plane do not intersect, parallel lines drawn upon the surface of a sphere will always intersect. In short, I am arguing that we need to change the ways in which we think about the world so that we can change the ways we act in the world. However it is no small task to do this. One is destined to fail by taking the line that "everything you know is wrong." This is the case even, and perhaps especially, if "everything you know" *is* wrong. We like our traditions and habits for better or for worse.

It seems better then to work towards the overturning of a system by some other means than direct assault. The system—the norms and institutions of society along with the epistemological and ontological assumptions behind them—is designed to counter this kind of direct attack by moving the battle onto its own grounds. It is far too well defended, in all kinds of subtle and not so subtle ways, against a frontal assault. It is better to undo a flawed system (not that there is such a thing as a perfect one) from within, on its own terms. This is the spirit and benefit of what is often called immanent critique. Such a critique, to paraphrase the language of Ken Booth, seeks to move forward not on the basis of some utopian teleology, but rather on the basis of the unexplored and unfulfilled possibilities latent within the existing circumstances.[6] In this book I work within the bounds of a certain canon of Western political thought precisely because I want to do more than replace one tradition with another (as yet largely unformed) one. I want to show how even if the "evidence" remains the same, its meaning does not have to.

This re-thinking of thinking itself is in part a response to the challenge of globalization. As a phenomenon the definition of globalization is still a subject of some debate. For the time being I will abide by Booth's definition of globalization as being a twofold process. He sees as first a politico-economic project, synonymous with the growth of the world economy with the United States taking the lead. This is globalization as neoliberal, capitalist triumph. Second he sees it as a techno-cultural process marking a multitude of "complex interpenetrations of the local and the global . . . Globalization is the set of processes constructing a smaller world."[7]

I believe that globalization does more than call for a streamlining of operations. It is more the demand that we do things more efficiently, or faster, or with more, and better technology. It is more than the expansion of an old border problem that has confronted the state for centuries. It is more than an economic or political issue. Rather it is a wholesale challenge, not only to the capabilities of our economic, political, cultural, and even spiritual institutions, but to all of the logical—and even the ontological—assumptions upon which they are based. In short, none of the "common sense" ways of understanding we have been using to comprehend the world around us are working. The situation is such that it has moved beyond the commonsensical. This does not mean that the world has gone mad, although surely it may be experienced this way. It would be far too easy to deal with if it had. All that would be called for is a reestablishment of order.

Of course, this is exactly the kind of response we have seen in recent decades, especially after the conclusion of the Cold War and the collapse of the "evil empire," the Soviet Union.[8] Since that time there has been a desperate hunt for a new "bad guy." This can be seen throughout the 1990s when seemingly out of nowhere inner-city crime and gang warfare became a problem. The White separatist movement in the United States and the neo-Nazis abroad became a problem. Japan became a problem. Human trafficking, AIDS, and famine in Africa became a problem.[9] The future of NATO became a problem. Even the Teletubbies became a problem.[10] Above all, we were repeatedly reminded, "the enemy is unpredictability. The enemy is instability."[11] In all these cases the audience of the media outlets through which these problems were presented was reassured that what was required, and what was most appropriate was a clampdown, a re-imposition of law and order, a reassertion of "traditional family values."[12] To do anything else would be to invite complete and utter disaster. Or so the story goes.

Security, Speech Acts, and the Shield of Achilles

The story to which I refer has a name. It is "security." This story has a long, multivalent and multifaceted history, some of which intersects with the topic of this book. Its central features typically include an "us" threatened by some "them" in a life-or-death challenge. What is understood to be at stake here is "our" security, the assumption being that this is a simple thing to define. And yet this is far from the case. It has been widely noted that security is what W. B. Gallie called an "essentially contested concept."[13] This indicates not just that it is difficult to define, but that the meaning of the term is inherently disputable. There is no neutral ground upon which to establish a firm definition. This in turn speaks of the fact that security is also a derivative concept. Different theories about how to best understand world politics will produce different understandings of what is to be secured, and how to best do it. That being said, there is a general understanding that security at least minimally implies a freedom from threat and danger. For nearly half a century, questions of security were predominantly focused on the bipolarity of the Cold War. There is a great irony then in the fact that the end of the Cold War has not achieved the expected triumph of "us" over "them." Rather we have once again found ourselves is a state of deep insecurity.

The threat of nuclear annihilation at the hands of a hostile global superpower has been replaced by the threat of annihilation at the hands of a hostile global network of radical terrorist groups, or by the prospect of another global economic depression, or by the threat of an uncontrollable warming of the planet with all of its attendant disasters. In any case the threat of annihilation remains very much in place. On top of that there has been a bombardment of issue areas vying for attention as issues of security. No longer is security a question of who the military should be preparing to fight, or how many missiles "they" have compared to "us," but it is now a question of the economy, the environment and global warming, drugs, immigration, crime, poverty, AIDS and other diseases, computer hackers and the control of information, accident, and even natural disasters. The Cold War may be over, but we are hardly to be considered more secure for it. In fact the very way that we think, talk, and act about these issues is directly implicated in their rise as areas of concern.

Although the number of issue areas clamoring for attention as matters of security exploded, almost literally, in the 1990s, the stage had been set for this kind of expansion quite some time beforehand. Prior to the 1990s the orthodoxy of security studies focused largely on military concerns. Security was a matter of *state* or *national* survival. It was, in the long-disused vernacular, "high-politics." This orthodoxy was challenged by Barry Buzan's 1983 publication *People, States, and Fear* in which he argued that security should be examined on at least three levels of analysis; the individual, the state, and the international system.[14] Buzan also argued that matters of security should be broadened to include not just military matters, but also economic, societal, political, and environmental concerns. Buzan's arguments for both broadening and deepening research into the subject formed the basis for what later became known as the Copenhagen school of security studies.

The Copenhagen school is best known for its concept of securitization. This is the idea that issues of security should be understood first and foremost as speech acts. In the words of Ole Waever:

What then is security? With the help of language theory, we can regard "security" as a *speech act*. In this usage, security is not of interest as a sign that refers to something more real; the utterance *itself* is the act. By saying it, something is done (as in betting, giving a promise, naming a ship). By uttering "security" a state representative moves a particular development into a specific area, thereby claims a special right to use whatever means are necessary to block it.[15]

In short, securitization is the process through which an issue becomes a matter of security precisely through its representation as such. Any "securitizing move" operates through the establishment a "referent object" which is existentially threatened by some issue, event, or circumstance. The nature of this threat calls for the adoption of urgent and immediate action. Furthermore, this emergency calls for a departure from, or suspension of the rules of normal, non-emergency politics.[16]

One of the consequences of securitization is that the issue areas that could count as security matters are not limited. This implies a second consequence. If too many issue areas become "security matters" then the term begins to lose its meaning. "The concept is thus reduced to its every-day sense, which is only a semantic *identity*, not the *concept* of security."[17] Not only that, but the logic of securitization can go so far as to displace the rule by the exception. Hence there is concern among adherents to this approach not only with how issues are set on the security agenda, but also with how they might be taken off of it.

To understand security and securitization as speech acts is to highlight the fact that they are always the result of a deliberate political choice. The success or failure of any "securitizing move" depends ultimately on the willingness of the audience to accept the given representation. The primary emphasis of "de-securitization" is therefore aimed at calling into question the willingness of the audience to accept any given representation of an issue as a matter of security. It is on this point that the argument presented in this book is the closest to the Copenhagen school. This is particularly the case given Waever's call for "less security, more politics!"[18]

The central metaphor that this book will employ is the Shield of Achilles, drawn from the pages of Homer's *Iliad*. The Shield of Achilles as a metaphor calls attention to a kind of logic that bears very close resemblance to the process of securitization. It too designates a speech act that tends to bring about the very world it purports only to describe. If the task of the security discourse is "to turn threats into challenges; to move developments from the sphere of existential fear to one where they could be handled by ordinary means"[19] then the shield as a metaphor allows for an understanding of the use of fear as a political tool that operates in the exact opposite direction. Shield logic left unchallenged is designed to firmly establish and secure developments within the realm of "existential fear." An understanding of its logic is intended precisely to short-circuit the tendency of its audience to accept it on its own terms. The motivation behind the use of this metaphor shares the concerns of the Copenhagen school with de-securitization and takes them one step further by providing the beginnings of a methodological, or at least tactical, approach with which the *individual* can manage his or her own "security agenda."

Inherent in this position is a shift in focus away from the state or the nation and onto the individual as the "referent object" of security. This is similar to the position of what is called the Welsh school or the Critical Security Studies project. A group of scholars influenced by the critical theoretical insights of the Frankfurt school have argued that to focus on the individual is not simply a matter of altering the level of analysis, but instead a radical alteration of the logic of security itself.[20]

For adherents to the Welsh school, security is primarily a matter of emancipation. This concept can be understood as being measured against a fixed and pre-existing teleological standard, as is typical of the ideologies of the Enlightenment project, most notably Marxism and Liberalism. As such the concept of emancipation may be rightly criticized for its complicity in the bloodshed, suffering and atrocities committed in its name. It can however be understood in a more abstract way as a sensitivity to "the possibility of progressive alternatives to the status quo."[21] In this guise, some concept of emancipation is to be found in all critical discussions of security. The argument presented here is not concerned with outlining the parameters of Emancipation,[22] but certainly holds a loose conception of emancipation very close. I am most definitely concerned with heightening awareness or sensitivity to "possibilities of progressive alternatives to the status quo."[23]

The current status quo is the politics of fear. Fear as a tool of motivation and manipulation. Fear as a method of control. It has already been mentioned that this fear stems from a variety of sources, so many that it can be difficult to make sense of it all. The apparent manic chaos of threat upon threat from all directions at once makes a thoughtful analysis of those threats difficult. It is overwhelming and paralyzing. The individual runs the very real risk of becoming the proverbial deer in headlights. What is needed is a way to make sense of the noise and this is precisely the role filled by the metaphor of the Shield of Achilles. Using the metaphor allows for the identification of a certain logical structure, shield logic, that underlies all of these apparently disparate threats. The noise is therefore quieted, allowing a bit more room for critical reflection.

The resistance to shield logic begins with the use of its identifying metaphor. The metaphor derives from what is commonly considered to be the oldest text of the Western tradition, Homer's *Iliad*. The logic in question was as much in use then as it is today. Its persistence over time may be indicative of some permanent and fixed feature of human nature. This line of argumentation has been pursued in much of the literature of the past millennia in far greater detail than this project could ever attempt. Instead, I will begin with a focus on another aspect of this metaphor, namely its mythical origins. While it could be that the shield suggests the persistence of a fixed human nature, it also suggests that each articulation of its logic is a further articulation of a persistent myth. A myth is a story that we tell ourselves to make sense of the world in which we live. One of the features of a myth is that it can be told and retold in a variety of ways without each retelling jeopardizing its status as being the same myth. A story that can be told in a variety of ways can be responded to in a variety of ways, even if the language of its telling ostensibly restricts a "proper" response to only a single option.

Another central feature of the metaphor resides in its literary origins. By making sense of the logic of a fear through a metaphor borrowed from a work of fiction, I am suggesting that each instance of shield logic is equally fictive. Just as we can draw on the tools of literary criticism to better understand Homer, so too can those same tools be used to gain some critical distance from the logic of the shield. In particular, I will argue for the use of ekphrasis as a tool useful in the analysis and critique of political speech.

Ekphrasis is the verbal representation of a non-verbal representation. It most commonly refers to poetry that describes a work of art. Its classical and archetypical example is, coincidentally, Homer's description of the Shield of Achilles in *The Iliad*. Employing ekphrasis as a critical tool, one can argue that any example of the logic of the shield is at best a representation of a representation. This places tremendous pressure on both of the central claims of shield logic; "this is the way it is" and "there is nothing (else) to be done about it." Ekphrasis as a critical tool exposes the "this is the way it is" claim as, at best, the equivalent of "this is something like something it is like." The corresponding second claim then becomes "it is something like it is like there is nothing to be done." Ekphrasis as a critical tool allows for the two claims to be rephrased as "this is the best we can make of it at the moment" and "there is always something else to be done." Armed with ekphrasis as a critical tool, the individual need not be paralyzed by the logic of fear.

Summary: Plotting the Course

My concern in this book is to identify, analyze and then counter a certain logic of fear. I will begin with a discussion of the metaphor of the Shield of Achilles. Through a close examination of those passages from *The Iliad* in which Homer describes the shield, I will show how the shield works to paralyze its audience, suspending that audience between beauty and terror, repulsion and attraction. I will argue that the shield makes a double claim: "this is the way it is" and "there is nothing (else) you can do about it." This double claim comes complete with divine sanction so that to resist it becomes an act of hubris. Furthermore the paralyzing logic of the shield tends to replicate the truth conditions of this double claim, effectively generating the world it purports only to reflect. My discussion of the logic of the shield will be fleshed out through an example of it at work in the contemporary world. The example is to be found in the language of the Bush Administration regarding the War on Terror. The second part of Chapter 2 will look at the speech given by President George W. Bush to a joint session of Congress on the evening of September 20, 2001. The boldest statement of shield logic in this particular example can be summed up in the phrase "you are with us or you are with the terrorists."[24]

This claim, like all shield logic, works to close off all avenues of response but one. It leaves no room for debate or discussion of alternatives. It is politically paralyzing. Its effects are pernicious, and call out for some kind of critical response. What is one to do with a claim like this? Can its logic be resisted, and if so, how? I will argue that shield logic most certainly can be resisted, and I will argue for a particular way that this can happen.

A variety of responses have been formulated by some of the greatest figures of the Western intellectual tradition. Not all of these responses are stated explicitly as reactions to the logic of the shield, but they are clearly discernible nonetheless. Chapter 3 will examine one of the first responses, which offers a warning regarding the hazards of bearing the shield. I will address this response first by staying as close to the Homeric tale as possible. The fate of the shield after the death of Achilles is a central feature in particular works of Sophocles. Both his plays *Ajax* and *Philoctetes* offer clues as to what it means to bear the shield after the death of Achilles. Of particular importance is the observation that along with the appearance of the shield comes a shift in the way the relationship between language and the world can be understood. This shift challenges the simple notion of correspondence between word and world, a feature highlighted by the fact the Odysseus is named the rightful heir to the shield.

A warning about the bearing of the shield is also to be found in the writings of Thucydides. Chapter 3 continues by pointing out the historian's juxtaposition of events as a form of critique. He identifies a consistent mentality of shield logic among the Athenians, and then demonstrates the catastrophic results of such thinking. I will pay particular attention to three components of his work, namely the introduction, Pericles' funeral oration, and the Melian dialogue. Each of these much-read passages is matched with a subsequent undoing, thereby serving as a warning to the audience about the hazards of shield logic.

The third section of Chapter 3 will briefly discuss Machiavelli. Although he never mentions it by name, Machiavelli recognizes the Shield of Achilles as a potent tool in any prince's political toolbox. He provides example after example of its successful use, along with the hazards of its overuse.

As useful as warnings may be, they do not constitute the sole response to the logic of the shield, nor do they in themselves challenge that logic. Given that the shield operates in part by rendering its presented (non) options as pressing and acute concerns, thereby disallowing the time needed for a closer consideration of those options, what is called for is critical distance. One response that does offer a direct challenge to the logic of the shield is the concept of mimesis. Chapters 4 and 5 will proceed through a discussion of mimesis as it appears in Plato's *Republic* and, in a modified form, in the work of Jean Baudrillard. However the concept of mimesis as articulated by Plato in the *Republic* and by Baudrillard's notions of simulacra and the hyperreal falls short of its intended goal. Rather than repudiating the logic of the shield, their respective arguments perpetuate it.

If mimesis as a critical tool is not capable of providing the critical distance it claims to provide, this does not mean that the insights it can offer are to be ignored or jettisoned in an offhanded way. Is there a concept that embraces these insights, and yet does not fall prey to the same defects? To best answer this question, Chapter 6 will return to Homer and specifically to a discussion of the character of Odysseus, the rightful inheritor of the shield after the death of Achilles. Odysseus is a very difficult figure in that he is a constant and purposeful disturber of his own identity. He gives rise to what is, for Freidrich Nietzsche, the true "Homeric Question." Nietzsche sees Odysseus, and by extension Homer himself, as problematic not because his contradictions indicate an untenable standpoint—a fatally flawed "this is the way it is"—but because his contradictions render it exceedingly difficult, and perhaps impossible, to attribute any standpoint to him, once and for all. In fact, Nietzsche understands all of life to be this way. Nietzsche departs from an ontological reliance on a "way things really are" as it appears in Plato or indeed in the Enlightenment project, or even, for that matter, in Baudrillard's work, (albeit in a clandestine way). Instead he insists on life itself as a constant interplay between what he calls the Apollonian and the Dionysian drives. Any outcome of this interplay is to be held suspect and cannot be understood as being "the whole truth" in any kind of final way.

Nietzsche blurs the distinction between reality and imagination, between the natural and the constructed, and allows for the broad scope of life to be understood as poetic. Following the clues left by Plato's use of mimetic poetry against itself, by Nietzsche's linguistic turn, and by the deconstructive techniques of reading a text from its margins utilized by both Baudrillard and Derrida, it is advisable that one treat the Shield of Achilles as a literary construct. Hence it is from the field of literary criticism that an alternate to mimesis can be found.

The alternative I offer is the concept of ekphrasis, the verbal representation of a non-verbal representation. Coincidentally, the archetypical example of ekphrasis is Homer's description of the Shield of Achilles. I will discuss its import and application in Chapter 7. The argument will outline the four components of ekphrasis as Andrew Sprague Becker identifies them. I will argue that each of these four components should be identifiable in any political speech that employs the binary logic of the shield. In identifying these components it is possible to open a space for debate and political action that may be, and often is, explicitly closed off by the ostensible content of the speech itself. I will make the point that *the politics of fear may be undone through an understanding of the poetics of fear.*

Finally, the use of ekphrasis as a tool for the critical analysis of political speech will be demonstrated through a real world example. I will offer an exegesis of a speech given by President Barack Obama in March of 2009 on the topic of Afghanistan and Pakistan. I will demonstrate how this speech is an example of shield logic at work, and then show how each of the four components of ekphrasis can be found within it. By treating the speech as an example of ekphrasis rather than a straightforward retelling of the facts, the audience need not remain paralyzed by its logic and space is opened up for further debate, precisely where that space would appear to have been closed off.

Notes

[1] Hayward Alker, "Emancipation in the Critical Security Studies Project," in *Critical Security Studies and World Politics*, ed. Ken Booth, Critical Security Studies (Boulder, CO: Lynne Reinner Publishers, 2005).

[2] Nietzsche, Friedrich Wilhelm, Keith Ansell-Pearson, and Carol Diethe. *On the Genealogy of Morality.* Rev. student ed. *Cambridge Texts in the History of Political Thought.* Cambridge (New York: Cambridge University Press, 2007), 66.

[3] Plato, *Republic*, in *Plato: Complete Works*, ed. John M. Cooper (Indianapolis, IN: Hackett Publishing Company, 1997), 368d.

[4] Lene Hansen, *Security as Practice: Discourse Analysis and the Bosnian War*, The New International Relations (London: Routledge, 2006), 18.

[5] Friedrich Wilhelm Nietzsche, *Twilight of the Idols and the Anti-Christ*, trans. R. J. Hollingdale, Penguin Classics (Harmondsworth: Penguin, 1968), 199.

[6] Ken Booth, and Tim Dunne, eds *Worlds in Collision: Terror and the Future of Global Order* (New York: Palgrave Macmillan, 2002), 11.

[7] Ibid., 31.

[8] Reagan first used this phrase in a 1983 speech, which is itself an excellent example of the politics of fear at work. Ronald Reagan, "President Reagan's Speech to the National Association of Evangelicals" (1983).

[9] Boutros Boutros-Ghali, "An Agenda for Peace: Preventative Diplomacy, Peacemaking and Peace-Keeping," *International Relations* 11, no. 3 (1992): 201–18.

10 "Gay Tinky Winky Bad for Children," (1999). This article is a sample of some of the public uproar sparked by Moral Majority leader Jerry Falwell's claim that the character was "a gay role-model" and therefore a threat to children.

11 This was a mantra for both President George Bush (Sr.) and President Clinton. James Der Derian, "The Value of Security: Hobbes, Marx, Nietzsche, and Baudrillard," in *On Security*, ed. Ronnie D. Lipshutz, New Directions in World Politics (New York: Columbia University Press, 1995), 25.

12 Larry Hunter et al., "Republican Contract With America," (1994).

13 W. B. Gallie, "Essentially Contested Concepts," *Proceedings of the Aristotelian Society* 56 (1956): 167–98. One of the easily overlooked implications of this is that to come to a settled definition is anathema to the concept itself. "Security" defined once and for all is no longer security, which is an essentially contested concept. Whatever we have to say about it, we cannot claim to have the last word.

14 Barry Buzan, *People, States, and Fear: The National Security Problem in International Relations* (Brighton: Wheatsheaf Books, 1983). Buzan's work is strongly influenced by the observations made in Kenneth Waltz, *Theory of International Politics* (New York: Random House, 1979).

15 Ole Waever, "Securitization and Desecuritization," in *On Security*, ed. John Gerard Ruggie, New Directions in World Politics (New York: Columbia University Press, 1995), 55.

16 Barry Buzan et al., *Security: A New Framework for Analysis* (Boulder, CO: Lynne Rienner Publishers, 1998).

17 Ole Waever, "Securitization and Desecuritization," 50. Waever argues that security must be understood through the lens of the state, a point that I tend to disagree with.

18 Ibid., 56. Waever says "to act politically means to take responsibility for leaving an impact, for forcing things in one direction instead of another . . . Politics is inherently about closing off options, about forcing the stream of history in particular directions." (76) I want to point out his understanding of politics thus requires an ever present range of options to be "closed off." It is for this reason, as we shall see, that the politics of fear is anti-political, or rather politics disguised as non-political.

19 Ibid., 55. He is paraphrasing Egbert Jahn.

20 Andrew Linklater, "Political Community and Human Security," in *Critical Security Studies and World Politics*, ed. Ken Booth, Critical Security Studies (Boulder, CO: Lynne Reinner Publishers, 2005); Rens Van Munster, "Security on a Shoestring: A Hitchhiker's Guide to Critical Schools of Security in Europe," *Cooperation and Conflict: Journal of the Nordic International Studies Association* 42 (2), no. 2 (2007): 235–43.

21 Richard Wyn Jones, "On Emancipation: Necessity, Capacity, and Concrete Utopias," in *Critical Security Studies and World Politics*, ed. Ken Booth, Critical Security Studies (Boulder, CO: Lynne Reinner Publishers, 2005), 218.

[22] The capitalization of the term is intended to denote it in its permanent, fixed, universal, once-and-for-all guise that is predominant in the usage of the term by the Enlightenment thinkers.

[23] Of course this calls for some discussion of what counts as progress. A thorough examination is well beyond the scope of this book, but let it suffice for the moment to say that progress need not be measured against a fixed and pre-existing telos. It may instead be related to a broadening awareness that things could, put simply, be otherwise. This is not to say that there are no utopias to be articulated, but rather to say that there are always others, no matter where one stands in regards to the realization of any particular one.

[24] George W. Bush, "President Bush Speaks to United Nations," (2001).

2

The God of Fire's Gift: The Shield of Achilles and the Logic of Fear

The plethora of issue areas that employ fear as a tool for the mobilization of political action can be overwhelming. It can be difficult to make sense of them all. It is not stretching the point to suggest that the potential for critical thought is greatly reduced in such circumstances, thereby rendering the sense of fear all the more irresistible, and hence politically effective. What is called for is a means by which to simplify the field; a model or framework, if you will. Fortunately, just such a model is in easy reach. It is to be found in one of the basic and highly influential texts of Western culture, namely Homer's *Iliad*.[1]

The 30-Second *Iliad*

"Rage—Goddess, sing the rage of Peleus' son Achilles . . ."(1:1)[2]

The opening line of Homer's *Iliad* is very clear as to its main topic. The enraged Achilles, greatest of all Greek heroes, makes the decision to stop fighting after King Agamemnon publicly humiliates him. In his absence, the war goes badly for the Greeks. As the Trojans are about to reach the Greek ships, Achilles' friend Patroclus pleads with him to return to battle. Achilles refuses, still consumed by his rage towards Agamemnon, but permits Patroclus to don his armor so that the Trojans might believe Achilles has returned. Patroclus manages to frighten away the main force of the Trojans, but is then killed by Hector, son of the Trojan king and mightiest of the Trojan warriors. Hector strips Patroclus of Achilles' armor, taking it for himself. When Achilles hears of the death of Patroclus, he decides to redirect his rage away from Agamemnon and towards the Trojans. Before he can reenter the battle, his mother, the goddess Thetis, makes him promise not to fight until she returns with a new set of armor for him. Thetis flies up to Mount Olympus where she begs Hephaestus, the god of fire, to make this gift. Achilles accepts the arms from his mother— a breastplate, a helmet, greaves, and most significantly, a shield—and plunges back into the bloody thick of the fight. His murderous rampage eventually results in the death of Hector. After killing Hector, Achilles ties the body to the back of his war cart and drags the fallen hero through the Greek camp. Having thus offended the gods, Achilles is ordered to return the body by a messenger from Zeus. Priam, the Trojan king, sneaks into the Greek camp with the help of the gods and begs for the return of his son's body. The epic concludes with the reconciliation between Achilles and Priam and the funeral of Hector.

The Shield of Achilles

The shield that Thetis provides to her son is notable in Homer's epic. Nowhere else does he devote so many lines to the description of a single object. Homer is quick to point out the terrible power of the shield saying that at its mere presence "a tremor ran through all the Myrmidon ranks— none dared / to look straight at the glare, each fighter shrank away" (19:17–18). Despite the reaction of his allies and kinsmen, the images do not appear on the surface to be fearful at all. The shield depicts the earth and sky, sun and moon and the constellations. There are also images of a city at peace and a city at war. The former is complete with wedding celebrations and court cases. The latter contains the expected depictions of carnage and strife, but these should not have been overly frightful to veteran soldiers in the tenth year of an ongoing war. Aside from this there are images of a more pastoral nature—the plowing and planting of fields, a king's estate, the growing and harvesting of barley and grapes, a herd of cattle set upon by lions, a dancing circle filled with young dancers and tumblers. Largely absent are the standard images of terror to be found on other shields described by Homer.[3] There are no mythical beasts, no Gorgons or Griffins, no serpents or Sphinxes, nor even that much straightforward gore.

Another notable feature is that Homer's description of the shield is more of a narrative than an exposition. He does provide some detail as to the materials and expert craftsmanship of the various scenes, but most strikingly and most engagingly he retells the story of each scene.

The audience is drawn into these stories to an extent that it is quite easy to forget that the poet is describing a particular object. The shield is an interesting feature within Homer's epic and it raises equally interesting questions. Foremost among these questions is, "why is the shield so terrifying?" An answer to this question can be discerned through a closer examination of both the wording and the implications of Homer's text.

The shield as an object has multiple functions, not all of them equally obvious. First, it is a tool for providing physical protection—a mobile wall behind which the body of its carrier may take shelter. Yet it is important to remember that all but the heel of Achilles is invulnerable, his mother having dipped him in the river Styx as an infant.[4] But if this is the case, what is the purpose of this new armor? Its purpose cannot be strictly protection as this would be redundant. Nor, for that matter does the armor provide any form of protection for his single vulnerable part. It must therefore have another function. An indication of this other function is provided in the text when Thetis says to Achilles "Hector *glories* in your armor, strapped across his back" (18:156).[5] The clear indication is that what the armor primarily protects is not the body, but the status of its bearer. Hector glories in the armor as an outward sign of his superiority over Achilles, and therefore over all the Achaeans.[6] The armor serves to situate the bearer within a social order. Agamemnon's armor is a useful model and comparison in this respect.[7]

The Arms of Agamemnon

The king's armor, described in some detail by Homer (11:19–52) has an obvious function in its protectiveness, but it also serves to show Agamemnon's status. The exquisite craftsmanship of the object itself speaks to the wealth and nobility of its bearer. Furthermore, the Gorgon's head emblazoned on a glittering shield echoes the Shield of Athena, the warrior goddess of wisdom. In carrying the shield then, Agamemnon is staking a claim to a status above that of all other kings, a status bordering on divinity. Such a claim suits the character of Agamemnon whose hubris, it must be recalled, was at the very root of the conflict between himself and Achilles. In the very opening lines of the epic, Homer says:

What drove them to fight with such a fury?
Apollo the son of Zeus and Leto. Incensed at the king
he swept a fatal plague through the army—men were dying
and all because Agamemnon spurned Apollo's priest. (1:9–12)

If Agamemnon's armor, crafted by human hands, hints at the likeness to divinity (and perhaps also the hubris) of its bearer, the divine origin of Achilles' new armor specifically serves to encase him in a sheathing of divinity. It is created with the specific intent of being "armor that any man in the world of men will marvel at through all the years to come—whoever sees its splendor" (18:544–6). It thereby all but guarantees the permanent glory of its bearer.

The relationship between the Shield of Agamemnon and the Shield of Achilles within the structure of *The Iliad* helps to reveal yet another function of the shield. The shield is also a medium for the transmission of a message intended (though not exclusively) for those faced with its advance. M. W. Edwards notes that in *The Iliad*:

> Often . . . a short form of a type-scene (or other structural pattern) precedes a fuller version, as if to familiarize the hearer with the concept before its most significant occurrence.[8]

Such is the case with the two shields in question, the former serving as an introduction to the latter. Thus the Shield of Agamemnon is of the same type as the Shield of Achilles and can be of considerable assistance in understanding how the latter works to produce its effects. The Shield of Agamemnon echoes the Shield of the goddess Athena and hence offers a significant clue as to how the Shield of Achilles works. Athena had lent her mirrored shield to the hero Perseus to aid him in his quest to kill the Gorgon, Medusa. Medusa, once beautiful, had been cursed by Athena so that whomsoever looked upon her would be instantly turned to stone. Perseus was able to avoid her gaze, thanks to the reflective properties of the shield, and decapitate her. The hero then returned the shield and the severed head to Athena, who in turn affixed the terrifying visage upon the shield.[9]

Homer describes the shield Agamemnon carries as being decorated with "the Gorgon's grim mask— / the burning eyes, the stark, transfixing horror— / and round her strode the shapes of Rout and Fear" (11:39–40). The Gorgon's head on his shield threatens to paralyze the viewer, to remove from him the possibility of resistance.[10] The production of fear and reverence (anticipating "shock and awe") is intended both for enemies and subjects alike. This kind of psychological warfare is easily found in both historical and contemporary settings. As a later example, the Spartan hoplites were known to have their shields uniformly embossed with the single character Λ (lambda) for "Lacedaemon." This sent a distinct message to their opponents and allies alike that the Spartans fought, moved, and were victorious as a single unit. This was extremely powerful within the context of phalanx based warfare. To face such a uniform wall without the benefit of being part of one oneself must have been daunting indeed. This effect *on its own* contributes to the very efficiency and efficacy of which it speaks. An intimidated opponent is a more easily defeated opponent. Intimidation lends itself to panic and poor decisions on the part of the intimidated. The Shield of Achilles works in much the same way.

Homer is quick to tell the reader that the Shield of Achilles was a terrifying sight. Even the allies of Achilles could not look at it directly. Only Achilles himself was capable of this. Where others "shrank away" (19: 18), the more Achilles looks, the deeper his anger goes, fearful not for his own life, but that the body of his lover Patroclus "may rot to nothing" (19: 33).[11] It is clear that an important function of the shield is to enthrall its audience into inaction. Thus there is a genealogical relationship of sorts between the paralyzing gaze of Medusa, the Shield of Agamemnon, and the Shield of Achilles. It does not perform this function in the expected way, as exemplified in the cold-eyed stare of the Gorgon depicted on Agamemnon's shield. Yet its paralyzing effect is more powerful. How then does it enthrall?

The links between Medusa and the shields of Athena, Agamemnon, and Achilles indicate the importance of fear in their respective operations. Certainly each of them work, at least in part, by paralyzing their audience through fear. Yet at the same time there is more going on. The reader is introduced to the Shield of Achilles as "a world of gorgeous immortal work" (18:564). Agamemnon's shield is introduced as "beautiful blazoned work" (11:35). Even Medusa herself was once very beautiful before being cursed by Athena.[12] Both beauty and fear are central in the operation of the shield. There is an immense and irresolvable tension between repulsion and attraction built into the shield. Homer captures this tension when he describes the shield as "gleaming bright as the light that reaches sailors out at sea, . . . " (19:443–4) Such a light may be a beacon, guiding the sailors home. But it may also be a warning, telling of treacherous waters and unsafe passage.

Graves notes that Athena affixes the Gorgon's head onto her shield doubtless to warn people against examining the divine mysteries hidden behind it. Greek bakers used to paint Gorgon masks on their ovens, to discourage busybodies from opening the oven door, peeping in, and thus allowing a draught to spoil the bread.[13]

These descriptions, too, make note of an underlying tension between repulsion and attraction. Were Athena's shield and the mysteries hidden behind it not attractive, there would be no need for the warning visage. Were it not a matter of attractive curiosity as to what is happening in the unseen confines of the baker's oven, the doors would remain unadorned. To inquire into these mysteries, to seek to reveal that which is hidden is to disrupt their power and to destabilize their operation. If one wants to sustain the mysteries of the gods, they must remain unknowable. If one wants to make a loaf of bread, the oven door must remain closed. By extension, if one wants to represent an interpretation of events, a particular strategy, or particular policy such as the "War on Terror" as inevitable, all other options must remain closed. The power of the shield is the power to close off the other options.[14] The shield enthralls by suspending its audience between beauty and fear, between attraction and repulsion, between the known and the unknowable, between life and death. The shield paralyzes by destroying hope.

Beauty, Hope and Fear

The majority of Homer's description of the shield is taken up by events that take place away from the city at war. He dedicates relatively few lines to the description of war on the shield. Yet the intensity of the battle scenes cannot be denied. It is as if Homer is telling the reader, or that the shield is reminding the viewer, that the quieter life of abundance and the rule of law is the backdrop against which the sacrifices of war can make sense. Thus it would at first appear that war is but a relatively small part of a larger world. War can be seen as set against a backdrop of more civil, ordered modes or forms of living. For what soldier does not think of a return to the life he has left behind? This is very clear throughout Homer's epic. Note, for example, how quickly the Argives embrace Agamemnon's suggestion that they leave Troy (2:168–80). How else could Helen's mimicry of the voices of the wives of those hidden in the wooden horse be so compelling?[15] Or again, how else is it that the most intense fighting comes when the Achaean ships are threatened? These ships are nothing if not an ever present and necessary reminder of the possibility of return to a peaceful life beyond the battlefield. It is this possibility, this promise of a better world that the shield (understood as a claim) takes away.

The overwhelming power of the shield, its paralyzing effect, is achieved in a manner as subtle as the artwork embossed upon it. Although the battle scenes are a small part of the overall picture, they bleed into everything.

They absorb the background against which they appear. This takes place largely through the multiple parallels between the images on the shield and the lives led by its immediate audience, those faced with its advance on the battlefield. Some of these parallels are obvious. Clearly the language used by Homer in the description of the battle by the river could be taken from one of a thousand other places in the text of *The Iliad*. It is not difficult to see the fate of Hector in Homer's reference to "hauling a dead man through the slaughter by the heels, . . . " (18:625). This image bears a sense of the prophetic, but only in so far as the reader is already familiar with the outcome of the greater narrative. This "prophetic" character of the images on the shield becomes recognized as such only de facto. Retrospectively the events can be seen as fated, inevitable. Of course, Hector's corpse is not the only one to be accorded such treatment. Sarpedon, Patroclus, and a host of others are subjected to such indignity within the epic. This particular image on the shield both describes events that have happened and events that will happen. Indeed to the immediate audience, they are representations of events that *are happening*. This lends weight to the claim that the message of the shield is timeless and to its acceptability as an accurate reflection of the world.

The images of the soldiers in battle are those that most closely and obviously mirror the experience of the shield's immediate audience. Trojans and Greeks alike see themselves reflected in those figures, which,

> clashed and fought like living, breathing men
> grappling each others corpses, dragging off the dead. (18:627–8)

These lines simultaneously describe the craftsmanship of Hephaestus and the existential state of the combatants themselves. Due to this proximity of image and experience, the combatants, like the reader, see the blurring of the lines between the representations on the shield and their own realities. The soldiers and the reader (the audience) are taken in by the mirroring effect of the shield, forgetting that these images are representations, not reflections, and most certainly not the "things themselves." The immediate audience of the shield, Greek and Trojan alike, are caught in the ambiguity of the lines quoted above. In these lines, in this image, the viewers of the shield are told that they are already dead; that they are only "*like* living, breathing men" even as they appear—even to themselves—to live and breathe as men.

The obvious parallels are powerful, but they are far from exhaustive. Nor, for that matter, are they necessarily the most powerful inducers of paralysis on the shield. The direct parallels may suggest the impossibility of any combatant making it out alive, but they do nothing to disturb the backdrop of a peaceful life for the sake of which a continual, if ultimately fatal, struggle might make sense. That is, the unavoidability of death underscored by the obvious parallels between the images on the shield and the existential condition of its immediate audience does nothing in itself to remove the motivation to struggle on.[16] It is precisely this motivation that is eroded, and even erased by the subtler mirroring to be found on the shield.

Take, for example 18:676–85, which reads,

> …—a savage roar!—
> a crashing attack—and a pair of ramping lions
> had seized a bull from the cattle's front ranks—
> he bellowed out as they dragged him off in agony.
> Packs of dogs and the young herdsmen rushed to help
> but the lions ripping open the hide of the huge bull
> were gulping down the guts and the black pooling blood
> while the herdsmen yelled the fast pack on—no use.
> The hounds shrank from sinking teeth in the lions,
> they balked, hunching close, barking, cringing away.

Compare this image on the shield to the description of a Trojan assault in Book 15:

> Routed like herds of cattle or big flocks of sheep
> when two wild beasts stampeded them away in terror,
> suddenly pouncing down in their midst. (15:382–4)

Or again compare these lines to 17:69–75:

> Menelaus fierce as a mountain lion sure of his power,
> seizing the choicest head from a good grazing herd.
> First he cracks its neck, clamped in its huge jaws,
> mauling the kill then down in gulps he bolts it,
> blood and guts, and around him dogs and shepherds
> raise a fierce din but they keep their distance,
> lacking nerve to go in and take the lion on—
> the fear that grips their spirit makes them blanch.

Although nearly identical language is used to describe these events, the events themselves belong in the two opposing worlds of peace and war. With these passages one can begin to discern the erosion of the boundaries between the two worlds. But this is not all. Another of the more pacific scenes on the shield depicts,

> . . . a thriving vineyard loaded with clusters,
> bunches of lustrous grapes in gold, ripening deep purple
> and climbing vines shot up on silver vine-poles.
> And round it he cut a ditch in dark blue enamel
> and round the ditch he staked a fence in tin.
> And one lone footpath led toward the vineyard
> and down it the pickers ran
> whenever they went to strip the grapes at vintage—
> girls and boys, their hearts leaping in innocence,
> bearing away the sweet ripe fruit in wicker baskets. (18:654–663)

The images here bear a strong resemblance to the physical layout of the Achaean camp, surrounded by a trench filled with sharp stakes and accessible by a single gate (12:65–79). It is not overly difficult to see the similarities between the youths bearing away the vintage they have "stripped" and the Trojan soldiers carrying away the spoils they have stripped from the dead Argives within the gates of the encampment (15:409). With only a small amount of visual imagination, one can quite easily see the similarities between the baskets dripping with the dark juice of the grapes, and the spoils of the encampment, dripping with the dark blood of the Achaeans.

The similarities in this image work by placing the combatants in the dual role of both harvester and harvested. This is significant when one considers the number of agricultural scenes depicted on the Shield of Achilles. Elsewhere Homer compares the sound of battle to the thud of a timber cutter's axe when clearing a forest (15:736). The work of war and the work of peace are equated. They are made interchangeable. Thus within the context of the message of the shield, the reach of war extends that much further.

There is one particular scene on the shield that seems most removed from the bloody grind and feverish activity of the battlefield:

> And the famous crippled Smith forged a meadow
> deep in a shaded glen for shimmering flocks to graze,
> with shepherds' steadings, well roofed huts and sheepfolds. (18:686–8)

This scene is quintessentially pastoral. Quiet and still, it seems almost an antipode to the battle scenes. And yet one can find echoes of the imagery of this scene in the most pitched, most heated moments of the war. After the death of Sarpedon when both armies are in a desperate struggle to claim his corpse, Homer says,

> But they still kept swarming round and round the corpse
> like flies in a sheepfold buzzing over the brimming pails
> in the first spring days when the buckets flood with milk.
> So veteran troops kept swarming around that corpse,
> never pausing—(16:745–9)

Echoes of war are to be found even in the tranquility of the "deep shaded glen." The description of the death of Sarpedon contains within it one of the key images that work to confirm the universality of war. The message conveyed is that the reach of war is universal, its presence ubiquitous. What is more, the ensuing battle for his corpse is instructive in another way.

Sarpedon's Body

Immediately prior to the passage quoted above Homer says,

> Not even a hawk-eyed scout could still make out Sarpedon,
> the man's magnificent body covered over head to toe,
> buried under a mass of weapons, blood and dust. (16:742–4)

This is significant in that the ostensible rationale for the ongoing fight at that time and at that place is the recovery of Sarpedon's body either to gain glory by stripping it of its armor, or else to save it from such a fate. Yet the object of the struggle, the purpose for which it is waged becomes obscured by the struggle itself. This is true both in a literal sense in that the body is hidden from sight, and true on a grander scale in that it is during this fight that Patroclus is killed by Hector. Sarpedon's body as a *causus belli* is lost, just as are all such causes for war, and the fighting ultimately continues for its own sake. It is in this realization that the shield at last displays its most terrifying power.

It should by now be clear that the Shield of Achilles can be spoken of in many ways. It can be taken at face value as an object preexisting its description by Homer. It can be treated as existing only in its description. It can be treated figuratively and archetypically as a model for specific types of truth claims. The shield is therefore an object, a description, a truth claim, and a model of any such truth claims. It is to the parameters of this truth claim that the inquiry now turns. The shield makes a profound claim that "this is the way the world is," backed by the divine sanction of its origin. It carries with it the full weight of the realization that there is no quiet life to which one might return, there is no greater cause that makes the continuing struggle meaningful. The claim of the shield is that there is no cause for war at all, only war for the sake of its own perpetuation. Each and every one of the participants is already dead, and only "like living, breathing men" (18:627). The potency of the claim made by the shield, the veracity of its "this is the way it is" and its effectiveness as a tool of war, depends on the constant recreation of the context within which its claim is true. The shield presents its audience with an apparently inescapable and foregone conclusion that a life of peace "is not for you." The combatant, (the audience), is always irretrievably cut off from that other world to which the soldier hopes to return. Ironically enough, the shield achieves this by presenting the worlds of war and peace as distinct.

The claim of the shield, its divinely sanctioned "this is the way it is," resonates with a preexisting framework of experience on the part of its audience. Every soldier faced with the advancing shield has distinct memories of a life before the war, and harbors hopes of a return to that life after the war. As the war drags on, these memories fade and these hopes diminish. It is likely that had Thetis given the shield to Achilles upon his departure for Troy, the claim thereon would have had less of an impact. The memory of the world of peace would still have been too fresh in the minds and hearts of the audience (the adversary) to be so radically excluded. Ten years on the same conclusion has come to bear significant weight. It has become utterly believable and thus utterly effective. In a way the shield works to alter the realities of its audience and its bearer alike. It takes what is obviously true—that war and peace are distinct; that a peaceful world does precede and will follow on the intermittent and limited eruption of war—and turns it into an illusion. It supplants that "reality" with its own claim to "reality."

Speaking anachronistically, the shield accomplishes something of a Copernican revolution. The empirical evidence remains the same, but its meaning is radically altered. The making of a claim is not the same thing as the truth of the claim. The shield may make a powerful "this is the way it is" claim, but this does not in itself make the claim true. However there are features of this claim that do work to recreate the conditions within which it is true, or rather *becomes* true. To simply state "this is the way it is" does not make it so. Yet if this claim is believed to be true and acted upon as if it were true, it does, after a time, become true. The claim, which presents itself as a reflection of the world, can and does work to shape the world in its own image. The claim becomes auto-catalytic and self-verifying. An example of this can be found in a discussion of the function of the paralysis induced by the shield.

What exactly is meant by "paralysis" in this context? Clearly this paralysis is not literal in the same way as the Gorgon's stare causes paralysis. Although the sight of the shield does not turn its audience into stone, its "blazoned glory" (19:16) does induce a momentary pause. It is, quite literally, *stunning* in its "well-wrought beauty" (19:23). This stunning takes place on both an experiential and existential level. The soldier faced with the images portrayed on the shield and the claim made by them that there is no peaceful life to which he might return is driven into a state of shock. It is in this moment of disorientation and despair that the audience (the enemy soldier) is most vulnerable. It is in this moment of inaction that the bearer's spear finds its mark. It is during this brief paralysis that the sword falls. The net result is that the momentary pause becomes the permanent paralysis of death. The claim of the shield thereby generates empirical evidence (in the form of a corpse) to back itself.

It is critical to note that this piling of corpses upon corpses—for the shield must constantly recreate the conditions of its own veracity—does not serve to hasten the end of the war, but to perpetuate it. When Achilles reenters the battle, shield in hand, he is not interested in winning the war, thereby bringing it to a close so that he might return to a life of peace. He is fully aware that such a life is, truly, not for him. Having been told by his father's horse, Roan Beauty, that his death is imminent:

> Achilles burst out in anger,
> "Why, Roan Beauty—why prophesy my doom?
> Don't waste your breath. I know, well I know—
> I am destined to die here, far from my dear father,
> far from mother. But all the same I will never stop
> till I drive the Trojans to their bloody fill of war!" (19:496–501)

Rather than desiring an end to the fighting, Achilles says,

> —what I really crave
> is slaughter and blood and the choking groans of men! (19:254–5)

In other words, Achilles is not interested in bringing the war to an end but in its perpetuation.

The Shield in a Modern Context

The Shield of Achilles is being discussed because of its usefulness as a metaphor for understanding the logic of fear. As such, it is helpful to see how it is used in a contemporary context. The shield produces paralysis in its audience by the subtle manipulation of fear. There are elements of what might be called "shock and awe," but the greatest share of its power is achieved more insidiously. It is frightful because it presents a divinely sanctioned worldview in which there is no place for hope. The same can be said of the early rhetoric surrounding the War on Terror. It is obviously ridiculous to suggest that President Bush went around ducking behind an enormous golden artifact from the ancient world. Nonetheless it can still be said that he carries the Shield of Achilles if he is seen as making the same kind of claim as is embodied by the shield. Just as the shield purports to reflect a world of perpetual warfare in which the struggle to keep hope alive is that which makes its absence more palpable, so too did President Bush's speeches render conflict inescapable, hope impossible and resistance to his particular plan of action futile. In short, both Achilles and George W. Bush move forward behind the divinely sanctioned claim "this is the way it is" and its counterpart "there is nothing (else) you can do about it."[17]

Evidence for this is not at all difficult to find. Almost any speech by a Bush administration official on the topic of the War on Terror is replete with examples.[18] One early and thematically archetypical example is President Bush's address to a joint session of the congress delivered only nine days after the fall of the World Trade Centre Towers and the burning of the Pentagon. The speech was given was within context in which there was a profound sense that the world had changed, that nothing would ever be the same again:

> In the normal course of events, Presidents come to this chamber to report on the state of the Union. Tonight, no such report is needed. It has already been delivered by the American people.[19]

From the outset there is a clear demarcation between competing worlds, one normal, one not. The opening lines of the speech both recognize the exceptional circumstances in which they are delivered and subsume the exception with the parameters of an accepted and established tradition. This modified State of the Union address proceeds to offer a portrayal of the current condition as replete with cooperative and coordinated action, compassion, piety and orderliness. There is no overt mention in these early lines of the chaos and confusion against which these manifestations appear. Here, even in the most dire of circumstances the American union is orderly, structured, and adherent to the rule of law. It is notable that in re-establishing the hegemony of the normal, the usual roles of leader and led are reversed. It is not the President who reports on the State of the Union, but the people themselves. In this way, the role of the people as the primary locus of authority is highlighted. This is not unexpected in a liberal democratic state, and is in fact a restatement of the core feature of such a state. The audience is subtly reassured that political power, of which America is the greatest contemporary example, is in their hands.

More than this, President Bush's reference to "the unfurling of flags, the lighting of candles, the giving of blood, the saying of prayers"[20] presents a series of symbolic images all indicating a sense of belonging to and partaking in a life beyond the self. Each of these actions may be highlighted as especially significant in a time of crisis, but the symbolic and material infrastructures upon which they depend are not themselves reflex responses to crisis. For these acts to be meaningful, the symbolic frameworks within which they are meaningful must already be in place. That is, the unfurling of a flag in a time of crisis relies upon an already existing sense of political unity. The lighting of candles obtains its symbolic power from a pre-existing framework of memorial practices. The giving of blood and the saying of prayers require an already existing means of doing so through hospitals and churches. None of the gestures are selfish. All are other-directed, selfless. Each of these gestures, in other words, is indicative of a selflessness that was already institutionalized prior to the crisis in which such gestures are highlighted. They are indicative of "the decency of a loving and giving people who have made the grief of strangers their own."[21] It is not that the September 11 attacks have made us this way. It is who we were already. More than once, and in no uncertain terms, the audience is reminded that this is the "city at peace."

The images of orderliness and compassion are extended beyond the boundaries of a single country. Indeed the reflections on the similarly orderly responses offered in various locations and settings around the globe—lawmakers singing on the Capitol steps;[22] the American national anthem playing in London, Paris and Berlin;[23] prayer services outside the embassy in South Korea and inside a mosque in Cairo;[24] moments of silence in Australia and Latin America[25]—all tend to indicate the presence of a greater "civilized" world with America at its head.[26] This greater *polis*, like that portrayed on the Shield of Achilles, is both concerned with and representative of justice. This is made abundantly clear in the statement "whether we bring our enemies to justice, or justice to our enemies, justice will be done."[27]

Against this enlarged "city of peace" there is a corresponding "city at war." The shift from the "city at peace" to the "city at war" comes with the declaration: "On September 11, enemies of freedom committed an act of war against our country."[28] This "city at war" is characterized by a complete lack of compassion, an inability, or worse, an unwillingness to recognize and respect the rule of law. Evidence for this is indicated by the institutionalized lack of a distinction between civilian and combatant. Just as in Homer's description of the shield, it is here that the most blatant images of terror are to be found.

> The terrorists' directive commands them to kill Christians and Jews, to kill all Americans, and make no distinction among military and civilians, including women and children.[29]

Immediately, there are clear lines established: freedom versus enslavement, justice versus cruelty, rationalism versus radicalism, civilization versus barbarity, good versus evil. It is true that much of the gore to be found in Homer's account of the city at war is absent, but no less shocking to the contemporary audience—and perhaps more so—is the revelation that "you can be jailed for owning a television. Religion can be practiced only as their leaders dictate. A man can be jailed in Afghanistan if his beard is not long enough."[30] There is a double move in Bush's litany of abuses to be found in Taliban-controlled Afghanistan. He provides a glimpse into a particular legal code, a particular social order, yet his purpose is to expose it as pure disorder. Murder and the arbitrary display of power is the only "rule" here. Just as the "the citizens of 80 other nations who died with our own"[31] are united in a single event, so too are "thousands of these terrorists in more than 60 countries"[32] united by a single unified purpose; to hasten the downfall of civilization itself. The sides are clearly demarcated. There is no room for any other consideration. The choice, if it can be considered that, is stark: "Every nation, in every region, now has a decision to make. Either you are with us, or you are with the terrorists."[33]

Bush's speech, much like the Shield of Achilles, presents itself as an accurate reflection of the world. There is nothing particularly surprising in his demarcation of a line between peace and war. Such a distinction is obvious from a common sense perspective. Yet by marking this distinction, he establishes a framework within which the attacks can be nothing else but acts of war. In doing so, he also establishes the parameters of an appropriate response. He says at one point "by sacrificing human life to serve their radical visions—by abandoning every value except the will to power—they follow in the path of fascism, and Nazism, and totalitarianism."[34] By directly equating the terrorists with fascists, Nazis and Communists, the President is translating the threat of militant Islam into a symbolic, *mythological* language that bears considerable weight for those portions of the population who lived through the later half of the last century. Not only is he representing this threat in terms that can be easily understood, he is also implying an already patterned response to that threat.[35] If militant Islam is equated with Nazism and Communism, it should be fought in the same way, namely wholeheartedly, in all places, at all times, with all necessary sacrifices:

> Americans are asking: How will we fight and win this war? We will direct every resource at our command—every means of diplomacy, every tool of intelligence, every instrument of law enforcement, every financial influence, and every necessary weapon of war—to the disruption and to the defeat of the global terror network.[36]

Thus the struggle against terrorism becomes just another episode in a perpetual war between "freedom and fear."[37] Within this formula, one cannot "come to terms" with the enemy. One can only destroy the enemy outright. "The only way to defeat terrorism as a threat to our way of life is to stop it, eliminate it, and destroy it where it grows."[38]

The Shield of Achilles accomplishes something of a Copernican revolution. It presents its audience with familiar observations, but radically alters the meaning of those observations. Although President Bush's speech makes repeated reference to "the values of America" and repeatedly reinforces the priority of peace over war, the measures he proposes in the speech work to invert that relationship and to redefine those values. In specific terms, Bush speaks of "our freedom of religion, our freedom of speech, our freedom to vote and assemble and disagree with each other."[39] The operational term is "freedom." As his opening lines imply this freedom resides in the fact that each individual is the primary locus of power. Political power is not centralized in the institutional hierarchies of government officials, but resides in the people themselves. It is notable that in the name of defending this freedom, President Bush proposes a centralization of power by creating an Office of Homeland Security. In the name of securing freedom, his policies, which he deems "essential,"[40] are more appropriate to the establishment and operation of a police state. In the name of securing freedom he proposes "to give law enforcement the additional tools it needs,"[41] "to dramatically expand the number of air marshals on domestic flights,"[42] to "strengthen our intelligence capabilities"[43] so that—hopefully—"in the months and years ahead, life will return to almost normal."[44]

If "remaking the world—and imposing [their] radical beliefs on people everywhere"[45] is a goal of al Qaeda and its supporters, then President Bush appears to be conceding at least partial defeat. If a return to life that is "almost normal" is at best—"hopefully"—years away, then the terrorists have indeed remade the world. "All of this was brought upon us in a single day—and night fell on a different world, a world where freedom itself is under attack."[46] And yet there are strong indications in the speech that the world has not changed, only our awareness of it has. In describing America as "a country awakened to danger," the President implies two things. First, he points to the presence of danger in the world well before the September 11 attacks. Second, he implies that America's security in its freedoms was an illusion. More precisely its sense of "normal" was a *daydream*. In his statement, "normal" is rendered illusory. In so far as the "city at peace" is representative of that normalcy, he inverts the priority of peace over war. From now on, we are awake to the fact that war is the norm, just as it will be for the foreseeable future, *and just as it always has been*. This is indeed one of the key functions of the shield; to perpetuate the war it depicts as perpetual. In the end, the bearing of the shield itself creates the world it purports only to represent.

In the discussion of Homer's epic, the body of Sarpedon was said to represent an ever self-perpetuating *causus belli*. Although beyond the parameters of the September 20 speech, a similar loss of the *causus belli* can be seen in the execution of the War on Terror.[47] Active American involvement in the war began in Afghanistan and was a retaliatory strike in response to the September 11 attacks. The purpose was to destroy al Qaeda training camps known to be there. This cause for war overlapped with the stated aim of liberating the Afghani people—most especially its women—from the oppression of Taliban rule. In January of 2002, the scope of the war widened with the identification of the so-called "axis of evil."[48] As the focus shifted to weapons of mass destruction, multiple and ever broader causes for war became apparent. Just as the cause of the fight shifts in Homer's epic from the recovery of Sarpedon's body to the recovery of

Patroclus' body, to Achilles raw craving for "slaughter and blood and the choking groans of men" (19:254–5), the cause for the War on Terror shifts from the September 11 attacks to the liberation of oppressed peoples,[49] to the halting of the spread of weapons of mass destruction, to the mere presence of evil in the world.[50] As the cause for the war becomes more abstract, its scope increases. With a stated aim of the eradication of evil itself, the war becomes an existential feature of the world. Just as in the image on Achilles' shield, there is no option but perpetual, universal warfare. Bush forthrightly announces this in his speech of September 20, 2001: "Americans [read the civilized world] should not expect one battle, but a lengthy campaign unlike any we have ever seen."[51] Even the appearance of peace is no indication of its existence because the possibility of ongoing "covert operations, secret even in success" cannot be ruled out.[52] Indeed, the ubiquity of this war is made quite clear by observing that Bush is speaking as commander-in-chief when he says, "I ask you to live your lives, and hug your children."[53] Even the mundane becomes the action of a dutiful soldier. In the same breath as he condemns the enemy for a lack of regard for the civilian/combatant distinction, he eradicates the same boundary. "Like flies in a sheepfold," indeed.

Achilles and Priam: Setting aside the Shield

The Shield of Achilles and the rhetoric of the Bush administration differ in at least one key aspect. One of Homer's central points, as is readily discernable in the depictions on the shield, is to mark the similarities between the combatants. They are not radically different, but rather nigh unto undifferentiated. The Greeks under Agamemnon and the Trojans under Priam worship the same gods, speak the same language, and hold the same standards of proper conduct. In the narrative, it is easy to become lost in a blur of names of the dead of both armies. The dead are simultaneously marked as different and subsumed as a mere fraction of an increasing mass of corpses. All different, all the same. It is on this point that one of the main differences between the Homeric myth and the War on Terror is to be found.

The Bush administration and the neoconservatives around it have gone to great lengths to mark clear and untransgressable boundaries between "us" and "them," the (good) "citizen" and the (evil) "terrorist." The effort to mark the distinctions between combatants as absolute and diametrically opposed has the effect and express intent of rendering any reconciliation impossible. It is obvious that given an adversary who is not subject to the jurisdiction of logic or diplomacy, an adversary who cannot be appeased, then the only remaining option (and because of it, no option at all) is to fight. Given that "they" are not even beholden to the rules of a "fair fight," one has no choice but to bend those rules in return.[54]

Achilles provides a good example of this when he re-enters the fight rearmed. In his bloodlust he willfully abandons the conventions of what might be called "civilized" behavior. The death of Patroclus changes Achilles for the worse. Patroclus is the beloved of Achilles. He is that which is valued above all, even above Achilles' own life. Ironically the return to combat, motivated by the cherished value of friendship and close human connection, reveals the animalistic aspects of Achilles' character. He is angrier, more likely to kill a defeated enemy,[55] less likely to recognize and respect the bounds of honor and civility,[56] more prone to hubris.[57]

Achilles is magnanimous in his suffering. He spreads his suffering out to make it universal. A comparison can be made to a common theme of the Bush administration's rhetoric, encapsulated in Paul Wolfowitz's statement that "the way to defeat extremism is to demonstrate that the values we call Western are indeed universal."[58] The logic employed by Achilles, and implied by Wolfowitz, is that "if I must suffer, so shall you all." Certainly this suffering and these values are not universal until they are made so in the press of battle, by the application of force.

The one whom Achilles makes suffer the most is Priam, Hector's father. If Achilles' treatment of Hector's body marks his furthest foray from his own humanity, it is also the precondition of his return to it. The encounter between Achilles and Priam has been noted repeatedly as the moment when Achilles returns to the fold of humanity.[59] In this encounter two enemies recognize themselves in each other and are united by a common bond of suffering and loss. This leads in turn to a further forging of mutual respect when Achilles is convinced to return the body of Hector, and to offer Priam safe passage out of the Greek encampment. Achilles comes once again to recognize his place as one human being among many. The hubris he had displayed in his combat with the river god Scamander is wiped clean in the restraint he shows in not killing Priam.

This case of recognition and respect for a divine order is important. Achilles is farthest removed from his own humanity when he returns to battle armed with the shield. The claim of that shield is that war is omnipresent and perpetual. To challenge that claim, even by defending one's self when one is already only "like [a] living breathing [man]," is an act of hubris. It is to directly contradict the voice of the gods. Yet Achilles himself challenges that claim by making peace with Priam. There is no small irony in this. His rage unleashed, Achilles is guilty of hubris, as evidenced by his combat with Scamander (21:264–434), and by the outrage of the Olympian gods at his actions (24:25–60). His rage in check and his humanity regained, he is also guilty of hubris as he exposes the gods as liars.[60] His peace with Priam is a direct rejection of the divinely sanctioned "this is the way it is" of the shield. His actions prove that there is more to life than killing. There is a broader suggestion in the truce forged between the king and the warrior that war can come to an end. Figuratively, the reconciliation flows from and displays the eternal possibility that any universal claim of the type "this is the way it is" can be mistaken. He puts an end to war, even if temporarily, thereby making the counter claim "this is not the way it is," effectively placing the authority of his will above that of the gods. The deeper irony is that he achieves this only by recognizing the authority of the gods.

Achilles does this in two stages. The first recognition is more a matter of course than conviction. Having been instructed by the gods to return Hector's body:

The swift runner replied *in haste*, "So be it.
The man who brings the ransom can take away the body,
if Olympian Zeus himself insists in all earnest." (24:168–70)[61]

This recognition of divine authority can be seen as bearing the hallmarks of hubris. Specifically, the conditional aspect of the remark suggests that if it were not the case that "Zeus himself insists in all earnest," then the act would not be done. Such a conditional agreement is more to be expected in a negotiation between equals than in an exchange between god and man. In making these remarks Achilles places himself on par with the king of the gods. He remains therefore in a precarious position, trapped by his own arrogance.

The second stage comes later, and in a much quieter, more thoughtful way. In the presence of Priam, Hector's father, Achilles is reminded of his own father. As Priam begs for the return of his son's corpse, Achilles warns him,

Don't stir my raging heart still more.
Or under my own roof I may not spare your life, old man –
suppliant that you are—may break the laws of Zeus! (24:667–9)

And again, having agreed to return Hectors body to Priam, Achilles does not permit Priam to see his son before the body is washed, for,

> He feared that, overwhelmed by the sight of Hector,
> wild with grief, Priam might let his anger flare
> and Achilles might fly into a fresh rage himself,
> cut the old man down and break the laws of Zeus. (24:684–7)[62]

Here, Achilles is fully aware of his tenuous grip on his own anger and because of this he is better able to control it. This recognition of the laws of Zeus is not an off the cuff, automatic reply delivered in a heated mood. In the second instance, where Homer makes the reader privy to the private thoughts of Achilles, it is clear that this is a genuine recognition of those laws. There is a sincerity and palpability to his deference to those divine laws. It is this second stage that saves Achilles from the precarious heights of arrogance and hubris. But this is not to say that Achilles has found his footing in a place *beneath* the gods.

Zeus does not stay the hand of Achilles from killing Priam. Rather, Achilles restrains *himself.* It is up to him to follow the will of the gods or not. It should be noted that Achilles is fully aware of his own fate and that his death must closely follow that of Hector. He cannot therefore seek to avoid offending Zeus for fear of his own life. To give deference to the divine for the sake of one's own skin may be prudent, but it is not honorable. By not killing Priam, Achilles adheres to the dictates of a divine order out of a sheer sense of unambiguous honor (*tîmê*). He does not spare Priam in order to save his own life, but because it is what he believes is the right thing to do. This display of *tîmê* in turn renders the immortality of Achilles possible. It is what makes him a hero. Simply by having this choice, to follow the laws of the gods or not, he is not, strictly speaking, *bound* by the laws of the gods. Put differently, he is not a participant in the cosmological/ethical matrix of "this is the way it is" and "there is nothing (else) to be done." It is more appropriate to say that this matrix is a tool useful in the furthering of his own will: a will that is equal to or greater than the will of the gods. Thus in gaining control of his anger, and restraining his animalistic instincts he elevates himself above the station of the gods and simultaneously terminates his hubris.

This conclusion appears to be borne out by Homer himself as the scene immediately following what I have called the second stage recognition describes a meal shared by Priam and Achilles. Two points make this notable. First, Achilles suggests that Priam dine with him, retelling the tale of Niobe, a woman punished for her hubris.[63] This certainly brings the subject of hubris to the foreground of the audience's (reader's) attention. Second, the description of the meal itself is notably devoid of the usual offerings of the first cuts of meat as a sacrifice to the gods. In other parts of the epic, such an omission is a near certain way to garner the wrath of the gods. Here, however, the context is such that the gods are assuaged.

Achilles' reconciliation with Priam, his laying aside of the shield, not only saves the life of Priam and the dignity of Hector, but elevates the station of Achilles above that of the gods. He outstrips the power of the gods by recognizing and respecting that power, (much as Odysseus will do repeatedly in *The Odyssey*). He transcends himself in a way that the gods cannot do. Without his reconciliation with Priam, it is clear that the wrath of Achilles would destroy him. Without it, the world that is his rightful domain and creation would utterly debase and consume him. Were he to become beholden to his own portrayal of the world, were to be taken in by his own artificial "this is the way it is," it would devour him. The risks of believing one's own spin are serious indeed. It is his ability to set aside the shield, to escape its illusory effects, that makes Achilles a suitable bearer of it.[64]

The recognition of sameness in the other is a critical part of Achilles' decision to follow the laws of Zeus, thereby elevating himself above those laws. It is precisely such a recognition that is overtly disallowed by the rhetoric of the war on terror. Without the possibility of reconciliation, the claim of the shield, that is the parameters within which the war is understood as a necessity, cannot be challenged. So long as these parameters remain unchallenged both the speaker and the audience of these claims are doomed to live and die by them. There is a quiet usurpation in which the creator becomes subject to the creation. The author surrenders authority, the agent surrenders agency. Having abdicated authoritative power, the author can make the argument that he or she bears no responsibility for "things being the way they are."

The radical othering of the enemy, so prevalent in the rhetoric surrounding the War on Terror during the Bush administration, renders reconciliation impossible, along with any redemptive qualities it might contain or imply. On the ground, and in a more contemporary setting, this translated into a pervasive message that opposition to the Bush administration's policies was somehow dangerous, unpatriotic, and even traitorous.[65] Achilles overcomes this limitation precisely by setting the shield aside. The implication is that so long as the shield is being borne, the bearer remains unable to recognize the possibility that its "this is the way it is" claim might be mistaken.

Notes

1 It should be noted that the reference to "Western culture" is in this instance a mere convenience. It is made in full awareness that there is a tendency to treat "the Western World" as a unified entity simply by naming it, which is not necessarily an accurate depiction.

2 Homer, *The Iliad*, trans. Robert Fagles (New York: Penguin Books, 1990). Throughout the book, all references to Homer's epic are taken from Robert Fagles' translation. Given the preponderance of available translations, all references will be provided in parentheses within the text using the format: (Book:Line(s)).

3 Or many other ancient writers, for that matter. Of particular note is Hesiod's description of the Shield of Heracles. This shield is notable for its similarities to the Shield of Achilles, but even more so for its differences. In short, the Shield of Heracles is a far more blatantly fearful object. Hesiod, "The Shield of Herakles," in *The Poems and Fragments Done Into English Prose With Introduction and Appendices By A. W. Mair* (Oxford: Clarendon, 1908).

4 Alternately it is said that his mother held him over the fire of immortality in order to burn away all mortal parts of him. See Robert Graves, *The Greek Myths* (New York: George Brazillier, Inc, 1955).

5 Emphasis added.

6 By wearing the armor, Hector claims his superiority, but as anyone familiar with the events of the epic will immediately recognize, the making of the claim and the veracity of the claim are not one and the same.

7 The intimate connection between the notable individual and their specific armaments is to be found throughout *The Iliad*. Witness Telamonian Ajax's tower shield, Nestor's chariot, Pandarus' bow, Hectors "flashing helm." See Blair Campbell, "The Epic Hero as Politico," *History of Political Thought* 11, no. 2 (1990); Ian C Johnston, *The Ironies of War: An Introduction to Homer's Iliad* (Lanham, MD: University Press of America, 1988).

8 Mark W. Edwards, and G. S. Kirk, eds *The Iliad: A Commentary*, vol. 5: Books 17–20 (Cambridge: Cambridge University Press, 1991).

9 See Robert Graves, *The Greek Myths*.

10 Of course, as with Hector's claim to superiority over Achilles, Agamemnon's message that resistance is impossible is not entirely true. The conflict between Agamemnon and Achilles is explicitly based on Achilles' promise to the seer Calchas to defend him against the wrath of Agamemnon (1:85–98). Were it the case that resistance to the authority of Agamemnon was as impossible as he

claims, then whole of the epic would be groundless. This is a critical point and will be addressed in much more detail, albeit in a slightly different context, later in the argument.

[11] In keeping with the overall themes of this book, there is an opening here to examine the parallels between Patroclus as a symbol of the core values of friendship and other-connection and the present challenges to traditional notions of family, national pride and other "core values" especially as they are perceived by social conservatives. Could it be that there is a fear that these conservative "core values" may also "rot to nothing"?

[12] Consider that after her death, Pegasus, the very symbol of beauty, is born from her corpse.

[13] Ibid., 129.

[14] And to disrupt that power is to allow for alternatives. The later chapters of the book will discuss ways in which this power can be disrupted.

[15] Homer. *The Odyssey*. Translated by Robert Fagles. New York: Penguin Books, 1996.

[16] One could argue that on the contrary it is precisely the inevitability of death that renders possible the ethical code by which the Homeric heroes operate. Glory is to be found in the accomplishments of one's life and the way in which one chooses to face an unavoidable death. See Zanker, 1997, 228.

[17] This is not to say that it is only these two parties that advance behind the shield. It would not be difficult to demonstrate that the same sorts of claims are made by bin Laden and representatives of al Qaeda. Indeed these types of claims are very widespread, but no less problematic for it.

[18] For a brief sample of these speeches, taken from Secretary and Undersecretary of Defense, see Donald H. Rumsfeld, "A New Kind of War" (2001); Donald H. Rumsfeld, "Remarks to the Heritage Foundation" (2004); Donald H. Rumsfeld, "Secretary Rumsfeld Remarks At the International Institute for Strategic Studies" (2004); Paul Wolfowitz, "Bridging the Dangerous Gap Between the West and the Muslim World" (2002); Paul Wolfowitz, "Building a Better World: One Path From Crisis to Opportunity" (2002); Paul Wolfowitz, "The Gathering Storm: the Threat of Global Terror and Asia/Pacific Security" (2002); Paul Wolfowitz, Georgetown Iden Lecture: "Winning the Battle of Ideas: Another Front in the War on Terror" (2003); Paul Wolfowitz, "America's New Allies in the War on Terrorism", U.S. Dept. Of Defense (2004); Paul Wolfowitz, "A Strategic Approach to the Challenge of Terrorism" (2004).

[19] George W. Bush, "Address to a Joint Session of Congress and the American People, 20 September, 2001" (2001).

[20] Ibid.

[21] Ibid.

[22] Ibid.

[23] Ibid.

[24] Ibid.

[25] Ibid.

26 One effect of this is to reassert the continued viability of American hegemony
    which had been so recently shaken by the profound sense of helplessness and
    uncertainty that followed the September 11 attacks.

27 Ibid. There is a discrepancy between the transcript of the speech and the audio
    record of it. The quote is taken from the transcript, but in the audio record
    the President says "whether we bring our enemies to justice, or *injustice* to
    our enemies, justice will be done." This slip of the tongue, if it is one, is instruc-
    tive because when stated this way, the President implies an adherence to a
    Hammurabic code of justice; an eye for an eye, a life for a life, injustice repaid
    by injustice. Given his consistency in adhering to a "fight fire with fire" response
    to the attacks, this may not be far off the mark.

28 Ibid. The declaration begins the description of "city at war," but also establishes
    a framework within which the attacks can make sense – as acts of war. The
    confusion as to how to respond is reduced, since "Americans have known
    wars." This patterning of responses is a common semiotic theme of the speech,
    and more will be said of it below.

29 Ibid.

30 Ibid.

31 Ibid.

32 Ibid.

33 Ibid. The corresponding "identity formula"(see above) is less apparent in this
    early speech by President Bush than it is in the work of Frum and Perle, where
    it is effectively stated as "Islam = Radical Fundamentalist Islam = Chaos." See
    David Frum, and Richard Perle, *An End to Evil: How to Win the War on Terror*
    (New York: Random House, 2003). Of course to choose to be "with us" means
    to "choose" to take part in a global, all out war against those who have chosen to
    fight a global, all out war.

34 George W. Bush, "Address to a Joint Session of Congress and the American
    People, 20 September, 2001."

35 See Cyril Buffet, and Beatrice Heuser, eds *Haunted By History: Myths in Inter-
    national Relations* (Providence, RI: Berghahn Books, 1998). For another
    discussion of this rhetorical technique see Maja Zehfuss, "Writing War, Against
    Good Conscience," *Millennium: Journal of International Studies* 33, no. 1 (2004):
    91–121.

36 George W. Bush, "Address to a Joint Session of Congress and the American
    People, 20 September, 2001." Note that there is an ambiguity in the language
    here. While obviously true that some Americans are asking this question, this
    is also a suggested definition of what it means to be an American. By this inter-
    pretation, if you are not asking this question, and therefore if you have not
    accepted the framework that dictates the events of September 11 as acts of
    war, you are un-American.

37 There are affinities between this effect and Philip Bobbit's argument.
    Philip Bobbitt, *The Shield of Achilles War, Peace, and the Course of History*

(New York: Anchor Books, 2002). His title selection seems odd for a book in which Homer scarcely appears in the index, but if the argument of this chapter is correct, (that the message of the shield is the inevitability of war), it is not an accidental choice. I would disagree with Bobbitt that al Qaeda is best understood as a "virtual state" (that is to say "as good as a state") as this leads to the perpetuation of a state-centric model within which one epochal war must follow another. Bobbitt too is trapped by his own mirrorings.

[38] George W. Bush, "Address to a Joint Session of Congress and the American People, 20 September, 2001."

[39] Ibid.

[40] Ibid.

[41] Ibid.

[42] Ibid.

[43] Ibid. One begins to suspect that the "we" referred to in this passage is not the same as the "we" that hold the freedoms enumerated earlier. If the latter "we" refers to the people as a whole, the former appears to refer more to the institutions of a government over and above the people.

[44] Ibid.

[45] Ibid.

[46] Ibid.

[47] Although a detailed analysis of this phenomenon would certainly prove fruitful, it is beyond the scope of the present argument. For the time being a few salient points will have to suffice.

[48] George W. Bush, "State of the Union Address" (2002).

[49] As has been the case, to date, in both Afghanistan and Iraq, with an eye to North Korea, Iran, Syria, and possibly Saudi Arabia.

[50] For a detailed discussion of the war in such terms see David Frum, and Richard Perle, *An End to Evil: How to Win the War on Terror*.

[51] George W. Bush, "Address to a Joint Session of Congress and the American People, 20 September, 2001."

[52] Ibid.

[53] Ibid.

[54] It is for this reason that the Iraqi prisoner abuse scandal should not come as a real surprise. It is the same with revelations that the legal council for the Bush Administration has been implicated in giving the green light to the use of torture.

[55] See Achilles' treatment of Lycaon (21:38–155). Lycaon, a son of Priam, had been captured "in Priam's well fenced orchard" by Achilles 12 days before, then immediately ransomed back to his family. He is caught again by Achilles, and as Lycaon grasps Achilles knees, begging for mercy, he is run through and killed. His death is strikingly similar to that of Leodes in *The Odyssey*. Homer, *The Odyssey*, 22:324–45.

56 This is particularly evident in his treatment of the corpse of Hector (22:465–76).

57 One of the most notable examples is his open combat with Scamander, the river god (21:240–320).

58 Paul Wolfowitz, "Building a Better World: One Path From Crisis to Opportunity." As in President Bush's speech of September 20, 2001, Wolfowitz does not spell out exactly what these values are. This gives him a certain flexibility in his proscriptions. The logic of spreading suffering, of responding to force with force, may be guided by a sense of (Hammurabic) justice, or by a kind of egalitarianism. It may even be guided by a variation of the so-called "Golden Rule." ("Do unto others as you would have them do unto you.") The variation coming in the doing unto others *as they have already demonstrated* they would have done unto themselves. Thus by causing suffering, the terrorists wish to be made to suffer.

59 See Mark W. Edwards, and G. S. Kirk, *The Iliad: A Commentary*.

60 This means he has also exposed himself as a liar. In making the shield, the gods make a "this is the way it is" claim, the specific content of which is "all is war." In bearing the shield, Achilles makes the same claim. His reconciliation with Priam however puts an end to war, even if only temporarily, thus exposing both himself as a bearer of the shield, and the gods as guarantors of its "this is the way it is," as liars.

61 Emphasis added.

62 It may also be argued that by the time Achilles reconciles with Priam he has already exacted his revenge by killing Hector, hence exhausting his propensity for hubris. In this case he would be best understood as exhibiting exhaustion rather than restraint. The quotes just offered speak against such an interpretation. So too does the fact that even after the death of Hector and the funeral of Patroclus, Achilles "kept on raging, shaming noble Hector" (24:25). Even Apollo notes that "his temper can never bend and change" (24:48). It is not altogether surprising that twelve days would not be enough to exhaust Achilles' anger and pride, given that it has not been exhausted, but rather increased, from the very opening line of the poem as a whole.

63 Even in the depths of her suffering, Niobe had to eat. Consider Nietzsche's comment that "the abdomen is the reason why people are not so quick to consider themselves gods." Friedrich Wilhelm Nietzsche et al., *Beyond Good and Evil : Prelude to a Philosophy of the Future*, Cambridge Texts in the History of Philosophy (Cambridge; New York: Cambridge University Press, 2002), 68.

64 Despite his transcendence of both himself and the gods, it can be argued that Achilles does not escape his fate. There is a subtle alteration in this fate however. In his reconciliation with Priam, Achilles' fate is less laid out for him than it is chosen by him. Just as his acceptance of the laws of the gods comes not at the behest or the command of the gods, but by his own volition, so too has he risen

above his fate by *willing* it. His death becomes not that which is presented to
him by the gods, but that which he has chosen for himself. Achilles becomes
the master of his own fate, even if the fate he chooses does not differ in content
from that given him by the gods.

[65] It is seen in the 2004 Republican presidential campaign theme that to choose
any other course of action (never mind choosing a new commander-in-chief)
is to risk catastrophe. A similar theme was pursued by the Republican party in
the early part of the 2008 Presidential campaign as well.

3

Unheeded Warnings

Achilles was quite unique as a bearer of the shield. In the first place, he was half divine. He already straddled the border between humanity and divinity. As such, he was capable of what appears to be extra-human accomplishments, not the least of which was his setting aside of the shield. Second, as has been argued here, he was a suitable bearer of the shield precisely because he had the ability to put it down, to set it aside. The message put forward by the logic of the shield, whatever its specific content, is meant to convey a sense of invulnerability and incontestability. It is not meant to be questioned or challenged. Indeed, it operates in such a way as to explicitly deny the very possibility of contestation. It has been demonstrated that the logic of the shield poses a clear hazard to its audience. And yet its dangers do not end there. The death of Achilles shows that not only is the shield hazardous for its audience, but for its bearer as well. It does not deliver on the promise of impenetrability or invulnerability it offers. What is more, its appearance of invulnerability can diminish the bearer's awareness of his or her own vulnerabilities. There is a series of obvious questions that arise here. How is one to resist, sidestep, or even undo the power of the shield? How is one to avoid falling prey to its paralyzing message? How is one to contest the "incontestable" or challenge the "unchallengeable?"

These are questions that have been answered in many ways by many different people. This chapter will examine the responses of three different authors who are united in the fact that their respective responses to the logic of the shield offer a warning of its dangers to any potential bearer of it. Given that the metaphor of the shield is drawn from a mythological context, the first author to be discussed will not stray far from that context. The chapter will begin with the playwright Sophocles. The focus will be chiefly on two of his plays, *Ajax* and *Philoctetes*, both of which address the events that follow the death of Achilles. The armor of the fallen hero takes on an important role in each of the plays.

Sophocles addresses the shield and its problems in a literal way. The next two authors do so much more abstractly. Neither the historian Thucydides, nor the political theorist Machiavelli make any explicit mention of the Shield of Achilles, but both can clearly be understood as critically engaging with exactly the kind of logic the shield metaphorically represents. Furthermore, both thinkers are typically associated with the tradition of "realist" thought, which because of its insistence on "telling it like it is" can itself be understood as an embodiment of shield logic. It will be demonstrated however that both can be read in such a way as to undermine the tradition they are so closely associated with.

Sophocles

Ajax

After the death of Achilles, his armor, including the shield, becomes the prize in a contest between heroes. The question to be asked is what the respective characters of those vying for its possession can tell us about what it means to bear the shield. Keeping in mind the central question of how one can resist or undo the power of the shield, can they show us anything about what it means to bear the shield after Achilles?

The two contestants reaching for this prize were Odysseus and Ajax, son of Telamon, also known as Greater Ajax. Achilles had identified both as "my dearest friends in all the Achaean armies, even in my anger" (9:238–9).[1] As such, both had a legitimate claim to the arms. Yet the two contestants could not have been less alike in character. Ajax, a blood relative of Achilles, is most like Achilles in his redoubtability on the battlefield and in his transparency of motivation and purpose. Ajax is self-sure, steadfast, laconic, honest to a fault (even to his own detriment, as when he angers Athena).[2] Odysseus on the other hand is much more mercurial.[3] He is a "great tactician" with a profound sense of the mutability of context, the fluidity of the battlefield, and how those changing circumstances call at various times for a wide range of sometimes contradictory responses. Odysseus is as likely to be found charging into the thick of battle as he is to be found leading a clandestine night raid, or disguised as a beggar in his own house, depending on the requirements of the circumstances. Where Ajax is known for his "wall-like shield," Odysseus is one of the only major characters in *The Iliad* not to be associated with a particular piece of battle gear. Yet he is portrayed as a master of them all.[4] He is renowned for his "cleverness," relying as much, if not more, on his wit than his weapons.[5]

Based on the respective characters of these two heroes, what would it mean for each to win the shield? It should be apparent at this point in the argument that to bear the shield is a hazardous enterprise, both for its audience and its bearer. The power of the shield is such that its claim "this is the way it is" can be utterly enchanting. This is to say that its bearer, and its audience alike are prone to believing its message as the indisputable truth. Its claim is entirely believable and it is only by virtue of a super-human act of will that Achilles, for whom the shield was made, is able to break that spell, even if only temporarily.[6]

Given the character traits of Ajax, it is doubtful that he would have been able to release himself from this spell. Were Ajax to have won the shield, there is little doubt that it would have been borne into battle, and would have become instrumental once more in an unstoppable and irresistible slaughter. There is little doubt that, in the name of piety, Ajax would have been reduced to a mere animal killing machine, a position he barely manages to hover above even without the shield.[7] Unable to break free of the "this is the way it is" of the shield, (the specific content of which in his case is a continuation of the Achillean "all is war"), Ajax would be doomed to an incessant re-creation of the conditions of its veracity.

It is for the better then that Ajax did not win the right to bear the shield. Despite the fact that Odysseus has a more tenuous claim to be the rightful recipient, he does in the end win the shield. After the death of Achilles, and perhaps even more so after Odysseus wins it, to carry the shield is always already a tainted exercise. Achilles exposes the subtle fraud perpetrated by the claim of the shield when he reconciles with Priam. Achilles has demonstrated that to bear the shield is to be a dissimulator, or more bluntly, a liar. Odysseus, renowned for his craftiness, his ruses and deceptions, wins the right to bear the shield. It seems fitting that he, and not the overly transparent Ajax, is given the prize. The shield does indeed go to its most fitting successor. It is not that the formerly simple truth claims made by the shield become inverted in the form of outright lies, rather it is that the language used to express such claims becomes less certain in its grasp on the world. It becomes possible to both deceive and to tell the truth in the same statement. Odysseus, as is to be expected, provides a very clear example of this when he gives his name "Udeis" ("nobody") to the cyclops, Polyphemus. This name that he provides conceals him and permits his escape—"nobody is killing me!"—and yet "Udeis" can also mean "hero."[8] Odysseus thus truthfully reveals and identifies himself as a hero, while at the same time denying his very presence. Odysseus in a single word accomplishes a simultaneous concealment and revelation of himself. This shift is not applicable only to Odysseus, however. It is a global change. We can see this in the most improbable and unlikely place; the character of Ajax.

Sophocles' *Ajax* tells the tale of Ajax after he has lost the bid for Achilles' arms. The play opens with Ajax outraged, in much the same way as Homer's *Iliad* opens with Achilles outraged. He is so slighted that he devises a plan to slaughter the entire upper echelon of the Achaean army, including Agamemnon and Odysseus. His plan is thwarted by the intervention of Athena who tricks him into killing the livestock instead. Having been doubly humiliated, Ajax resolves to kill himself. He says to the chorus,

> But now I am going to the bathing place
> And meadows by the sea, to cleanse my stains,
> In hope the goddess' wrath may pass from me.
> And when I've found a place that's quite deserted,
> I'll dig in the ground, and hide this sword of mine,
> Hatefulest of weapons, out of sight. May Darkness
> And Hades, God of Death, hold it in their safe keeping.[9]

His words are taken by the chorus to mean that the disgraced hero has set aside his thoughts of self-destruction and their fears for his safety are assuaged. Yet at the same time, Ajax has described in detail the means by which he intends to kill himself. [10]

There is a kind of slippage between what is said, what is meant, and what is heard. In Book 9 of *The Iliad*, Achilles says to Odysseus "I hate that man like the very Gates of Death/who says one thing but hides another in his heart" (9:378–9). When Achilles first carries the shield into battle, there is a direct line of communication. There is no mistaking the content of his "this is the way it is" claim. All is war, there is no peaceful life to return to, and you are already dead. However, after Achilles reconciles with Priam, and especially after the death of Achilles, this changes. The "this is the way it is" claim no longer corresponds to what *is* in any transparent or unproblematic way. What is said may or may not reveal what is meant. Neither is there any clear ground upon which to ensure that the audience hears what is said or meant. That is, there is no vantage point from which to discern the difference between what is said and what is "held in [the speaker's] heart." The shield in many ways ceases to be a mirror, although it certainly retains the appearance of one, and becomes recognizable as a tool, a means by which to obtain some other end. This change is confirmed when the shield is given to Odysseus, for who better to wield this tool of deception than the master tactician and dissimulator himself?

Philoctetes

After Odysseus gains possession of the shield, its fate (as an artifact or object) becomes somewhat unclear. He certainly does not arrive home to Ithaca with it. Given that all his spoils of war are lost at sea, one could conclude that the shield was lost at sea. Were this the case it would certainly support the argument that Odysseus's ability to recognize and respond to the constant change in the world around him makes him a suitable bearer of the shield. In other words, Odysseus is well aware that the claim "this is the way it is" is just another bit of flotsam in a vast sea of change.[11] The loss of the shield at sea would also dovetail nicely with the image on the outer rim of the shield. All of the images on the shield are bounded by a depiction of the "great ocean river" (18:708–9). Thus the depiction of the world thereon is revealed as an island of comparative stability against a backdrop of uncertainty and constant change.[12] Its loss at sea is therefore a testament to the fragility and transience of that stability.

Traditionally, however, it is thought that Odysseus passed the shield on to Neoptolemus (a.k.a. Phyrrus), the son of Achilles. Interestingly enough, this also offers evidence that to bear the shield, to make the claim "this is the way it is" is not what it seems to be. Following the story of Sophocles' *Philoctetes*, the Achaean army learns that victory over Troy can only come once both Neoptolemus and the bow of Heracles (then in the hands of Philoctetes) reach the battlefield. Odysseus is charged with the task of bringing them both to Troy. Odysseus had abandoned Philoctetes on the island of Lemnos ten years earlier after he had been bitten in the foot by a serpent. Alone on the island, suffering in pain, Philoctetes had fostered a deep hatred of Odysseus. Having already brought Neoptolemus aboard his ship, Odysseus develops a plan to wrest the bow from Philoctetes by guile. Neoptolemus is to be the operative party in this deception. Odysseus encourages the young man to befriend Philoctetes under the pretense that Neoptolemus too hates Odysseus. There is a telling exchange between the two on this point that is worth quoting at some length:

> Odysseus: I know, young man, it is not your natural bent
> to say such things nor to contrive such mischief.

But the prize of victory is pleasant to win.
Bear up: another time we shall prove honest.
For one brief shameless portion of a day
give me yourself, and then for all the rest
you may be called most scrupulous of men.
Neoptolemus: Son of Laertes, what I dislike to hear
I hate to put into execution.
I have a natural antipathy
to get my ends by tricks and stratagems
So, too, they say, my father was…
I would prefer even to fail with honor
than win by cheating.
Odysseus: You are a good man's son.
I was young, too, once, and then I had a tongue
very inactive and a doing hand.
Now as I go forth to see the test, I see
that everywhere among the race of men
it is the tongue that wins and not the deed.
Neoptolemus: What would you bid me do but to tell lies? . . .
Do you not find it vile yourself, this lying?
Odysseus: Not if the lying brings our rescue with it.
Neoptolemus: How can a man not blush to say such things?
Odysseus: When one does something for gain, one need not blush.[13]

This exchange shows Odysseus instructing Neoptolemus on how to craft a convincing "this is the way it is" claim. Odysseus is teaching him what he must do in order to carry his father's shield. He is telling him how to bear the shield in a figurative sense without falling under the spell of its particularly potent enchantments. Neoptolemus must learn how to bear the shield knowing its claim to be a ruse. He must learn to utilize its so-called "truth" claims to suit his own purposes. In the context of the exchange, and as a first test, Neoptolemus must lie to Philoctetes so that the fighting in Troy can stop. It is important to note that the pretext of this ruse is that Odysseus has refused to hand over the arms of Achilles to Neoptolemus. Yet there is some uncertainty as to whether or not Odysseus has actually handed them over. The position taken here is that Neoptolemus will earn his father's arms, including the shield, once he has proven himself worthy of them by deceiving Philoctetes.

Neoptolemus proceeds to deceive Philoctetes under the tutelage of Odysseus, who tells him that tricking Philoctetes will increase his reputation as "a wise man and a good [man]." The young man gains the trust of the suffering hero by means of a tale of betrayal at the hands of Odysseus and the Atridae, Menelaus and Agamemnon:

> I, his mourning son, wept for him [Achilles];
> then, in a while, came to the two Atridae,
> my friends, as it seemed right to do, and asked them
> for my father's arms and all he had else.
> They needed brazen faces for their answer:
> "Son of Achilles, all that your father had,
> all else, is yours to take, but not his arms.
> Another man now owns them, Laertes' son."[14]

Philoctetes, operating on the principle that "the enemy of my enemy is my friend," aligns himself with Neoptolemus. The hero begs the young man to take him off of the island of Lemnos where he has been stranded, and back to his homeland of Pios. Neoptolemus agrees, and in so doing places himself in an existential quandary, an aporetic juncture from which there is no easy path. Prior to looking more closely at the parameters of this juncture, the conditions under which he enters it should be examined. Specifically, it should be noted that his agreement to transport Philoctetes away from Lemnos comes only after an exhortation from the chorus that he do so.

> [I] would carry him
> in your quick, well-fitted ship
> to his home and so avoid offence before the face of god.[15]

Just as he was motivated to deceive Philoctetes by a promise of glorification by his peers, so too is he motivated to help him by a sense of shame at being out-done by his peers.

> I should be ashamed
> to be less ready than you [the chorus] to render a stranger service.[16]

The irony of these lines is that, given that they are a response to an expressed readiness to offer service, Neoptolemus is already exposed as "less ready than you to render a stranger service." The irony of this moment comes into play again as Neoptolemus' situation works itself through.

The critical moment for Neoptolemus comes when Philoctetes, wracked with pain, goes to sleep while the young man is in possession of the

bow of Heracles. As Philoctetes sleeps, the chorus urges Neoptolemus to
abscond with his prize. As Philoctetes awakens, Neoptolemus says,

> Now is the moment, what shall I do from now on?[17]

The next lines from Neoptolemus detail the parameters of his situation:

> All is disgust when one leaves his own nature
> and does things that misfit it. . .[18]
> I shall be shown to be dishonorable:
> I am afraid of that.[19]

Thus the situation is shown to have existential import. His decision will
have implications for what kind of person he is to be both now and in the
future. He is in a moment that will redefine his very identity. The second
quote shows the paradox to be one of honor. Neoptolemus is honor bound
in two incompatible directions. First, he is bound by the authority of
Odysseus and the princes who sent him. Odysseus, as if aware of the young
man's impending identity crisis, is careful to remind him at the very outset
of the play "it was to serve you came here."[20] From what might be called
the Odyssean perspective, the honorable course of action here would be
to return to Troy with the bow, giving no further thought to the plight
of Philoctetes. This is what leads Neoptolemus to refuse to return the bow
to the suffering hero:

> Justice and interest
> make me obedient to those in authority.[21]

Second, he is bound by his promise to Philoctetes. The honorable course
of action here, on the other hand, is to reject the mission he has been
given; to not go to Troy but instead return Philoctetes to his homeland
as he has promised to do. Philoctetes' exhortations are very pointed:

> Give it [the bow] back. Be your true self again.[22]

And again:

> You are not bad yourself; by bad men's teaching
> you came to practice your foul lesson.[23]

Neoptolemus finds these pleas compelling, and just as he is about to return the bow, Odysseus himself arrives. In the ensuing scene, Neoptolemus recedes to the background as the two rivals for his identity vie with each other. Philoctetes is most forward with his invective and his accusations of hubris:

> Hateful creature,
> what things you can invent! You plead the Gods
> to screen out your actions and make the Gods out liars.[24]

Uncharacteristically—and yet, at the same time, not entirely against his nature—Odysseus does not reply to these accusations.[25]

> If I had the time, I have much I could say to him.
> As it is, there is only one thing. As the occasion
> demands, such a one am I.
> When there is a competition of men just and good,
> you will find none more scrupulous than myself.
> What I seek in everything is to win
> except in your regard: I willingly yield to you now.[26]

Odysseus then takes the bow and leaves. Here again there is a tremendous irony. Odysseus "willingly yields" for more than one reason. First, Odysseus would be hard-pressed to defend himself against Philoctetes' charges. Indeed he has just proven the hero right in simultaneously claiming the capture of Philoctetes to be his own doing—"I and no other"[27]—and entirely at the behest of Zeus—"I am only his servant."[28] Second, Odysseus yields because he knows it is an empty gesture. He has the bow. He is free to leave. Odysseus has already won. Furthermore, if Philoctetes is to cast an accusation of hubris towards Odysseus, he is far from clean of it himself. When asked by the chorus to come to Troy, Philoctetes responds,

> Never, never! That is my fixed purpose.
> Not though the Lord of the Lightning, bearing his fiery bolts,
> come against me, burning me
> with flame and glare.
> Let Ilium go down and all that under its walls
> had the heart to cast me away, crippled![29]

These are words that Philoctetes will choke on as his departure for Troy is occasioned not by the greatest of the gods in all his power, but by a mere ghost of a comparatively minor deity (Heracles). Once Odysseus and Neoptolemus leave Philoctetes, a second and final exchange of views takes place. Neoptolemus is still torn as to his next course of action. Having decided to deceive Philoctetes, he has heard the hero's exhortations as to why he should not continue on that path. Now, in deciding to undo what he has done, he hears the exhortations of Odysseus. Odysseus had promised a double prize to Neoptolemus; an increase in his reputation both as a wise man and as a good man. In this exchange, he takes away both by promising that the hatred and enmity of the Greeks would come down upon Neoptolemus, and by denying the cleverness of his actions.

What Neoptolemus fails to realize is that the change in himself that he seeks to undo is already accomplished, an irredeemable fait accompli. This is implied in a simple question, posed by Odysseus:

> Neoptolemus: I did wrong when I obeyed you and the Greeks.
> Odysseus: What did we make you do that was unworthy?
> Neoptolemus: I practiced craft and treachery with success.
> Odysseus: On whom?[30]

This simple query highlights Neoptolemus' position. With his success in obtaining the bow from Philoctetes, he has proven himself treacherous and an accomplished liar. In returning the bow, he does not erase that treachery, but compounds it, for now he has betrayed the Greeks, too.[31] The best he can do is to deny his own agency in the matter, and thus maintain a sense of himself as honorable—a good man that has been taught by bad men.[32] Yet in doing this he only renders himself treacherous and deceitful *even to himself*. A single deception has been multiplied threefold. Neoptolemus remains a deceiver a liar, and a dissimulator, but unlike Odysseus, not a conscious one. The young man's "transparency" masks his duplicity.

The lesson that Odysseus has to teach is not one that Neoptolemus—whose name translates literally as "new war"—can learn. He becomes like his father prior to the reconciliation with Priam. Indeed it is Neoptolemus who kills Priam before the altar of Apollo, along with "scores" of other Trojan defenders.[33] The extent to which he is enthralled by the claim of the shield is made apparent in Odysseus's retelling of his actions while within the Trojan horse. As the soldiers wait for nightfall inside the hollow belly of the great wooden horse, Helen walks around the outside of it, calling each soldier by name in the voice each of their wives.[34] Where all others are tempted to the breaking point by this call from a peaceful life left behind, Neoptolemus alone does not flinch. Unable to distance himself from the claim of the shield, he is unmoved by a call from a life that does not exist. If all is war, there is no peaceful life to return to, so that call has no import to him whatsoever. Furthermore, even after the conclusion of the war in Troy, Neoptolemus continues in his violent ways. He sacks the temple of Apollo at Delphi when the god refuses to side with him in a dispute. He meets his final end when he is ritually murdered after refusing to allow the priests of Apollo to take the cattle he has slaughtered in offering. In short, having taken up his father's shield, he is unable to put it down again. Since he cannot—or will not—recognize its portrayal of permanent warfare as an effect(ive) tool for the furthering of a specific goal, within a specific context, he becomes locked into the world it creates.[35] He yields his authority to the shield, which then rules him.

Neoptolemus provides an object lesson in what it means to bear the shield after the death of Achilles. He bears the shield, but not in the same way his father did. Unlike Achilles, Neoptolemus takes up the shield, but never puts it down again. In this sense he provides an a lesson in abjection—an *abject* lesson if you will, for he bears the shield at his own peril. He becomes locked into his own illusion, unable to maintain any distance from it. He remains convinced of the correctness and justice of his own claims, to the point of demonstrating an extreme level of hubris. His inflexibility in this regard renders conflict with others unavoidable.[36] Sophocles, in his recounting of the dramatic events surrounding the pass-ing of the shield from father to son can be understood as offering his audience a clear warning about its use. To remain unaware of its operation as deception is deeply and tragically hazardous. Neoptolemus bears the shield both literally and figuratively. He may be the last to bear it literally, but he is far from the last to do so figuratively. Thus the power of the shield, which is from the outset based more in its figurative than its literal operation, remains undiminished long after the disappearance of the physical object.[37] Hence the problem posed by the shield, namely the question as to how one can resist or undo its power, also remains. Sophocles does not stray far from the mythological context within which the shield was introduced, but it should not be assumed that the logic of the shield has an effect only within the bounds of a mythological tale. The playwright offers a warning, but he is far from the only one to do so. An example is to be found in one of his contemporaries, the historian Thucydides.

Thucydides: The Shield in Athenian Hands

Thucydides wrote at a time when Western traditions of thought tended to understand themselves as emerging from the mythological fog of the past onto the solid ground of empirical facts. You can see this in a comparison between the work of Thucydides and Herodotus.[38] The latter often drifts off into the more fanciful realms of quasi-mythology, where the Thucydides explicitly states his intent to stick to the facts. He departs from Sophocles in a number of ways, and yet both can be understood as critically engaging with the logic of the shield. Where Sophocles remains in close proximity to the shield in its mythological origins, Thucydides concerns himself with what might be called a real world example of it in operation. He is very clear about his intentions from the very outset of his historical account of the war between Athens and Sparta:

> On the whole, however, the conclusions I have drawn from the proofs quoted may, I believe, safely be relied on. Assuredly they will not be disturbed either by the verses of a poet displaying the exaggeration of his craft, or by the compositions of the chroniclers that are attractive at truth's expense; the subjects they treat of being out of the reach of evidence, and time having robbed most of them of historical value by enthroning them in the region of legend. Turning from these, we can rest satisfied with having proceeded upon the clearest data, and having arrived at conclusions as exact as can be expected in matters of such antiquity. To come to this war: despite the known disposition of the actors in a struggle to overrate its importance, and when it is over to return to their admiration of earlier events, yet an examination of the facts will show that it was much greater than the wars which preceded it.[39]

From the outset, Thucydides clearly separates himself from both the poets and more "attractive" historians. He sets himself apart from those that have come before him, self-consciously declaring his project to be something quite new. He provides a clear demarcation of his methodology and is therefore a precursory model for contemporary standards of research. Much of his account is given through the retelling of speeches given by the actors directly involved. He is careful to state however, that

> With reference to the speeches in this history, some were delivered before the war began, others while it was going on; some I heard

myself, others I got from various quarters; it was in all cases difficult to carry them word for word in one's memory, so my habit has been to make the speakers say what was in my opinion demanded of them by the various occasions, of course adhering as closely as possible to the general sense of what they really said. And with reference to the narrative of events, far from permitting myself to derive it from the first source that came to hand, I did not even trust my own impressions, but it rests partly on what I saw myself, partly on what others saw for me, the accuracy of the report being always tried by the most severe and detailed tests possible. My conclusions have cost me some labor from the want of coincidence between accounts of the same occurrences by different eye-witnesses, arising sometimes from imperfect memory, sometimes from undue partiality for one side or the other. The absence of romance in my history will, I fear, detract somewhat from its interest; but if it be judged useful by those inquirers who desire an exact knowledge of the past as an aid to the interpretation of the future, which in the course of human things must resemble if it does not reflect it, I shall be content. In fine, I have written my work, not as an essay which is to win the applause of the moment, but as a possession for all time.[40]

It is clear that he is interested in "telling it like it is" rather than how it should be, ought to be or how his audience would like to hear it. It is for just this reason that Thucydides is often cited as a key figure in the canon of realism.[41]

Given the fact that one of the central tenets of realism as an approach to understanding the political world is its insistence on "telling it like it really is," Thucydides can get us much closer to showing just how the mythological Shield of Achilles can be of relevance when attempting to explain "the way things really are." That is, he can ease the transition from myth to reality. Irving Kristol, the self-avowed "Godfather of Neoconservativism" has said, "the favorite neoconservative text on foreign affairs, thanks to professors Leo Strauss of Chicago and Donald Kagan of Yale, is Thucydides on the Peloponnesian War."[42] If it can be demonstrated that the shield is a concern to one of the fathers of "realism," whose observations have had a clear influence on contemporary (neoconservative) policy, then the transition from understanding the shield as purely mythological to an item of practical import can be furthered.

It has already been indicated that the shield is a container capable of carrying a multitude of different messages. Thucydides appears to be addressing a particular form of that message. In a variety of places in his text he speaks of an attitude of the Athenians that seems to be particularly prominent at the time. This attitude can be summed up in a variety of ways, and is voiced in a variety of ways within his text. It is directly addressed multiple times in the history and can be understood as an example of the logic of the Shield of Achilles. The Athenians have undergone a period of time in which their political prestige has been massively inflated. This is due to their success against the encroachments of the Persian empire, particularly in the battles of Marathon, Salamis and Palataea. Having driven back the Persians, the Athenians have come to be a focal point for all of the surrounding Greek city-states who are themselves threatened by the enormous empire to their east. As a measure of self-protection, they turn to Athens. This is the origin of the Athenian empire. As might be expected, Athens comes to regard itself very highly in these circumstances. It is this high regard for itself that concerns not only the Spartans and a variety of other Greek states allied with them, but Thucydides himself.

In his recounting of the opening days of the war between Sparta and Athens, Thucydides speaks of a congress of the Peloponnesian League in which Sparta debates as to whether or not to embark on a preemptive war with the expanding Athenian empire. In the debates, a number of speeches, notably that of the Corinthians, had stirred the doubts and fears of the Spartans. It is at this point that a delegation of Athenian merchants speaks to the assembly. A member of the delegation says,

> [It] was not a very remarkable action, or contrary to the common practice of mankind, if we did accept an empire that was offered to us, and refused to give it up under the pressure of three of the strongest motives, fear, honor and interest. And it was not we who set the example, for it has always been law that the weaker should be subject to the stronger. Besides, we believed ourselves to be worthy of our position, and so you thought us till now, when calculations of interest have made you take up the cry of justice—a consideration which no one ever yet brought forward to hinder his ambition when he had a chance of gaining anything by might. And praise is due to all who, if not so superior to human nature as to refuse dominion, yet respects justice more than their position compels them to do.[43]

The fears of the Spartans are indeed well founded. It is also obvious that the Athenians have come to be metaphorical bearers of the Shield of Achilles. The Athenians do not put forward the same message as does

Achilles when he bears the shield, but the underlying structure remains the same. They make a "this is the way it is" claim in no uncertain terms. What is more, the Athenian claim comes complete with a cloak of divinity. This is not always an overt declaration of godliness, but can be seen in their insistence that "it was not we who set the example." This allows the Athenians to deny their own responsibility for things being the way they are, just as Achilles can pass off responsibility for the message that "all is war" to the gods.

The funeral oration delivered by Pericles at the end of the first year of the war provides yet another example of the kind of thinking that was predominant in Athens at the time. This speech, given by a man "of approved wisdom and eminent reputation," [44] can be fairly read as expressing a message that should not be taken as outside of the realm of the commonly understood. Pericles is not saying anything that will shock or surprise his audience. He is not making any radical pronouncements. What he does do is to paint a picture of a city that is greater than the legacy of its ancestry, that is greater than any of its enemies in its conduct and institutions, that is "greater than her reputation."[45] There is an unmistakable air of hubris about his words. He is not presenting a portrait to be challenged and debated. Pericles simply reflects back to the city that which they already think about themselves. He makes a point of contrasting his description of Athens as what amounts to the pinnacle of human goodness with the eulogies of Homer, "whose verses might charm for the moment only for the impression which they gave to melt at the touch of fact."[46] Yet again, there is evidence here of the logic of the shield at work. Athens is the best city, and its people the best people. To live best, one must live as an Athenian. This observation is furthermore stated as an observation of fact, and not poetic fancy. It is not to be challenged as there is no room for doing so. It can only be challenged by those who are already beyond redemption, and the challenge itself is indication enough of that.

The attitude of the Athenians is not a momentary thing. It was present prior to the outbreak of hostilities with Sparta, and indeed was instrumental in the outbreak of war. It is very much present after the first year of war, as evidenced in Pericles' funeral oration. Furthermore, it is an attitude that persists long after this as well. Thucydides offers a number of examples of its longevity, but none so pointed as when he recounts the events at Melos in the 16th year of the war. The exchange between the Athenian generals and the representatives of Melos is one of the most famous and oft-cited passages in his entire work. Once again, Thucydides highlights the same domineering mentality that seems to define the Athenians throughout his history. The details of this exchange are well known, and need not be recounted here, but certain salient points should be noted. First, it is quite obvious that this is a definite example of the logic of the shield at work. The Athenians are self-certain in their position and do not allow for any interpretation of events other than their own:

> We shall not trouble you with specious pretenses—either of how we have a right to our empire because we overthrew the Mede [Persians], or are now attacking you because of wrong that you have done us—and make a long speech that would not be believed; and in return we hope that you, instead of thinking to influence us by saying that you did not join the Spartans, although their colonists, or that you have done us no wrong, will aim at what is feasible, holding in view the real sentiments of us both; since you know as well as we do that right, as the world goes, is only in question between equals in power, while the strong do what they can while the weak suffer what they must.[47]

It is by no means difficult to identify the double claim of the shield in this (in)famous statement. However, it remains to be seen whether or not Thucydides is presenting each of these examples of the shield at work in the hands of the Athenians as simple fact, as a straightforward telling of things "as they really are," (and hence guilty of replicating its logic yet again) or if he is up to something else. It is tempting to say that Thucydides, through his association with traditional realism, is himself a bearer of the Shield of Achilles. However it is equally valid to say that he is critical of its operation. His criticism of the shield, much like that offered by Sophocles, takes the form of a warning.

It is important to note that most often the critique offered by Thucydides is quite subtle. To quote Francis Cornford, "much as a set of volcanic islands might heave themselves out of the sea, at such angles and distances that only to the eye of a bird, and not to the sailor cruising among them, would they appear as the summits," so too is the critique Thuydides offers easily overlooked by a pedestrian examination of his work.[48] Every writer must, in the process of writing, make editorial choices regarding what to include and what to exclude from a finished manuscript. The critical commentary offered by Thucydides appears in these editorial choices. It is useful to look not only at the events he describes, but also at the context within which they are described. It can be helpful to look not only at what he says, but also at the order in which he says it.

For every example of what has been identified as shield logic in Thucydides' account, there is a corresponding event that provides a larger context and commentary. This commentary works to undo much of the apparent message of the logic of the shield and the hubris associated with bearing it. For example, Pericles' funeral oration, with its unbounded praise for the indomitability of the Athenian spirit, is immediately followed by an outbreak of the plague. This "pestilence of such extent and mortality [as] was nowhere remembered" claimed as some of its first victims the physicians of Athens.[49] Not only that, but its severity exposed the limits both of "human art" and "supplications in the temples, divinations and so forth."[50] Thucydides makes a point of describing the physical effects of the illness that are remarkable in that they almost directly undo the exact characteristics Pericles extols in his funeral oration. These include a "fatal weakness" and "an entire loss of memory" so that its victims "did not know either themselves or their friends."[51] The ravages of the plague leave Athens in a generalized state of lawlessness, dishonor and godlessness. Among the victims of the plague was Pericles himself. It is as if by juxtaposing these two events, Thucydides is offering an account not only of the bearing of the shield, but the consequences thereof. And this is far from an isolated occurrence.

In the case of the speech of the Athenian delegation to the Spartans at the outset of the conflict, it is the words of the Athenians that prove to be the final and deciding factor in the decision by the Spartans to go to war. And this is a decision that in the end proves fatal for the Athenian empire. Yet another example of this contextualization of events is to be found in the pairing of the Melian dialogue with the disastrous Sicilian campaign. Sicily is the rock upon which the wave of Athenian power breaks and subsides. Again and again, Thucydides notes examples of the logic of the shield and the costs of employing it. In effect he is letting his readers know that while it is both possible and even easy to make shield type claims, it is always hazardous to do so. Perhaps this is what he is getting at when he declares his work to be "a possession for all time." To understand his work in this way is also to disturb his placement within the confines of traditional understandings of political realism. However, his placement there can be considered suspect from the very outset.

One of the notable features of the operation of the shield is that it works to conceal its fictiveness behind a screen of "objectivity." When Achilles carried the shield, its apparent claim that the peaceful world did not exist was, for all intents and purposes, make-believe, and yet presented itself as indisputable fact. Something similar is to be found in Thucydides' history.

There is a difference in that he is more concerned with offering a critique of the logic of the shield than in perpetuating it, but the precautionary steps he takes in that regard are often overlooked. In his introduction, Thucydides lays out his methodology and in doing so he makes a very troublesome admission for those who would think him to be a straightforward "realist." He says of the speeches he recounts,

> it was in all cases difficult to carry them word for word in one's memory, so my habit has been to make the speakers say what was in my opinion demanded of them by the various occasions, of course adhering as closely as possible to the general sense of what they really said.[52]

When it comes to the speeches, Thucydides provides his readers not with what the speakers actually did say, but with an account of what Thucydides thought they should have said given the circumstances. In other words, he made them up. In this admission, the careful reader is reminded that the very project of "telling it like it is" is suspect. There is always more than meets the eye.

Machiavelli: The Prince as Shield Bearer

The argument thus far has moved from myth to the more tangible realm of historical reality while holding the operation of the shield as a constant. If the shield moves out from the realm of mythology in the quiet criticisms put forward by Thucydides, Machiavelli places its operation squarely at the centre of practical political concerns. Machiavelli, like Thucydides before him, is writing in the midst of political upheaval. Italy in his time was a political hotbed. It was a checkerboard of small states, generally centered on larger cities such as Genoa, Milan, Venice, Florence and of course Rome. Rome was the seat of the Pope, who wielded direct political power over a sizeable chunk of the Italian peninsula, not to mention his almost immeasurable political clout across the entirety of Christendom. To the north was the kingdom of France, which would on occasion venture down into the Italian peninsula to claim new territory for itself before going back again. To the west was Spain, an absolute powerhouse with supreme naval hegemony. The Italian states themselves were constantly full of the political machinations of rival families, each with their own (usually mercenary) armies. It was the age of intrigue, conspiracy, and assassination. Families such as the Borgias and the Medicis were constantly jockeying for power and establishing new Cardinalships within the church in the hopes that "their man" would be elected Pope.

Machiavelli was a Florentine who spent much of his adult life in public service. Prior to 1512, Florence was a republic under the direction of Piero Soderini. Machiavelli was in his service and in charge of the city's militia.[53] However, in 1512 the Florentine militia was resoundingly defeated by a group of Spanish mercenaries, leading to the utter collapse of the republic. After the fall of the Florentine republic, Machiavelli was put on trial for his part in the debacle and tortured before being quietly exiled to the countryside. While he was in this semi-exile, he composed *The Prince* as a means of currying favor with the new ruler of Florence. [54]

Even though *The Prince* is a tiny book, it has earned its author an enormous reputation, and not necessarily a good one. He has been widely vilified as an immoralist, and atheist, even as evil incarnate.[55] One of the most (in)famous maxims attributed to Machiavelli is "the ends justify the means." The general meaning is taken to be that so long as you get the outcome you are after, anything goes. There is of course the issue that Machiavelli does not actually say this. What he does say is that,

> In the actions of all men, and especially of princes who are not subject to a court of appeal, we must always look to the end. Let a prince, therefore, win victories and uphold his state; his methods will always be considered worthy, and everyone will praise them, because the masses are always impressed by the superficial appearance of things, and by the outcome of an enterprise.[56]

This quote has considerably more qualifiers built into it than its far more universal (mis)interpretation as "the ends justify the means."[57] It also bears a strong family resemblance to the admonitions Odysseus gives to Neoptolemus in the *Philoctetes*. Odysseus was concerned with instructing Neoptolemus in the proper way to use the shield, namely as a tool for the furthering of some other end. He cautions the young man that to bear the shield is to be a dissimulator. One cannot be both a bearer of the shield and transparent at the same time. To attempt to do so is to fall under the enchantments of the shield itself. It is to forget that its message is but a ruse to facilitate the attainment of some other goal. Machiavelli hopes to instruct the new prince in exactly this same lesson.

There is no question that fear plays an enormous role in *The Prince*. Machiavelli talks almost incessantly about it. He talks about the fears of the prince, the fears of his subjects, the fears of his internal enemies, and the fears of his neighboring princes. He has an entire chapter entitled "On Cruelty & Clemency: Whether it is Better to be Loved or Feared." He is very clear in his treatment of it as one of the primary motivators of human action. His concern with the logic of the shield is also evident, although not always in the most obvious of ways. Amidst the imbroglio of politics on the Italian peninsula, Machiavelli treats the question of the emergence and stabilization of a(ny) particular city-state against the backdrop of the universal aspirations of the Catholic Church. Although he does not use the term at all, he can be understood as seeing in the universalist language of the church a clear example of the bearing of the shield. He addresses this in a very interesting manner.

Turning to Chapter XI, "Of Ecclesiastical States," we can get a better idea of what he is doing. This chapter can be read as having a tremendous sense of irony about it. He opens by saying that ecclesiastical states "present their worst difficulties before one takes possession of them" and that "they are gained either by *virtu* or fortune."[58] He then says that "they are sustained by the ancient principles of religion, which are so powerful and of such authority that they keep their princes in power whatever they do, however they live."[59] These "ancient principles of religion" are exemplary of the logic of the shield. This can be seen in Machiavelli's own admission regarding such states that "instituted as they are by God, and sustained by him, it would be a rash and imprudent man who ventured to discuss them."[60] He is giving a nod to the implied dual claim of religious authority, which is the dual claim of the shield. Machiavelli recognizes that the divine authority of the ecclesiastical state is directly comparable to the shield's claim that to question its "this is the way it is" claim is to challenge the authority of the gods, thereby rendering such questioning entirely *verboten*.

To point out the fact that the church makes use of the all or nothing logic of the shield is not overly surprising. What is unusual is that having just said that it is a rash and imprudent man who ventures to discuss such states, Machiavelli goes on to do just that. What stands out most in the discussion that follows is that Machiavelli does not treat the ecclesiastical prince as someone actually chosen by God to lead, but as just another politician. Furthermore, he does not do this in just this short chapter. He discusses the rise of Cardinals and Popes as examples of effective politicking over and over again. Similarly, he discusses the declining fortunes of such figures as exemplary of the hazards of political inefficiency. It should be noted that such examples do not sit well with his claim that those who claim religious authority can govern however they please, for better or worse. The net effect is that these ecclesiastical figures cease to be untouchable and unquestionable representatives of God and become instead savvy political actors who have special access to a particular and particularly powerful kind of political defense. He is in short reframing the discussion. By treating the ecclesiastical prince in this way he is sidestepping the power of the shield as it is borne by the Church. He is recognizing it as one tool among many, even if it happens to be an incredibly potent one.

Given the obvious power of the Church, Machiavelli is not at all hesitant to point out the efficacy of its methods of political control and influence. If the Church bears the Shield of Achilles, and if it has proven to be a successful tool, then it makes no sense from Machiavelli's perspective to discard it. Where Sophocles and Thucydides warn us, Machiavelli seeks to educate us on how to be better bearers of the shield. He would be remiss if he did not acknowledge the hazards of bearing the shield, but he would be equally remiss if he did not recognize it as an important component of every good politician's toolbox.

Machiavelli sees the value of the shield as an instrument of politics, but he puts rather strict qualifications on its usage. In example after example he demonstrates to the new prince that *virtú* resides in the ability to both make this kind of apparently unchallengeable claim and to back off from it as the need arises. R. B. J. Walker makes note of this in his essay "The Prince and 'the Pauper'."[61] Walker comments that Machiavelli is far more context sensitive than his placement in the realist tradition might suggest.[62] In that chapter the fortress itself can be understood as metaphorically standing in for the logic of the shield; the unassailability of the one reflected in that of the other. Machiavelli is happy to point out the benefits of the fortress when utilized in the proper circumstances, but he is also quick to condemn those who use them in all cases thinking they will inherently work to further his or her safety.

> All things considered, then, I may approve of those who build fortresses or those who do not, depending on the circumstances; but it is a foolish man who, because he puts trust in fortresses, thinks he need not worry about the enmity of his people.[63]

His examples tend to problematize the simple distinctions between good and bad behavior, between right and wrong conduct, between true and false statements and impressions. This is particularly clear in his praise for Cesare Borgia. In one particular instance, Machiavelli recounts the tale of

Messer Remirro de Orco, who was put in charge of the newly acquired state of Romagnia by Borgia and set with the task of reigning in the lawlessness that held sway there. De Orco did manage through the application of excessive force and fear to get the population back into line, but became the object of a generalized hatred in the process. Of course the fact that he was now the primary locus of the hatred of the population meant that Borgia himself no longer filled that role. De Orco's message of "get in line or die," which is of course an example of the shield at work, is countered or rather outdone by Borgia's next actions. Noting that the kind of excesses of authority displayed by de Orco were bound to weigh heavily on the population, Borgia had de Orco arrested and executed. His severed corpse was left on public display in the town square. The message not to be missed was that it was not the word of de Orco that mattered, but that of Borgia. In a single act of undeniable cruelty Borgia vaulted himself into the position of protector of the people and established himself as a truly formidable foe. Borgia was now the indisputable master, and this was not to be questioned under penalty of death. This threat need not be legislated as it could be presumed to be literal. There is yet another example of the logic of the shield at work here. The claim "this is the way the it is" carries the content "Borgia is the protector of the people and not to be challenged as the leader." The corresponding "nothing (else) to be done about it" is backed by the presumed and actual threat of death.

Borgia's action is clearly not for the sheer aggrandizement of the prince. Nor is it cruelty for its own sake.

> Cruelty can be described as well used (if it is permissible to say good words about something evil in itself) when it is performed all at once, for reasons of self-preservation; and when the acts are not repeated after that, but rather are turned as much as possible to the advantage of the subjects. Cruelty is badly used, when it is infrequent at first, but increases with time instead of diminishing.[64]

One of the primary limits placed on the use of the shield by Machiavelli is that it must always be carried so as to benefit the population as a whole. It is the stability of the state that must be bolstered and not the aggrandizement of the prince. The statement "the end justifies the means" carries with it the implication that so long as a prince is successful in his endeavors, be they aimed at the public good or at the enlargement of his own reputation, then his methods are justified. Yet the much more nuanced claim that

Machiavelli makes differs rather significantly from this. The justification of a prince's action is not determined by reference to the success or failure of his endeavors, but by the benchmark of the stable state. To bear the shield is permissible, but only in so far as doing so furthers the goal of attaining and maintaining a stable state. Furthermore, to bear the shield is always an extremely hazardous exercise as the bearer must somehow navigate a course between the Scylla of over-confidence and the Charybdis of becoming hated by his people.

> It is good to appear merciful, truthful, humane, sincere, and religious; it is good to be so in reality. But you must keep your mind so disposed that, in case of need, you can turn to the exact contrary.[65] (48)

Compare these lines to those spoken by Odysseus in the *Philoctetes*:

> As the occasion
> demands, such a one am I.
> When there is a competition of men just and good,
> you will find none more scrupulous than myself. [66]

Machiavelli draws the attention of his audience to the distinction between appearance and reality. He is concerned with the power of the image. He is intent on the power of the image, not to disrupt it but to better make use of it. Machiavelli recognizes just how potent the image can be in the mobilization of political behavior, and he hopes to harness it for the benefit of the state. He wants to expose its power to the prince, but importantly, not to his subjects. To educate the prince in the operation and effect of the image is central if the prince is to make use of this most potent of tools. However to expose those workings to the general public is to render those images less potent and the prince's job more difficult. It is this point that may prove of use in the present inquiry into the logic of the shield and how to overcome it.

Notes

[1] I am adopting the standard interpretation that these lines are spoken to Ajax and Odysseus. For a different interpretation, see Gregory Nagy, *Homeric Questions* (Austin, TX: University of Texas Press, 1996). Nagy argues that of the three intermediaries sent to him by Agamemnon, namely Ajax, Odysseus and Phoenix, Achilles pointedly excludes Odysseus in this greeting.

[2] See David Greene et al., eds *Sophocles 2 / Four Tragedies, The Complete Greek Tragedies* (Chicago, IL: University of Chicago Press, 1957).

[3] Especially if taken literally, based on the etymology of the term being traceable back to Mercury, the Roman counterpart of Hermes. Hermes is of course renowned as a trickster, and Odyssesus, can name him as an ancestor. This is mentioned by Plato in the *Republic*. See also Robert Graves, *The Greek Myths* (New York: George Brazillier, Inc, 1955).

[4] Graham Zanker, *The Heart of Achilles: Characterization and Personal Ethics in The Iliad* (Ann Arbour, MI: The University of Michigan Press, 1997).

[5] This is not to say that his prowess with a variety of weapons, is not a central aspect of Odysseus' character. Weapons (the spear, the discus, and especially the bow), remain important for him. One can imagine the limited success he would have had in overcoming the suitors with words alone.

[6] I describe this overcoming of himself as super-human as it requires a remaking of himself. It is at the same time super-divine as this self-remaking (*autopoiesis*) is beyond what even the gods can do.

[7] The pun here is not entirely unintentional, as after losing the shield he does become an animal killing machine. See Sophocles, "Ajax," in *Sophocles 2*, ed. David Greene, and Richard Lattimore (Chicago, IL: University of Chicago Press, 1957).

[8] Max Horkheimer, and Theodor Adorno, *Dialectic of Enlightenment*, Cultural Memory in the Present (Stanford: Stanford University Press, 2002), 47.

[9] Sophocles, "Philoctetes," in *Sophocles 2*, ed. by David Greene, and Richard Lattimore (Chicago, IL: University of Chicago Press, 1957), 665–60.

[10] He does find a hidden spot where he buries the hilt of his sword in the ground before falling on its blade.

[11] Not that this renders it any less useful. More than once Odysseus saves himself by grasping onto a bit of flotsam. For example, when Charybdis sucks down his raft, Odysseus manages to grasp the overhanging branches of a fig tree:

> I hung there, staunch in my hope that when she spewed again, she'd throw up keel and mast. And to my joy they finally appeared. Homer, *The Odyssey*, trans. Robert Fagles (New York: Penguin Books, 1996), 12.571–3.

[12] The relative stability of this "island" must be stressed given how strikingly dynamic Homer's depictions are. The world he describes on the shield is in constant flux and is not stable at all, except when compared to the utterly unpredictable character of the great Ocean River that surrounds it.

[13] Sophocles, "Philoctetes," l.79–111.

[14] Ibid., l.360–68.

[15] Ibid., l.512.

[16] Ibid., l.524. Emphasis added.

[17] Ibid., l.894.

18 Ibid., l.902.
19 Ibid., l.904.
20 Ibid., l.7.
21 Ibid., l.925.
22 Ibid., l.950.
23 Ibid., l.971.
24 Ibid., l.991.
25 It is simultaneously uncharacteristic that Odysseus would back down from a challenge, and yet true to form in that his non-response (which typically for him takes the form of a pointed response) is in line with his awareness that any further confrontation with Philoctetes will not further his goal of obtaining the bow of Heracles, which he has already obtained.
26 Ibid., l.1048–52.
27 Ibid., l.980.
28 Ibid., l.990. This simultaneous acceptance and denial of responsibility is also evident in the opening lines of the play when Odysseus explains the abandonment of Philoctetes to Neoptolemus. There, Odysseus says,

> I had orders for what I did:
> My masters, the princes, bade me do it. (l.7)

The same is also the case when, in *The Odyssey*, he meets the ghost of Ajax. Odysseus says to the fallen hero:

> For your death we grieved as we did for Achilles' death—
> we grieved incessantly, true, and none's to blame
> but Zeus, who hated Achaea's fighting spearmen
> so intensely, Zeus sealed your doom. (11:637–40)

29 Ibid., l.1196–201.
30 Ibid., 1226–9. Emphasis added.
31 Curiously, a contemporary example of this kind of compounding of error can be found in the character of Uppam in Steven Spielberg's *Saving Private Ryan*. By the conclusion of the climactic battle, Uppam has demonstrated himself to be a coward. When he shoots the German prisoner he had befriended earlier in the film, he does not redeem his cowardice, but exposes himself as a murderer as well. His utter decline of character comes in the very next moment when he unilaterally releases the remaining prisoners, exactly as the man he has just murdered was released earlier in the film (only to return to the battlefield as the agent of death for Captain Miller, the film's major protagonist). Stephen Spielberg, *Saving Private Ryan* (1998).
32 Neoptolemus' decision to take this course of action would lead him to place all of his decisions in the hands of the gods, and as such may go a long way in explaining the need for the deus ex machina at the conclusion of Sophohcles' play.

[33] Many of his deeds are recounted when Odysseus meets Achilles in the kingdom of the dead. See Homer, *The Odyssey*, 11:576–606.

[34] Ibid., 4:307–23.

[35] The neologism "effect(ive)" is employed here to highlight the fact that the shield operates through the generation of an effect—a convincing image—that in turn is efficacious in the furthering of the agenda of its bearer.

[36] This is not to say that the conflicts themselves are unavoidable, and even less to say that conflict in general is unavoidable. It may be that there is an irreducible possibility of conflict, but this does not mean that it is inevitable.

[37] Assuming, for the sake of argument that there ever was a physical object. Indeed the figural power of the shield is brought into further relief when one considers that it only ever existed in a notional sense, as a bit of textual fiction.

[38] See Robert B. Strassler, ed. *The Landmark Thucydides: A Comprehensive Guide to the Peloponnesian War* (New York: The Free Press, 1996); *Herodotus, Histories, Cambridge Greek and Latin Classics* (Cambridge: Cambridge University Press, 2002).

[39] Robert B. Strassler, *The Landmark Thucydides: A Comprehensive Guide to the Peloponnesian War*, 1.21. Given the preponderance of available translations, references to Thucydides will be to book and paragraph rather than page number. Strasslers' edition is most useful on this account.

[40] Ibid., 1.22.

[41] To be most precise, it is not the whole of Thucydides' text that is drawn upon. Most often it is Pericles' funeral oration and the Melian dialogue that garner the lion's share of the attention. Although officially beginning with the writings of E. H. Carr, the list of authors cited as the fathers or progenitors of realism usually includes, (inter alia), Clausewitz, Hobbes and Machiavelli. See Edward Hallett Carr, *The Twenty Years' Crisis, 1919–1939; an Introduction to the Study of International Relations*, 2nd ed., Harper Torchbooks. Academy Library (New York: Harper & Row, 1964); Carl Von Clausewitz, *On War* (IAP, 2008); Thomas Hobbes, *Leviathan* (Cambridge: Cambridge University Press, 1996); Niccolo Machiavelli, *The Prince*, trans. Luigi Ricci, Signet Classic (New York: Oxford University Press, 1999).

[42] Irving Kristol, "The Neoconservative Persuasion," *The Weekly Standard* 8, no. 47 (2003).

[43] Robert B. Strassler, *The Landmark Thucydides: A Comprehensive Guide to the Peloponnesian War*, 1.76. Emphasis added.

[44] Ibid., 2.34.

[45] Ibid., 2.41.

[46] Ibid., 2.41.

[47] Ibid., 5.89.

[48] Francis MacDonald Cornford, *Thucydides Mythistoricus* (London: E. Arnold, 1907), vii.

[49] Robert B. Strassler, *The Landmark Thucydides: A Comprehensive Guide to the Peloponnesian War*, 2.47.

50 Ibid., 2.47.

51 Ibid., 2.49.

52 Ibid., 1.22.

53 Much of his thought on the mater of civilian armies can be found in his work *The Art of War*, but it can also be found in his attitude towards mercenary armies in *The Prince*. See Niccolò Machiavelli, *Art of War* (Chicago, IL: University of Chicago Press, 2003).

54 It was originally composed for Guiliano de Medici, the third son of "Lorenzo the Magnificent," and rededicated to his son Lorenzo once Guiliano died. Machiavelli had hoped to find in the Medicis the same spirit as Lorenzo the Magnificent had shown. He hoped (in vain) that they might prove to be the leader needed to unite Italy into a single, stable state that was far better equipped to deal with the incursions from the similarly unified powers to the north and west.

55 The sort of duplicitous politicking he seems to advocate has drawn considerable attention from a range of historical figures, not limited to political thinkers. For example, the character of Iago in Shakespeare's *Othello* is the playwright's response to Machiavelli. In England, his disrepute has gone so far that one of the common appellations for the devil is "Old Nick" in direct reference to Nicolo Machiavelli.

56 Niccolò Machiavelli and Robert Martin Adams, *The Prince: A Revised Translation, Backgrounds, Interpretations, Marginalia*, 2nd ed. (New York: Norton, 1992), 49.

57 It is quite clear that Machiavelli establishes the stability of the state as the benchmark by which to judge the performance of the Prince. He remains adamant about this throughout the book.

58 Ibid., 31.

59 Ibid., 31–2.

60 Ibid., 32.

61 R. B. J. Walker, "The Prince and 'the Pauper': Tradition, Modernity, and Practice in the Theory of International Relations," in *International/Intertextual Relations: Postmodern Readings of World Politics*, ed. James Der Derian, and Michael J. Shapiro (New York: Lexington Books, 1989).

62 He is in other words more akin to the character of Odysseus than that of Ajax.

63 Niccolò Machiavelli and Robert Martin Adams, *The Prince: A Revised Translation, Backgrounds, Interpretations, Marginalia*, 60.

64 Ibid., 27.

65 Ibid., 48.

66 Sophocles, "Philoctetes," l.1050–2.

4

Mimesis as Resistance

The Shield of Achilles is a powerful physical instrument of war. And yet as powerful as it is, it is far more powerful in its figurative operation. The shield makes a dual claim, "this is the way it is" and "there is nothing (else) to be done." The bearing of the shield can be understood as a shorthand reference to any position making such a claim. The shield is in this way a container. Achilles filled that container with the message "all is war," as did his son Neoptolemus. It is important to note that this is not the only message the shield can put forward. It is capable of holding many and various contents.[1] The variety of possible contents does not alter the structural features or operation of the shield. Whatever its particular message, it remains a weapon of war, underpinned by violence. As such, the bearing of the shield can have deadly effects. A range of warnings on this point has already been demonstrated, but warnings can only go so far. They can alert us to dangers ahead, but is there some other response to the logic embodied in the shield? Can it be resisted? Given that the shield makes an apparently unimpeachable claim "this is the way it is," the simplest line of resistance to it would be the counterclaim "no it is not." From this point, the corresponding ethos, "nothing to be done" can potentially be called into question. But just how is one to gainsay the "this is the way it is" claim? What is more, is anything achieved by such a gainsaying?

This chapter will look at one particular avenue through which resistance has been sought. Specifically, the focus will be on the concept of mimesis as a critical tool and a countermeasure to the advancement of the shield. Mimesis, generally defined as representation or imitation, is a vast topic and has occupied the thought of many of the brightest minds in the Western intellectual tradition. A detailed examination of this tradition would, and does, take up volumes.[2] Such an examination is well beyond the scope of the present project. This chapter will therefore restrict its scope to a discussion of mimesis as it is developed by Plato in the *Republic*.

Having begun the present argument with Homer, Plato's *Republic* is an obvious choice for closer examination, as that is where he addresses the poet directly. Plato's concept of the Forms establishes a solid ontological background against which images—including those that comprise the "this is the way it is" of the shield—can be seen *as images*. As such they are simultaneously like and unlike that which they purport to represent. This chapter will not only look at how that promise of critical distance is extended, but whether or not it is a promise that he can keep.

Shields and Rings: Plato against the Poets

Figuratively speaking, the ill effects of the shield are of great concern to Plato, who sees Homer himself as a bearer of it. It is far from a controversial statement to say that Homer played a profoundly important role in ancient Greek culture. The ancients looked to the texts as the core of their educational systems,[3] and the Homeric heroes provided role models for the citizenry. His work provided a central worldview against which the actions of moral agents could be judged.

Athenian politics in Plato's time was defined in terms of public debate and the course of action taken by the *polis* was determined by these debates. In the broadest of strokes these topics of debate included the goals of the state and the means by which to best achieve those goals. The importance of these issues and the manner in which they were determined helps to explain the prominence of the art of public speaking, and of its teachers, the sophists. The sophist made his living by fees earned through educating the young men of Athens in the art of public speaking. The emphasis of these instructors, (at least as portrayed by Plato), was on the use of various rhetorical devices to evoke the passions and sympathies of an audience. The object was to win the argument, thereby affecting the policies adopted by the *polis*, hence the character and condition of the *polis* itself. As such the effectiveness of a sophist was best measured by the actions resulting from his speech. In an exchange with Adeimantus, Plato has Socrates say,

Do you too believe, as the masses do, that some young people are corrupted by sophists—that there are sophists, private individuals, who corrupt them to a significant extent? Isn't it, rather, the very people who say this who are the greatest sophists of all, who educate most effectively and produce young and old men and women of just the sort they want?

Adeimantus: When do they do that?

Socrates: When many of them sit together in assemblies, courts, theaters, army camps, or any other gathering of a mass of people in public, and with a loud uproar, object excessively to some of the things that are said or done, then approve excessively of others, shouting and clapping; when, in addition to these people themselves, the rocks and the surrounding space itself echo and redouble the uproar of their praise or blame. In a situation like that, how do you think—as the saying goes—a young man's heart is affected? How will whatever sort of private education he has received hold up for him, and not get swept away by such praise and blame, and go be carried off by the flood wherever it goes, so that he will call the same things beautiful or ugly as these people, practice what they practice, and become like them?

Adeimantus: The compulsion to do so will be enormous, Socrates.

Socrates: And yet we have not mentioned the greatest compulsion of all.

Adeimantus: What is that?

Socrates: It is what these educators and sophists impose by their actions if their words fail to persuade. Or don't you know that they punish anyone who is not persuaded, with disenfranchisement, fines, or death?[4]

Here then is Plato's understanding of what it means for Homer to bear the shield, for it is Homer who "seems to be the first teacher and leader of all these fine tragedians."[5] It is Homer who teaches the many what is to be considered good and bad, right and wrong. Homer's "this is the way it is," as Plato sees it, differs in content from that of Achilles' "all is war," being more akin to "everywhere among the race of men, it is the tongue that wins and not the deed."[6] The extended quote above also shows that Homer, as the first among the sophists according to Plato, makes a compelling "nothing to be done about it" claim. To resist is to be silenced. Recalcitrance is death. And it is not hard to see that Socrates himself was one of "the recalcitrant."

The death of Socrates gives rise to a problem. In one sense, his death is clearly a case of justice having been served. Socrates' case was heard before the *demos* and a judgment was made according to the applicable institutional standards and rules. And yet at the same time his death is clearly a travesty of justice. How is it that a just decision can be so utterly unjust? The question of justice motivates the *Republic*, and a possible resolution to this problem can be extrapolated from the arguments found there. This possible resolution is to be found in Plato's insistence on a distinction between justice and the appearance of justice. In order for Plato's argument to work, he requires a firm distinction between truth and its image. The concept of mimesis allows him to make this distinction.

According to Plato, the images, charms and enchantments of poetry are Siren-like, simultaneously profoundly alluring and profoundly dangerous. The poets and the sophists claim to have knowledge without having it at all. The power they wield is the power to foster and even impose ignorance while claiming to dispel it.[7] In short, Plato sees the poets as wielding the power of the shield, and as sharing in the hubris of doing so.[8] This power is disrupted by the distinction between the representation or image and the real, between dreaming and waking. Plato hopes to show that the power of the image is not derived from the image itself, but from the willingness on the part of the audience to grant it veracity, to accept it as real. He hopes to show that to rescind this acceptance is to short-circuit the power of the image and thus to escape the power of the shield.

Plato does not speak of the shield directly, but he does speak of the ring of Gyges, which functions in a strikingly similar way. The ring of Gyges, first mentioned by Glaucon in Book II of the *Republic*, allows its bearer to become invisible. Protected by this invisibility, the wearer of the ring is free to act with impunity. The wearer is free to disavow any and all responsibility for his or her actions, just as the bearer of the shield can disavow any role in creating the world the shield purports to reflect. The claim voiced by Glaucon is that,

> [If] there were two such rings, one worn by the just person, the other by the unjust. Now no one, it seems, would be so incorruptible that he would stay on the path of justice, or bring himself to keep away from other people's possessions and not touch them, when he could take whatever he wanted from the marketplace with impunity, go into houses and have sex with anyone he wished, kill or release from prison anyone he wished, and do all the other things which would make him like a god among humans. And in so behaving, he would do no differently than the unjust person , but both would both follow the same path.[9]

The proximity of the ring and the shield is evident through a number of clues in Glaucon's speech. Gyges is said to have obtained the ring from the hand of "a corpse, which seemed more than human size" buried inside "a hollow bronze horse."[10] It is difficult to read these lines without being reminded of the Trojan Horse that housed the Greek heroes who themselves "seemed of more than human size" in the eyes of Plato's less philosophically inclined contemporaries. The specter of Homer looms large indeed.

Plato sees the sophists, taking their lead from the tragedians, as measuring the goodness or badness (and by extension the rightness or wrongness, even the truth or falsity) of a given statement by the response it elicits within its audience.[11] Plato himself takes a much different stance. In the *Republic* the goodness or badness, rightness or wrongness, truth or falsity of a claim is measured by reference to a fixed standard, that is, by reference to the Forms and to the Good itself. The important distinctions made possible by Plato's introduction of the Forms are most clear in his (in)famous attack on poetry.

The sophist and the poet alike are not concerned with truth, as Plato understands it, but with eliciting a desired response in their audience. Plato identifies Homer as being "the first, the teacher and the leader of all those fine tragedians." Homer is therefore at the very head of the tradition that has resulted in the death of Socrates. In a move reminiscent of the actions of Perseus, Plato aims to decapitate this deadly foe. Already in Books II and III of the *Republic* Plato has expressed his deep dissatisfaction with the poets. His introduction of the Forms in Books VI and VII sets the stage for the sudden exclamation in Book X that "we usually posit some one particular form in connection with each set of many things to which we apply the same name."[12] This statement shows one of the key distinctions relied upon by Plato in his efforts, namely that between the particular (the object or article) and the universal (the Form or Idea).

> Socrates: For example there are, if you like, many couches and tables.
> Glaucon: Of course.
> Socrates: But the forms connected to these manufactured items are surely just two, one of a couch and one of a table.[13]

In addition to this two part distinction, Plato adds a third, that of the image. Where the object or article is a product of the craftsman with an eye to its Form—its perfection and true being—the image is a product of the poet or painter, or even simply the person carrying a mirror, with an eye to the object. Thus Plato claims that "an imitator is at three removes from nature."[14]

Plato's use of the concept of mimesis is not entirely consistent within the *Republic*, but clearly one of its key meanings is the production of images.[15] Since these images are disconnected from the truth they claim to reveal, they are censured (and censored) by Plato as dangerous and misleading. The danger posed by these mimetic images, including the word-image,[16] is heightened by another aspect of Plato's mimesis, which in modern parlance is best summed up in the actions of the mime. That is, the danger of the mimetic image is compounded by what Girard will later call the "mimetic instinct" of the audience of those images.[17] People will shape their behaviors to mimic the role models provided to them. In Book VI, Socrates says "do you think there is any way to prevent someone from associating with something he admires without imitating it?" to which Adeimantus replies "he can't possibly."[18] If the "things" one "consorts with" in Homer do not provide a consistent model of that which is to be admired, but rather contradict one another—as do equally admired tales of piety and impiety, moderation and excess—then the end result can "not possibly" be anything but a fragmented, self-contradictory and confused ordering of both the soul and the city.[19] An education based on what Plato sees as the Homeric "this is the way it is" can only produce a man "long suffering," constantly at odds with both himself and others.[20] An excellent example of this is provided very early in the *Republic* by Polemarchus:

> Socrates: It seems, then, that a just person has turned out to be a kind of thief. You probably got that idea from Homer. For he loves Autolycus, the maternal grandfather of Odysseus, whom he describes as better than everyone at stealing and swearing false oaths. According to you and Homer and Simonides, then, justice appears to be some sort of craft of stealing—one that benefits friends and harms enemies. Isn't that what you meant?
> Polemarchus: No, by Zeus, it isn't. But I do not know anymore what I meant.[21]

A city guided by such a model, according to Plato, cannot help but be in a constant state of strife and upheaval. This upheaval is precisely what Plato himself lived through in the war with Sparta. It is expressed in the collapse of the Athenian empire under the weight of its own hubris.[22] It is expressed in the rapid flux of the Athenian government from a democracy to an oligarchy and back again. The predominance of what Plato sees as Homeric models allows for the sophist, with the approval of the many, to "justly" murder the just man, Socrates.[23]

The primary exemplar of one beholden to such a model in the *Republic* is Thracymachus. For Thracymachus, "the just is nothing else than the advantage of the stronger."[24] Plato sees in this position the figural bearing of the shield. He is aware, as indicated earlier, that this position is illusory. Plato is equally aware that as such it cannot withstand logical scrutiny, but will instead maintain itself by force.[25] The entry of Thracymachus into the argument comes at exactly such a moment. Polemarchus, arguing the traditional position that justice is to help one's friends and harm one's enemies, has just been exposed as "[not knowing] any longer what [he] meant." The argument has come to the conclusion that "it is never just to harm anyone."[26]

> When we [Socrates and Polemarchus] paused after what I [Socrates] had just said, however, he [Thracymachus] could not keep quiet any longer: crouched up like a wild beast about to spring, and he hurled himself at us as if to tear us to pieces. Polemarchus and I were frightened and flustered as he roared into our midst.[27]

There are a number of features that are notable about these lines and the ones immediately following. First, the description of Thracymachus as "a wild beast about to spring . . . as if to tear us to pieces" echoes quite strongly a number of scenes in Homer's *Iliad*, especially those in his description of the Shield of Achilles.[28] Socrates subsequently comments that "his words startled me, and looking at him I was afraid. And I think if I had not seen him before he had looked at me, I would have been dumbstruck."[29] This comment is very appropriate to an exchange contextualized by references to the shield, as it provides an excellent example of its operation. The words of Thracymachus exemplify the paralyzing power of the shield. It is this stunned moment that would normally spell the end of resistance. Were it not for the good fortune of a glance in the right direction, the dialogue would have ended here, Socrates having been rendered "dumbstruck," leaving Thracymachus the de facto victor.

It is also notable that there is more going on here than a confrontation between Thracymachus the lion and Socrates the bull. Indeed the stage is set for a confrontation between Socrates and the entire tradition Thracymachus represents.[30] This becomes apparent through a number of subtle clues. Socrates refers to Thracymachus as one of the "clever people."[31]

This particular moniker is often applied to Odysseus, who had just been brought up in the discussion with Polemarchus. The allusion to Odysseus and his craftiness carries on. Thracymachus accuses Socrates of being "captious" and when asked if he believes that Socrates intends to trick him, he says,

> I know it very well, he said, but it will not do you any good, for I would be well aware of your trickery; nor would you have the ability to force my argument in open debate.[32]

In this comment, Thracymachus exposes himself even more clearly as being a figural descendant of Odysseus (as Plato understands him). For Thracymachus to know trickery when he sees it, he must also be adept at it. Following the logic of the exchange with Polemarchus, if Thracymachus is adept at trickery, he must also be adept at its opposite, honesty or truthfulness. It is fairly clear that Thracymachus believes this of himself. Socrates must therefore prove that Thracymachus is not even adept at trickery if he is to show the sophist's claim to knowledge to be false.[33] Plato has subtly established that this is not just a debunking of Thracymachus, but of Odysseus, and by extension, Homer himself.[34]

The scope of Plato's task is further expanded to include the replacement of even more cultural icons. Again this is done in a most subtle, almost sub-textual manner and begins with Thracymachus' evocation of Heracles. This in itself would be relatively unremarkable, were it not for the later statement of Socrates: "Do you think, I said, that I am crazy enough to try to shave a lion and quibble with Thracymachus?"[35] This rather odd saying, combined with the earlier portrayal of Thracymachus as a lion brings to mind the labors of Heracles. In a fit of insane rage—"craziness"—Heracles murdered his wife and children. As a way to redeem himself he was assigned twelve labors. The first of these tasks was to confront and conquer the Nemean lion, whose hide could not be pierced by any weapon. At this point, multiple parallels between this tale, and Plato's implicit criticism of the state of affairs under the guidance of the Sophists are readily apparent. Thracymachus, already a stand-in for the entire tradition of sophistry (which Plato identifies as being led by Homer), here becomes a stand in for the Nemean lion. The position of the Sophist, protected as it is from all attacks, a substitute for the lion's hide.[36] Socrates, then, takes the place of Heracles. Heracles succeeds in his task by stunning the lion with a club made of an olive tree, then strangling it to death. He defeats the beast without piercing its hide. He then proceeds to skin the lion using its own

razor sharp claws, taking the hide as armor for himself. It is exactly this
operation that Socrates performs on Thracymachus. First, Thracymachus is
forced to stay by the onlookers to the conversation,[37] then Socrates
turns the Sophists' own tools, his words, against him. This is to say that
Socrates out tricks the trickster. Rather than addressing the Sophist's
concept of justice directly, Socrates uses an oblique approach, discussing
ships' captains, doctors and musicians rather than tyrants or other political
rulers. Thracymachus finds himself in a position where his concept of
justice is no longer tenable, and his recourse to force has been sidestepped.
"And then I saw something I had never seen before—Thracymachus
blushing."[38] He is *shamed* into submission.

Thracymachus puts forward the suggestion that to understand trickery
is to avoid being caught by it. This is a suggestion that Plato embraces
when he befriends Thracymachus. It is Plato's intent to mitigate the
ill effects of sophistry and poetry—of what he sees as Homer's bearing of
the shield—by putting forth an understanding of how poetry operates
mimetically.

> Socrates: Between ourselves—for you won't denounce me to the
> tragic poets or any of the other imitative ones—I think all such poetry
> is likely to corrupt the mind of its hearers who do not have knowl-
> edge of what it is really like as a drug to counteract it.[39]

He offers the concept of mimesis as this antidote (*pharmakon*).[40] Plato
seeks to undo the paralyzing power of the shield by showing that power to
be illusory. His concept of mimesis (as the production of images) extends
the possibility of a properly educated audience of the shield to declare "that
is not the way it is." The paralyzing "this is the way it is" can be understood
as having nothing whatsoever to do with how "it is." Plato thus displays
the grounds upon which he can censure Homer (and hence an entire
ethico-political system) for providing "a bad image of [what] the gods and
heroes are like, just as a painter might paint a picture that is not at all like
the things he is trying to paint."[41]

The concept of mimesis as a critical tool is useful in showing that
the mimetic image cannot deliver what it claims to deliver. The image is
concerned with the object, which is not real within Plato's ontological
framework. The image is capable of expressing opinion but not knowledge.
The image cannot claim, "this is the way it is." Or rather it can, but the
referent of the claim, the "it", is "my opinion about the world" rather than
"the world itself." The corresponding ethos, "nothing (else) to be done

about it," can remain in force, but the implications of this statement too are altered radically. It is one thing to say that the world is as it is and there is nothing to be done to change it. It is quite another to say that my opinion about the world is what it is and there is nothing to be done to change it.

This observation is made more explicit using Plato's image of the line from Book VI. G. M. A. Grube presents this image as a diagram:[42]

The Line Analogy

noeisis understanding	B		forms, dialectic
dianoia reasoning	E		mathematical realities, science
	C		
pistis opinion			objects of sense
	D		
			images, reflections, (works) of art?
eikasia image-making or imagination	A		

Plato's critique of the poets is that they operate solely within the realm of the visible (line segment AC), and yet they argue as if they offered understanding, which is beyond the ream of the visible (line segment AB). But Plato's line does not permit the image (AD) to provide any kind of direct access to true understanding (BE). Thus to bear the shield, to make a "this is the way it is" claim, is to present an image that, *simply by being an image,* cannot be a representation of the Forms, which *are*. The image can say "this is the way it is" but the "is" can only ever be an opinion. It may be that this opinion is a reasoned opinion (EC) and reason is a guide to what is (BE), but a reasoned opinion is not reason itself, just as reason is not the Good itself.

The great promise of mimesis as a critical tool is that it can disrupt the paralyzing effects of the shield. It promises to provide critical distance from the images through which the message of the shield is transmitted. The "this is the way it is" can never be anything other than "this is *like* the way it is." Where the former does not allow for the possibility of things being different, the latter opens considerable space for such possibilities. "This it is like the way it is" implies similarity without identity. To be like is to simultaneously be unlike, for a perfect likeness ceases to be a likeness at all, as Plato notes in the *Cratylus*:

> Socrates: An image cannot remain an image if it presents all the details of what it represents. See if I am right. Would there be two things—Cratylus and an image of Cratylus—in the following circumstances? Suppose some god didn't just represent your color and shape the way painters do, but made all the inner parts like yours, with the same warmth and softness, and put motion, soul, and wisdom like your into them—in a word, suppose he made a duplicate of everything you have and put it beside you. Would there then be two Cratyluses or Cratylus and an image of Cratylus?
> Cratylus: It seems to me, Socrates, that there would be two Cratyluses.[43]

This reverberates through the "nothing to be done" claim of the shield, which can at best only ever be "it is *like* there is nothing to be done." The implication here is that there *is* something to be done. With this in mind, two questions emerge. First, it becomes imperative to ask "how is this image unlike that which it purports to represent?" Second, it is equally imperative to ask, "what can be done?" The imperative status of these questions is evident in Plato's discussion of the "true lie."

> Socrates: Don't you know that all gods and humans hate a *true* lie, if one may call it that?
> Adeimantus: What do you mean?
> Socrates: I mean no one intentionally wants to lie about the most important to what is most important in himself. On the contrary, he fears to hold a lie there more than anything.
> Adeimantus: I still do not understand.
> Socrates: That is because you think I am saying something deep. I simply mean that to lie and to have lied to the soul about the things that are, and to be ignorant, and to have and to hold a lie there, is what everyone would least of all accept; indeed they especially hate it there.
> Adeimantus: They certainly do.
> Socrates: But surely, as I was saying just now, this would be most correct to say that it is truly speaking a lie—the ignorance in the soul

of the one to whom the lie was told. For a lie in words is sort of an imitation of this affection in the soul, an image of it that comes into being after it, and not an altogether pure lie. Isn't that so?
Adeimantus: Yes, it is.
Socrates: A real lie, then, is hated not only by the gods, but also by human beings.[44]

Plato thus establishes a situation in which the inquisition of the image is vital if one is to avoid being hated by both gods and men alike.

Plato as a Poet

Given how harsh Plato is towards the poets, it would appear to be a damning critique to point out that Plato himself is an imitative poet par excellence. Consider that the entirety of the *Republic* is written as a dialogue between Socrates and a variety of more or less ignorant interlocutors.

Socrates: But when he [the poet] makes a speech as if he were someone else, won't we say that he makes his own style as much like that of the person he tells us is about to speak?
Adeimantus: We certainly will.
Socrates: Now to make oneself like somebody else in voice or appearance is to imitate the person one makes oneself like, isn't it?
Adeimantus: Of course.
Socrates: Then in a passage of that sort, it seems, he, and the rest of poets as well, produce their narration through imitation.[45]

Yet precisely in the act of critiquing such imitation, Plato is himself partaking of it. It is intriguing that Plato, in the voice of Socrates, states in the very next passage "if the poet never disguised himself, his entire poem would be narration without imitation," and "I am not a poet."[46]

There are two things that make this particular passage so interesting. First, by the standards set forth in the passages quoted earlier, none of the *Republic* is written as narration. Everything from the setting of the scene for the dialogue to the retelling of the Er myth at the conclusion of Book X are presented in the voice of Socrates or one of his (lesser) counterparts.[47] The text is devoid of (non-mimetic) narration; therefore Plato must be "disguising" himself everywhere.[48] He is, at least in this respect, wearing the ring of Gyges.[49] It may well be the case that Plato's use of Socrates as a mouthpiece for his own arguments was well known, even to his contemporaries, but this does not mean that Plato is not concealing himself. His dialogues carry on the same kind of questioning that the death of Socrates was intended to outlaw, but Plato has left himself a safety valve, if you will. If Plato finds himself brought before the court, he can claim that the words were not his, but those of Socrates, who has already been punished for them. This is certainly a measure of concealment on his part.[50] If it were not, then, by the very standards laid out in the *Republic*, none of Plato's works would be presented in dialogue form, as this necessitates the imitation of the other interlocutors. Indeed, the more faithful the author is to the comments of others, the better concealed the author is as an author of those words.

Plato is utilizing Socrates' transparency—the open rejection of any status as a poet—to conceal his own poetry. There is a certain distance here between the author and the subject that is being deliberately collapsed. Layers of removal are being effaced, but to what end? One reason to collapse this distance is to work towards the elimination of the ambiguities that such a distance can reveal. That is to say that a good deal of the power of a mimetic representation comes from its concealing itself as mimetic. Images are most powerful when they are most convincing, and less powerful when they are obvious as imitations.[51] This is what Thracymachus points towards when he says of himself that he is aware of Socrates' trickery, and therefore immune to it.

This is supported as well by the famous metaphor of the cave. For the prisoners chained in place, the dancing shadows on the wall are utterly real. They have no grounds upon which to say that they are anything but real. For the philosopher, however, these shadows are nothing but fleeting imitations of something that is itself an imitation. The philosopher is not convinced by the shadow play at all, having left the cave and turned his eyes towards the sun. To hear Socrates speak is one thing. To hear Plato tell us what Socrates said during a conversation where Plato was not even present is another. By hiding or disguising himself, Plato attempts to block questions about the accuracy or veracity of his account that might otherwise arise, just as the prisoners in the cave are chained so that they cannot turn to see the fire behind them. By concealing himself, Plato is in effect holding his audience prisoner, and amplifying the dream-inducing effects of his representations of the truth. And yet, "isn't it dreaming to think—whether asleep or awake—that a likeness is not a likeness but rather the thing itself that it is like?"[52]

The amplification of the dream-inducing power of the representation has two purposes. First, for those who are not by nature philosophical, it induces a powerful stupor from which they are unlikely to awake. In this dream-state the reader is more amenable to being led by the arguments being made, rather than paying attention to the problematic way in which they are made. Importantly, this dream-state is a vast improvement over their previous Homeric dreams by virtue of being dreams about, or at least oriented towards, the Good. Second, it is all too simplistic to say that Plato is attempting to imprison his audience, for he is at the same time offering a means of escape, at least for certain philosophical souls. It is as if Plato, in order to liberate his audience, must first imprison them. For those more philosophically inclined souls, this amplification of the dream also amplifies the distortions of the dream. It is as if Plato were exposing the flaws of an audio recording by playing it at a very high volume. In other words, by focusing so intently on the way in which the poets make their claims, while at the same time utilizing those methods, Plato invites the philosophically inclined reader to come and find him.

> [Plato speaking as] Socrates: There is one kind of style and narration that a really good and fine person would use whenever he had to say something, and another kind, unlike that one, which his opposite by nature and education would always favor, and in which he would narrate his story.
> Adeimantus: What kinds are they?
> Socrates: In my view, when a moderate man comes upon the words or actions of a good man in the course of a narration, he will be willing to report them as if he were that man himself, and he won't be ashamed of that sort of imitation. He will be most willing to impersonate the good man when he is acting in a faultless and intelligent manner, but less willing and more reluctant to do so when he is upset by disease, passion, drunkenness or some other misfortune. When he comes upon a character who is beneath him, however, he will be unwilling to make himself resemble this inferior character in any serious way—except perhaps for a brief period when he is doing something good. On the contrary, he will be ashamed to do something like that, both because he is unpracticed in the imitation of such people, and also because he cannot stand to shape and mold himself on an inferior pattern. In his mind he despises that, except when it is for the sake of amusement.[53]

The greater purpose of this playful game of hide-and-seek is that Plato wishes the philosophically inclined reader to follow him in his turn towards the Good.[54] To this end, he is quite happy to admit that he utilizes the same mimetic techniques as the poets, with one centrally important difference. Rather than pandering to the whims of the many, his imitations are oriented towards the Good.[55] He makes use of the loophole he has left for himself when he says,

> Socrates: All the same, let it be said that, if the imitative poetry that aims at pleasure has any argument to show it should have a place in a well-governed city, we would gladly welcome it back, since we are well aware of being charmed by it ourselves. Still, it is not pious to betray what one believes to be the truth. What about you my friend; aren't you also charmed by it, especially when it is through Homer that you look at it?
> Glaucon: Very.
> Socrates: Isn't it just, then, for her to reenter in that way, when she has defended herself in lyric or some other meter?
> Glaucon: Yes, indeed.
> Socrates: Then we will surely allow her defenders—the ones who are not poets themselves, but lovers of poetry—to argue without meter on her behalf, showing that she gives not only pleasure but also benefit both to constitutions and to human life. Indeed, we will listen to them graciously, since we would certainly profit if poetry were shown to be not only pleasant but also beneficial.[56]

Plato in his discussion of poetry is offering both a critique and a defense of it. He is banishing bad mimesis—that which distorts the truth and leads the audience away from the truth—and embracing good mimesis—which is oriented towards the Good.

Plato as a Shield Bearer

The poetry of Plato's writing turns out to be not so much of a problem for him as it first seems. The more serious problem facing Plato is that in his effort to distance himself and his audience from the paralyzing effects of the shield, he ends up bearing it. To bear the shield is to make a double claim: "this is the way it is" and "there is nothing (else) to be done about it." This double claim is structured so as to block critical analysis. It presents itself as unassailable. To resist its advance is to defy the gods, or in Plato's case, it is to live in a dream,[57] it is to live unfulfilled,[58] it is to wallow in one's own pettiness,[59] and to be hated by both gods and men.[60] His use of mimesis as a critical tool is useful in pointing out that the shield produces a dream for waking eyes, but it does nothing in itself to challenge the structure that underlies the operation of the shield. Plato, in short, replaces one "this is the way it is" with another. More specifically, at least in the *Republic*, he replaces what he sees as Homer's "this is the way it is" with his own "this is the way it *really* is."

If there remains any question that Plato is making such a claim in the *Republic*, consider Socrates' statements to Adeimantus at the conclusion of Book V:

Socrates: [W]hat about those who in each case look at the things themselves that are always in every respect? Won't we say that they have knowledge, not mere belief?
Adeimantus: Once again, we would have to.
Socrates: Shall we say, then, that these people are passionately devoted to and love the things with which knowledge deals, as the others are devoted to and love the things with which belief deals? We have not forgotten, have we, that the latter love and look at beautiful sounds, colors, and things of that sort, but cannot even bear the idea of the beautiful itself is a thing that it is?
Glaucon: No, we have not.
Socrates: Will be striking a false note, then, if we call such people "philodoxers" (lovers of belief) rather than "philosophers" (lovers of wisdom or knowledge)? Will they be very angry with us if we call them that?
Galucon: Not if they take my advice. It is not in accord with divine law to be angry with the truth.[61]

This passage shows quite clearly that there is a profound "this is the way it is" at work. The "things themselves" are what they are and they do not change. They are not therefore subject to alteration by any human action. The ontological status of "the things themselves" solidifies the claim "there is nothing to be done." Within this framework, knowledge, unlike opinion, is not challengeable or in any way contestable. It simply is. Furthermore, Adeimantus' observation that "it is not in accord with divine law to be angry with the truth" brings the coercive power of the state to bear against any that would question the pronouncements of the philosophers.[62] The tensions caused by the death of Socrates are therefore resolved by an inversion of the power relations that led to his death. Now it is the sophist who must defend himself in the language of the philosopher and not the philosopher who must defend himself as a sophist.[63]

Plato, like Perseus, is successful in his attempt to decapitate his foe. In Perseus' case it was Medusa and her paralyzing gaze. In Plato's case it is Homer as the head of a tradition that is epistemologically and politically paralyzing.[64] However unlike Perseus, Plato is unable, at least in the *Republic*, to come to the realization that his prize is still too dangerous to wield.[65] It is not difficult to imagine a situation in which the scene described by Plato in Book VI where he rails against the sophistry of the many is repeated as a mirror image of itself.[66] This would not at first glance seem to be a problem at all. In the first instance, the opinion of the many is based on nothing but itself, where in the second, this opinion is based on knowledge of the Good. Thus, on one hand, the inversion of the scene is also a corrective measure. On the other hand, this also reveals a difficulty for Plato.

Plato describes a situation in which the philosopher must either be divinely guided—as is the case with Socrates and his *daemon*—or be the end result of a proper public education.

> There is not now, never has been, nor ever will be, a character whose view of virtue goes contrary to the education these [the masses] provide. I mean a human character, comrade—the divine, as the saying goes, is an exception to the rule. You may be sure that if anything is saved and turns out well in the political systems that exist now, you won't be mistaken in saying that divine providence saved it.[67]

The establishment of the just city must therefore be accomplished by a philosopher of the second sort, for the city that could produce the uncorrupted philosopher by public education is already the city that such a philosopher would establish. Furthermore, the task of this philosopher-king is to "take the city and people's characters as their sketching plate . . . They would erase one thing, I suppose, and draw in another, until they had made people's characters as dear to the gods as possible."[68] This is problematic for two reasons. First, the erasing and redrawing process implies that errors will be made in the attempt to make "human characters as dear to the gods as possible." There will be moments in this process when the philosopher-king discovers that what he had thought was the correct measure turns out not to be. Yet this does not seem possible if the philosopher-king has the knowledge he claims to have. By Plato's own reasoning, the object of his knowledge—that which is—cannot change.

It cannot be the case that the errors of the philosopher reside in the changing nature of what is. They must reside in the philosopher's flawed understanding of what is. Therefore in so far as the philosopher errs in his policy measures, he does not have knowledge, but something else.

It is possible that the philosopher may have knowledge of the Good, but not of the human beings he hopes to shape into its likeness. Indeed, given that human beings are malleable in this way precludes there ever being knowledge of them until such time as they are perfected and no longer change.[69] Thus the errors of the philosopher are attributable to the deficiencies in the medium in which he works, and are not indicative of his knowledge, or lack thereof, of the model. This may help explain the process of drawing and redrawing, but it leads to a second problem.

The second problem is that for the philosopher to shape human characters so as to make them "as dear to the gods as possible," he must know what is dear to the gods. Yet how does one know unquestioningly what is dear to the gods without being a god? It has already been shown that the philosopher is prone to error in his policy decisions. In this respect he is most definitively human, as his opinions about what the best policy is to be will change from time to time. The philosopher is in a position where he both must be and cannot be a god.[70] Given that the philosopher remains a human being, he remains prone to error and to the altering of his beliefs. However, the city under the rule of the philosopher is organized so as to preclude any debate as to whether the beliefs of the philosopher-king are correct or not. Even though the philosopher can be wrong, and by Plato's own implication *via* the image of the draughtsman, sometimes *is* wrong, his correctness is both assumed and enforced.

There is a distinct danger that the power of this image—the correctness of the philosopher-king—could become bewitching even to the philosopher-king. This issue comes to the fore in light of another, albeit related, question. If the philosopher-king is a draughtsman drawing and redrawing the image of the human character so as to perfect it in the eyes of the gods, how is he to know when his task is complete? Plato is quite clear that "until the philosopher class gains mastery of a city there will be no respite from evils for either city or citizens," and that at such time there will be no further grounds for dispute.[71] One possibility therefore is that the philosopher may understand his task to be complete when there are no grounds for dispute, as this is an indication of social harmony. Interestingly however, for all of his vehemence against the power of the image, Plato (disguised as Socrates) then says, "they [those people who were straining to attack us] have become altogether gentle and persuaded; so that, *out of shame, if nothing else*, they will agree."[72] The qualifier "if nothing else" indicates that disagreement may not be resolved so much as the disagreeing party will become too ashamed to continue arguing the point.[73] It need not be the case that there is genuine accord among the citizenry as to what is correct, so long as there is the *appearance* of it. Recall that since human beings are changeable, they are not knowable, for strictly speaking, knowledge is of what is, and they are not. As it is not possible to have knowledge about human beings, one only has access to empirical observations of their comings and goings. The danger is that the philosopher-king, led astray by the appearance of social harmony and god-like human character may stop short of his goal of *actually* shaping such harmony and character.

What is worse, the possibility of this error being pointed out to the philosopher-king, either by another philosopher or anyone else, has been removed in the process of categorically rendering such challenges impious and illogical.[74] The "good" citizen will, by force of habit, remain within the parameters set by the philosopher.[75] Those that do not are subject to the coercive power of the state. Thus the parameters set by the philosopher, even if they are set in error, cannot be questioned. They are ultimately maintained by force.

It is apparent that Plato's attempt to disrupt the power of the shield has failed. He has succeeded only in overturning the particular content given to it by the sophists. This inversion does nothing to alter the structure and operation of the shield, but rather reinscribes and reinforces that power. Yet the promise of mimesis remains. Is it possible to expose the "this is the way it is" claim of the Shield of Achilles as never anything more than "this is *like* the way it is" without relying on a corresponding "this is the way it *really* is?" Perhaps a more developed understanding of the concept may prove better suited for the task?

Notes

[1] It is precisely this ability that renders the shield a useful metaphor for comprehending the various instances of the use of the logic of fear.

[2] For a brief sample of such literature, see Erich Auerbach, *Mimesis: The Representation of Reality in Western Literature* (Princeton, NJ: Princeton University Press, 2003); Barbara Fuchs, *Mimesis and Empire the New World, Islam, and European Identities, Cambridge Studies in Renaissance Literature and Culture* (Cambridge: Cambridge University Press, 2001); Gunter Gebauer, and Christoph Wulf, *Mimesis: Culture, Art, Society* (Berkeley, CA: University of California Press, 1995); René Girard, "To Double Business Bound," in *Essays on Literature,*

Mimesis, and Anthropology (Baltimore, MD: Johns Hopkins University Press, 1978); Wong Kwok Kui, "Nietzsche, Plato and Aristotle on Mimesis," *Dogma*; Mihai Spariosu et al., eds. *Mimesis in Contemporary Theory: An Interdisciplinary Approach,* vol. 1, Cultura Ludens: Imitation and Play in Western Culture (Philadelphia, PA: John Benjamins Publishing Company, 1984).

3 See Plato, *Republic*, trans. C. D. C. Reeve (Indianapolis, IN: Hackett Publishing Company, Inc, 2004), 606e–7a. In these lines, Plato openly recognizes those who see Homer as "the educator of Greece" and that one should learn from him "the management of human affairs and of education, and arrange one's life in accordance with his teaching."

4 Ibid., 492a–2d.

5 Ibid., 595c.

6 This could also be stated as "appearance is everything." See Sophocles, "Philoctetes," in *Sophocles 2*, ed. David Greene, and Richard Lattimore (Chicago, IL: University of Chicago Press, 1957).

7 It is no mistake therefore that Plato says "so our first task, it seems, is to supervise the storytellers." Plato, *Republic*, 377c.

8 Testimony to this power is given by Socrates in the opening lines of the *Apology*:

> I do not know, men of Athens, how my accusers affected you; as for me, I was almost carried away in spite of myself, so persuasively did they speak. And yet, hardly anything of what they said is true. Plato, *Apology*, in *Plato: Complete Works*, ed. John M. Cooper (Indianapolis, IN: Hackett Publishing Company, 1997), 17a.

Plato takes this distinction between persuasiveness and truth with him into the arguments of the *Republic*, where he challenges Homer directly. The issue of hubris is raised in a notable way in Socrates' conversation with Euthyphro. His failed attempt to discover a fixed definition of piety from one with a reputation for expertise on the matter calls into question the self-righteousness of those who have accused Socrates of impiety. How can one be accused of impiety when no one can say what piety is? To claim knowledge one does not have is hubristic. See Plato, "Euthyphro," in *Plato: Complete Works*, ed. John M. Cooper (Indianapolis, IN: Hackett Publishing Company, 1997). Similarly, the character of Gyges in the *Republic* serves as an example of the hazards of "bearing the shield" (or wearing the ring, as it may be).

9 Plato, *Republic*, 360b–0c.

10 Ibid., 359d.

11 It is exactly this *ad extensio* that Socrates challenges in the *Apology* when he decries the craftsmen as erroneously convincing themselves that their knowledge in a limited area was broadly generalizable.

12 Ibid., 596a. Julia Annas points out that this "accustomization" is something of a surprise given that all prior discussions of the Forms had been introductory.

The only thing that makes the utilization of the Forms "customary" is Socrates' (Plato's) declaration of that status. Julia Annas, *An Introduction to Plato's Republic* (Oxford: Clarendon Press, 1981).

13 Plato, *Republic*, 596b.

14 Plato, *Republic*, in *Plato: Complete Works*, ed. John M. Cooper (Indianapolis, IN: Hackett Publishing Company, 1997), 597e.

15 Gebauer and Wulf list different meanings of the term in the *Republic*. See Gunter Gebauer, and Christoph Wulf, *Mimesis: Culture, Art, Society*. Plato marks a distinction between the user, the maker, and the imitator that runs parallel to the distinction between the Form, the object and the image. He argues that the user is in the best position to judge the quality of an object, more so than its maker. The mimic is in the position of least authority in regards to the quality of an object. By this line of argument, the products of the mimetic poet are only ever images. However, Plato runs into a problem in regards to the word-image. In the case of the sophist or poet, the product is the word or text, which is both made and used by what Plato considers the imitator. It is the sophist or poet, therefore that is in the best position to judge the quality of their own products.

16 "The verbal lie is a mere reflection of that which exists in the soul, a reflection of it which comes later, and is not completely untrue." Plato, *Republic*, 382b. The verbal lie is not entirely untrue because it does not exist in Plato's ontological framework as real. The utterance is always removed from the reality behind it. Hence the verbal lie is like the true lie, which is entirely untrue, but it is not the true lie and thus not entirely untrue. More will be said on this point below.

17 See René Girard, "To Double Business Bound."

18 Plato, *Republic*, 500c.

19 It must be noted that Plato, through the character of Socrates, denies the very existence of "a Homeric manner of life." Ibid., 600b. Yet in doing so he is reinforcing its existence. George Lakoff reminds us that "evoking a frame reinforces that frame." George Lakoff, "Simple Framing: An Introduction to Framing and Its Uses in Politics" (2004). In denying the existence of "a Homeric manner of life," Plato is not only reinforcing the existence of such a way of life, but also denying that his objection to the poets, to the sophists, and to public life informed by the tragedians has any grounds whatsoever. (Could it be then that he is offering only a simulation of resistance to such a (non-)"manner of life?") Yet shortly thereafter, Plato turns back from this denial when he recognizes the existence of just such a thing. He speaks of

> admirers of Homer—who tell us that this is the poet who educated Greece, and for the management of human affairs and education in them, one should take up his works and learn them and live guided by this poet in the arrangement of one's whole life. Plato, *Republic*, 606e.

For what are such people espousing, if not a Homeric manner of life? See n. 4, above.

20 Homer in *The Odyssey* systematically refers to his protagonist as "long suffering Odysseus." Plato recognizes Odysseus as a key figure in Homer's epics, and he tends to equate the two figures. He is far from alone in doing this, as noted by Clayton. See Barbara Clayton, *A Penelopean Poetics: Reweaving the Feminine in Homer's Odyssey, Greek Studies: Interdisciplinary Studies* (Lanham, MD: Lexington Books, 2004). Odysseus is a critical figure, but he is also a tremendously difficult figure. More will be said about Odysseus and Plato's understanding of him in Chapter 5.

21 Plato, *Republic*, 334b.

22 See the discussion of Thucydides in Chapter 3.

23 In so far as Socrates represents the presence of justice itself in the Athenian polis, this is the truest tragedy. See Plato, *Apology*.

24 Plato, *Republic*, 335e.

25 The shield is, after all and above all else, an instrument of war.

26 Ibid., 335e.

27 Ibid., 336b–6c.

28 One can easily see Thracymachus filling the role of a lion in the following lines:

> —a savage roar!—
> a crashing attack—and a pair of ramping lions
> had seized a bull from the cattle's front ranks—
> he bellowed out as they dragged him off in agony.
> Packs of dogs and the young herdsmen rushed to help
> But the lions ripping open the hide of the huge bull
> Were gulping down the guts and the black pooling blood
> While the herdsmen yelled the fast pack on—no use! (18:675–83)

29 Ibid., 336e.

30 A tradition Plato would characterize as Homeric.

31 Ibid., 337a.

32 Plato, *Republic*, 341b. Reeve translates this same passage as, "it won't do you any good. You will never be able to do me evil by covert means, and without them, you will never be able to overpower me by argument." Plato, *Republic*, 341b.

33 Which he does as the exchange with the sophist proceeds.

34 A more detailed discussion of the connection between Homer and Odysseus will be taken up in Chapter 5.

35 Ibid., 341c.

36 Socrates: You knew very well that if you ask someone how much twelve is, and in putting the question you warn him: "Don't tell me, man, that twelve is twice six, or three times four, or six times two, or four times three; for I won't accept such nonsense from you"—it was obvious to you, I imagine, that no could respond to a person who inquired in that way." Ibid., 337b.

37 Ibid., 344d.

38 Ibid., 350d.

[39] Ibid., 595b.

[40] The pharamkon has come to be the subject of a good deal of later theorizing. Of particular note is Jacques Derrida's essay "Plato's Pharmacy" collected in Jacques Derrida, *Dissemination,* trans. Barbara Johnson (Chicago, IL: The University of Chicago Press, 1981). Derrida's opening words are,

> A text is not a text unless it hides from the first comer, from the first glance, the law of its composition and the rules of its game. A text remains, moreover, forever imperceptible. Its laws and rules are not, however, harbored in the inaccessibility of a secret; it is simply that they can never be booked, in the present, into anything that could rigorously be called a perception. Ibid., 63.

There is an implication here that Plato must also be invisible to the first comer, to the casual glance. Could it be that Plato himself is wearing the ring of Gyges? This possibility will be addressed below.

[41] Plato, *Republic,* 377e.

[42] This diagram is to be found in Plato, *Republic,* trans. G. M. A. Grube (Indianapolis, IN: Hackett Publishing Company, 1974), 167n16.

[43] Plato, *Cratylus,* in *Plato: Complete Works,* ed. John M. Cooper (Indianapolis, IN: Hackett Publishing Company, 1997), 432b–2c.

[44] Plato, *Republic,* 382a–2c.

[45] Ibid., 393c.

[46] Ibid., 393d.

[47] The Er myth of Book X comes closest to being narration, but it too is portrayed by Plato as being spoken by Socrates.

[48] Grube replaces "disguising" with "hiding" and makes the point even more clear. Plato, *Republic,* 393d.

[49] Or perhaps the cap of Hades, as Perseus wore before him. See Plato, *Republic,* 612b. Plato's mention of the cap of Hades is a further detail linking the ring of Gyges and the shield. After all, it was the cap of Hades that permitted Perseus to move within striking range of Medusa without being seen.

[50] Not to mention further evidence, by virtue of his ability to thereby deny his own responsibility for his writings, that Plato does indeed wear the ring of Gyges, or bear the Shield of Achilles, as will be discussed below.

[51] This point is not diminished by Plato's argument that observing an overtly mimetic performance is both "enjoyable" and dangerous as it provides a bad model of proper behavior. Ibid., Plato's Republic, 605d–6d. The tragic play is powerful in its potential to confuse and mislead the audience, but this power is somewhat tempered by its easy recognition as a mimetic performance. One can, in other words, relatively easily recognize that what happens in the theatre is not necessarily what ought to happen in the "real-world" outside of the theatre. (The phrase "real-world" is not Plato's. He gives the comings and goings of day-to-day life no ontological status in the *Republic.* This he reserves for the Forms alone.

It is intended simply to mark the boundary between the inside and the outside of the theatre; between the imaginative realm of the performance space and the (supposed) "reality" of life outside of it.) The larger threat, as Plato sees it, is that the sophists and politicians in this ostensibly non-theatrical "real-world" operate on exactly the same principles as do the tragedians. Both appeal to audience response rather than reference to a fixed and underlying Truth as the measure of goodness or badness. Both are concerned with appearance over reality. The problem is therefore not so much that the *demos* will be corrupted by tragedy and mimetic poetry, as it is that the *demos* has already been corrupted. Mimetic poetry has left the theatre and entered public life, concealing itself in the process. Plato tacitly notes this shift when he speaks of "admirers of Homer" as an educator and as one from whom to learn "the management of human affairs." Plato, *Republic*, 606e. He is breaking down the barriers between the "real-world" and the theatre, disparaging both as all too "un-real."

52 Ibid., 476c.

53 Ibid., 396c–6e. Grube translates this last part as "he despises them in his mind, except perhaps for the sake of play." Plato, *Republic*, 396e.

54 Plato has Socrates say to Glaucon:

> No free man must learn anything under compulsion like a slave. Physical labour performed under duress does no harm to the body, but nothing learned under compulsion stays in the mind—True.
>
> Do not, therefore, my excellent friend, I said, instruct the boys in these studies by force, but in play, so that you will also see better what each of them is by nature fitted for. Plato, *Republic*, 536e.

We shall see, below, the extent to which Plato departs from his own rule in this regard.

55 Plato's "good" mimesis, which is quite literally a mimesis of the Good, operates under the rubric of the "noble fiction" or "necessary untruth."

56 Plato, *Republic*, 607c–7d.

57 Ibid., 476c.

58 Ibid., 585d.

59 Ibid., 586d.

60 Ibid., 382c.

61 Ibid., 480a.

62 Concerning, for example, the structuring of familial relations, or the restrictions imposed on the educational system in the just city. It is true that Plato envisions very little in the way of policy pronouncements or legislation from the philosopher. Such legislation would largely be limited to the structuring of the educational system, especially in regards to the regulation of artistic and physical innovation. Ibid., 424b. The philosopher will not concern himself with the operations of the marketplace, the bringing of lawsuits and the like for "it would not be appropriate to dictate to men who are fine and good. For they

will easily find out for themselves whatever needs to be legislated about such things." Ibid., 425e. But importantly, the philosopher is charged with not only the maintenance of the goodness and truth of the citizenry, but of the creation of that status among them. Since the philosopher is not always in a position where he is working with "men who are fine and good" he is in a position where more legislation is required. The philosophers walk a very thin line then between leading the *polis* as Plato envisions it and "[spending] their lives continually enacting and amending such laws in the hope of finding what is best." Ibid., 425e.

[63] See Plato, *Republic*, 607c–7d. Thus the injustice dramatized in the *Apology* is corrected.

[64] The "paralysis" induced by the "Homeric manner of life" is implied in Plato's comment that the adherents of such a way of life "are as good as they are capable of being." Plato, *Republic*, 607a. The "paralysis" is therefore stasis at a given moral and rational plateau, well below the potential heights of both morality and reason. The "Homeric manner of life," as Plato sees it, can only ever leave its adherents shackled in the subterranean depths of Plato's cave.

[65] Perseus comes to this conclusion after his experiences in Ethiopia, where he petrifies the army belonging to Andromeda's father in a single motion. After doing the same to Polydectes and thus saving his mother, he immediately returns the Gorgon's head, along with the mirrored shield to Athena. See Robert Graves, *The Greek Myths* (New York: George Brazillier, Inc, 1955).

[66] Plato, *Republic*, 492b–2d.

[67] Ibid., 492e.

[68] Ibid., 501a,c.

[69] This is tantamount to the claim that knowledge of human beings is not possible until they cease to be human beings and become gods. See Ibid., 381a–1d. The possibility that the philosopher does not have knowledge of the medium through which he works, *vis.*, the human character, is given further support by Plato's claim that the affairs of men and the comings and goings of phenomena are of no interest to the philosopher. Ibid., 486a.

[70] One wonders to what extent the philosopher is Plato's *deus ex machina*. It is clear that the education of the guardians is the machine that produces this particular "deity." Plato's view of the *deus ex machina* will be discussed below.

[71] Ibid., 501e.

[72] Ibid., 502a. Emphasis added. There is a clear allusion to Thracymachus who blushes after suffering a logical reversal of his position. Not only that, but the careful reader is reminded of the inadequacy of such a result, as demonstrated by Glaucon's challenge from Book II.

[73] It is not shame alone, but fear that comes into play. Compare this to the punishment and disenfranchisement levied by the Sophists against those their words cannot convince. Ibid., 492d.

[74] Thus Glaucon's challenge at the beginning of Book II where he says "Do you, Socrates, want to appear to have persuaded us, or do you want truly to convince

us" is disallowed. Ibid., 357a. He makes this challenge based on what he sees as Socrates incomplete answer to the argument put forward by Thracymachus, who is no longer willing to pursue his case, less because he is convinced than because he is ashamed. Of course, almost the whole of the argument made in the *Republic* stems from Glaucon's challenge and the lessons contained therein would be lost were it not for this challenge.

75 For the problematic fate of these souls who are good by habit, see Ibid., 619b–c. The Er myth, which concludes the *Republic* is troublesome in a myriad of ways. Most notably, the selection by an immortal soul of a life that is already fated hollows out the role of education that has played such a central role in the rest of the text. The fate of the habitually good soul may even suggest that a good education, as defined by Plato through the text may prove harmful in the end. It is notable that Odysseus is depicted as choosing "the quiet life of a private individual", in other words, a complete nobody. Ibid., 620c. He has in the end become "Udeis" ("Nobody"). In his choice, he has relegated himself to what Plato would consider to be his (and by extension, Homer's) "proper" position, unheralded by anyone.

5

What Begins with *Cratylus*, Leads to Baudrillard

Despite the inability of Plato's concept of mimesis as presented in the *Republic* to follow through on its promise of critical distance, one can, at the very least, retain from it a sense of the promise itself. Plato's inability to undo the *thlexis* (total enchantment) of the shield is no reason in itself to abandon the promise of critical distance altogether. But from what direction might this promise be fulfilled? One avenue of pursuit begins with Plato's *Cratylus*. In that dialogue Plato offers one of the first extant treatments of language—how words have meaning. The key positions in the dialogue are held by Hermogenes, who sees language as operating on a purely conventional basis, and Cratylus who advocates a correspondence model in which words have meaning by hooking onto the world in an appropriate (or what might be called "good mimetic") fashion. Cratylus holds that words are likenesses or imitations of that which they name. Plato, in the character of Socrates, addresses each of these positions in turn. He counters the notion of language as purely conventional by saying that,

> Socrates: [If] speaking or saying is a sort of action, one that is about things, isn't using names also a sort of action?
> Hermogenes: Yes.
> Socrates: And didn't we see that actions aren't in relation to us but have a special nature of their own?
> Hermogenes: We did.
> Socrates: So if we are to be consistent with what we said previously, we cannot name things as we choose; rather, we must name them in the natural way for them to be named and with the natural tool for

naming them. In that way we'll accomplish something and succeed in naming, otherwise we wont.[1]

Thus it is established that language must make reference to an underlying "nature" in relation to which it has meaning. At the same time Plato, speaking through Socrates, counters Cratylus' position by insisting that language tends to reflect a cosmos that is in constant motion.[2] The problem with this is that it renders knowledge impossible:

> Socrates: Indeed, it isn't even reasonable to say that there is such a thing as knowledge, Cratylus, if all things are passing on and none remain. For if that thing itself, knowledge, did not pass on from being knowledge, then knowledge would always remain, and there would be such a thing as knowledge. On the other hand, if the very form of knowledge passed on from being knowledge, the instant it passed on into a different form than that of knowledge, there would be no knowledge. Hence, on this account, no one could know anything and nothing could be known either. But if there is always that which knows and that which is known, if there are such things as the beautiful, the good, and each one of the things that are, it doesn't appear to me that these things can be at all like flowings or motions, as we were saying just now they were. So whether I'm right about these things or whether the truth lies with Heraclitus and many others isn't an easy matter to investigate. But surely no one with any understanding will commit himself or the cultivation of his soul to names, or trust them and their givers to the point of firmly stating that he knows something—condemning both himself and the things that are to be totally unsound like leaky sinks—or believe that things are exactly like people with runny noses, or that all things are afflicted with colds and drip over everything.[3]

This dialogue ends in a suspended state of indeterminacy. Socrates has not been entirely successful in his attempt to convince Cratylus that words can at best reveal the prejudices of the name giver, nor has he succeeded in convincing Cratylus that names must be judged in their goodness or badness by reference to a fixed being, rather than a changing one.

The Shield as Simulacrum

Since Plato's time, mimesis has remained an important, even central topic of Western traditions of thought. Much of this thought has accepted the tacit premise of the argument stated above that there is "such a thing as knowledge" that becomes more and more perfected with further inquiry.[4] The basic argument is that words provide insight into the nature of that which they name. Over time the relationship between the word and the world is increasingly refined, more closely perfected. However with the advent of the linguistic turn in philosophy, this premise has come under increasing scrutiny and doubt.[5] One of the more notable contemporary developments of a counter-argument to this line of thinking is offered by the French semiotician and cultural critic, Jean Baudrillard. He is of particular interest here not only because of his thoughts on language, representation and the image, but because of the interesting relationship he has with Plato. As Christopher Norris notes,

> Philosophers and political theorists since Plato have taken it as axiomatic that thought must at some point distinguish between truth and falsehood, reason and rhetoric, essence and appearance, science and ideology. One way of describing Baudrillard's project is to see it as a species of inverted Platonism, a discourse that systematically promotes the negative terms (rhetoric, appearance, ideology) above their positive counterparts.[6]

The relationship between Plato and Baudrillard can be seen quite clearly against the backdrop of Baudrillard's four phases of the image, as detailed in *Simulations*.

> This would be the successive phases of the image:
>   —it is a reflection of a basic reality
>   —it masks and perverts a basic reality
>   —it masks the absence of a basic reality
>   —it bears no relation to any realty whatever: it is its own pure simulacrum.[7]

Plato's mimesis is exemplary of the first two phases, where Baudrillard's work is more closely associated with the last two.

In the first phase, the image, which, as in Plato and Saussure alike can be a sound-image, reflects a basic reality.[8] The image acts as a mirror, and it remains faithful to that which it represents. This is the kind of image in operation in Plato's good mimesis. It is also the putative image put forward by the unchallenged operation of the Shield of Achilles. The image in this phase serves to reveal the world behind it. An excellent example of this particular phase of the image is to be found in Cratylus' position in the Platonic dialogue that bears his name. There, Cratylus maintains, "the correctness of a name consists in displaying the nature of the thing it names."[9] It may be, however, that this mirroring function is only in place because there is no means by which to question the image.

This kind of questioning is made possible in Plato's challenge to Homer in the *Republic*. As has been demonstrated, Plato critiques Homer for offering a distorted representation—a bad mimesis—of the real. This is Baudrillard's second phase of the image. It is in this phase that the image becomes associated with the imitation or counterfeit, along with all accompanying negative connotations. Where the first phase of the image is more or less self-evident and uncritical in its approach, the introduction of the second phase allows for a measure of critical distance from the image. In terms of the bearing of the shield, the second phase of the image can be employed as a critical tool. Resistance is possible to the "this is the way it is" of the shield by way of the counter claim "this is the way it really is." (The implication being a precursory "no it isn't.") Viewed as a second phase image, the rhetoric of anyone who bears the shield, with all of its attendant claims to "tell it like it is" can be seen as a distortion of the truth. This is an important step in that it also brings a challenge to the attendant claim that "there is nothing (else) to be done." Thus, for example, when Perle and Frum state that we have no other choice but to fight the War on Terror, the arguments they put forward can be seen as misleading, as would be any conclusions drawn from them. [10] Such a strategy of resistance requires access to objectively "better" information, and is an inherently empirical counter-argument. Of course, resistance to a particular instance of the bearing of the shield made along these lines can do nothing to challenge the bearing of the shield itself.

The emergence of the second phase of the image is already implicit in Plato's *Cratylus*.

> Socrates: Perhaps it will seem absurd, Hermogenes, to think that things become clear by being imitated in letters and syllables, but it is absolutely unavoidable. For we have nothing better on which to base the truth of primary names.[11]

This position is a classic statement of a model of language that obtains meaning by mapping onto reality in what can be objectively called better or worse ways. Indeed, this is the argument that Plato, in the character of

Socrates, brings to bear against Cratylus. He says that most primary words portray a cosmos in constant motion, a portrayal Plato sees as incorrect. The objective classification of words, that is to say sound-images, as good or bad representations implies an unfettered, unmediated and, importantly, non-linguistic access to the real. Without such access, no such judgment is possible "unless you want us to behave like tragic poets, who introduce a deus ex machina whenever they're perplexed."[12]

The deus ex machina of the tragic poets is a headlong rush into the inscrutability of the gods, and exposes the limits of reason. Plato clearly sees this as an artificial limit, reflective more of the non-philosophic nature of the poet, indicative of a own lack of reason, than of an actual limit to reason itself. It is clearly not "the best answer we can give."[13] By invoking the inscrutability of the gods, the strategy of the tragic poets implies that there are aspects of the real that are not available to human perception or understanding. There are, in other words, places where the truth or falsity of a word, the goodness or badness of its imitation of the truth, becomes undecidable. Without decidability, especially in the case of the so-called "primary names," the entire system of meaning presented by Plato comes crashing down.

> And yet regardless of what kind of excuse one offers, if one doesn't know about the correctness of primary names, one cannot know about the correctness of derivative ones, which can only express something by means of those others about which one knows nothing. Clearly, then, anyone who claims to have a scientific understanding of derivative names must first and foremost explain the primary ones with perfect clarity. Otherwise he can be certain that what he says about the others will be worthless.[14]

In Plato's case, this phase poses a few distinct problems, as he himself operates as an "imitative poet." Just as the poets he criticizes mislead their audiences by distorting and therefore concealing the truths they purport to reveal, so too does Plato. This is most evident in his metaphors of the sun, the line, and the cave. These are well known and very powerful images, but their very power is what makes them problematic. Indeed it has been noted that the power of these images is such that they may even get in the way of understanding.[15] Plato is well aware that any representation of the Good must simultaneously distort that which it hopes to reveal. His images can never be the Good they strive to represent. With this realization, even his so-called "good mimesis" must bear a close kinship to "bad mimesis."

Indeed, the distinction between good and bad mimesis is paradoxical. Even the best mimesis is not the equivalent of that which it strives to represent. The problem is that the "better" the image is as a representation, the greater is its threat to keep its distortions concealed. It is easier and easier to take the "good" image as the thing itself, although it remains a distortion of its underlying reality (and therefore bad mimesis) simply by remaining an image. As the mimetic image more closely approximates the real, the more it threatens to obscure the real entirely by fostering the (false) belief that it *is* the real. The more realistic the image, the more likely it will simply be accepted as real, thus hindering further refinement of the image. Yet, as we are told in the *Cratylus*, the image cannot be perfected so long as it remains an image. If the image is falsely accepted as the real, then the unobstructed access to the real that underpins the status of the image as good or bad develops a fatal blockage. An unproblematic relationship to the real is no longer possible. Once this paradox becomes apparent, the image functions so as to conceal it, thereby circumventing, or at least postponing the ascendancy of absolute relativism and chaos. Once this paradox becomes apparent, the image has entered its third phase.

In Baudrillard's third phase, the image ceases to be either a representation or a distortion of a basic reality and comes to "mask the absence of a basic reality." Baudrillard's favorite example of this third phase of the image is Disneyland. The "Magic Kingdom" in Baudrillard's understanding makes use of its blatant non-reality to conceal the fact that the real "magic kingdom" is outside the gates of the park.

> Disneyland is there to conceal the fact that it is the "real" country, all of "real" America, which is Disneyland (just as prisons are there to conceal the fact that it is the social in its entirety, in its banal omnipresence, which is carceral). Disneyland is presented as imaginary in order to make us believe that the rest is real, when in fact all of Los Angeles and the America surrounding it are no longer real, but of the order of the hyperreal and of simulation. It is no longer a question of a false representation of reality (ideology), but of concealing that fact that the real is no longer real, and thus of saving the reality principle.[16]

This is a difficult phase to grasp, but an example is to be found in the Shield of Achilles. The images on the shield as it appears in Homer's epic, in the guise of a divinely sanctioned revelation of the world as it is, serve to mask the absence of the world as it is depicted. The claim of the shield is "all is war" and yet this is clearly not the case. This is evident not only by the remembered experiences and future hopes of the soldiers, but by Achilles himself in his reconciliation with Priam, and by the characters of Nestor, Menelaus and Odysseus, each of whom ultimately returns to a life beyond the confines of the battlefield. This is the Disneyland example reversed. The theme park, in its blatant fictiveness, imbues the backdrop of the larger society with a sense of solid reality. The shield in the hands of Achilles, with its insistence on its own unimpeachable realty, imbues the backdrop of life beyond the battlefield with a sense of fictiveness or illusion. This is a pattern that is repeated in all instances of the bearing of the shield.

The third phase of the image is both promising and threatening. Turning once again to the War on Terror, the possibility is opened that one might see in the rhetoric surrounding it a strategy of concealment. One could point to the clean lines between "us" and "them" or "good" and "evil" as an attempt to conceal the absence of any such clear divisions. The insistence that one take sides in the conflict, that there is no neutral ground, can be understood as masking the impossibility of a meaningful taking of sides, and that there is only "neutral ground." To flesh this out somewhat, one must ask the question, "what does it mean to take sides between fundamentalism and itself?" The War on Terror, whatever else it may be, is a clash of fundamentalisms. The key antagonists of its early years, Bush and bin Laden (although the latter has become more of a shorthand for a variety of shadowy figures than an actual antagonist) have both been locked into an ideological matrix that is totalizing in its reach. Their way is the right way, anything else is wrong. Both have seen the other as the very embodiment of evil. Certainly within such a matrix, there is indeed no neutral ground. But the third phase of the image, employed as a critical tool, can highlight that both parties have been attempting, by way of their images (the car bomb, the surgical strike, the sound-image of a broadcast speech or audio tape) to force the image back into its pre-contemplative first phase. This is an ironic gesture because the very engine behind the need for such images is the ascendancy of the "relativism" it hopes to ward off. It would be better to say that the images seek to hold the appearance of relativism at bay, although it can do nothing about the disappearance of the real (or what might torturously be called the reality of the absence of the real). It is not the ascendancy of relativism, but rather the generalized awareness of the ascendancy of "relativism" that is circumvented or postponed.[17] There is a profound shift then from the real to the perception of the real, the appearance of reality, as the condition of the image.

Here begins the fourth phase of the image. In this phase, images become strictly self-referential, and therefore not referential at all. They cease to have any connection "to any reality." Images become pure simulacra. The real becomes doubled in its perfected image so that the only remaining difference between the real and the image is their sameness.[18] Mimesis, representation, becomes its own opposite.

Representation starts from the principle that the sign and the real are equivalent (even if this equivalence is Utopian, it is a fundamental axiom). Conversely, simulation starts from the Utopia of this principle of equivalence, from the radical negation of the sign as value, from the sign as reversion and death sentence of every reference. Whereas representation tries to absorb simulation by interpreting it as false representation, simulation envelops the whole edifice of representation as itself a simulacrum.[19]

Baudrillard employs an analogy to clarify what has happened to the real. He says that the obsession with perfect reproduction has created a "stereophonic effect" akin to feedback,

which is produced in acoustics by a source and a receiver being too close together and in history by an event and its dissemination being too close together and thus interfering disastrously—a short circuit between cause and effect like that between the object and the experimenting subject in microphysics (and in the human sciences!).[20]

As in acoustic feedback, once this stage is reached, there is no way to tease apart the resultant tone into is original notes. Thus there is no way to distinguish between the real and its simulation. The real ceases to be what it was, as does the representation of the real. Both become *hyperreal*. In a way Baudrillard has come back to the Platonic notion of the apparent as a pastiche of dreamwork. But he does so not to highlight the surface/depth distinction, but to eradicate it. The model is perfected in its image and vice versa.

In conjunction with the four phases of the image, Baudrillard outlines three orders of simulacra. The purpose of discussing these three orders is not to offer a full and in depth analysis of them, but to trace the effacement of the real in concrete historical and material context.[21] The first order of simulacra, the counterfeit, emerges with the decline of the feudal system and the rise of the bourgeoisie during the European Renaissance. The caste system of feudalism maintained its symbolic power by the strict limitation of the diffusion of signs. That the sign remained privy only to select members of specific classes, where they were transmitted by ritualistic practices, ensured that the signs "are not arbitrary."[22] With the decline of the feudal order, the sign became emancipated from its ritual transmission. The sign is no longer obligatory. It becomes "unburdened of all restraint, universally available," and thus counterfeit. "Counterfeiting does not take place by means of changing the nature of an 'original,' but, by extension, through completely altering a material whose clarity is completely dependent upon a restriction."[23] This is to say that the first order simulacrum replaces the obligatory sign while continuing to play at being obligatory.

The second order simulacrum is closely related to serial production, and is coeval with the Industrial Revolution. Here signs are no longer counterfeit. Signs do not play at being obligatory, but rather override the question of "their uniqueness or their origin" entirely. With the advent of serial production, objects do not appear in an original/replica relationship, but in a series. "In a series, objects become undefined simulacra one of the other. And so along with the objects do the men that produce them."[24] There is a shift from a reliance on the skill of the individual, the craftsman, to a reliance on the machine, on the technological means of production. Just as the status of the craftsman is effaced by the technical capacity of the machine, the status of the original becomes entirely hollowed out in the infinite reproducibility of the object. Production becomes its own end. "Production itself has no meaning: its social finality is lost in the series."[25] Once this stage is reached, third order simulacra begin.

> There is no more counterfeiting of an original, as there was in the first order, and no more pure series as there was in the second; there are models from which all forms proceed according to modulated differences. Only affiliation to the model has any meaning, since nothing proceeds in accordance with its end any more, but issues instead from the model, the "signifier of reference," functioning as a foregone, and the only credible, conclusion.[26]

Here is the realm of the hyperreal.

The primary symbol for the triumph of the hyperreal and of the power monopoly of capital is, or rather was, the World Trade Center in New York City.

> The effigy of the capitalist system has passed from the pyramid to the punch card. The buildings are no longer obelisks, but trustingly stand

next to one another like the columns of a statistical graph. This new architecture no longer embodies a competitive system, but a countable one where competition has disappeared in favor of correlation ... This architectural graphism belongs to the monopoly: the World Trade Center's two towers are perfect parallelepipeds, four hundred meters high on a square base; they are perfectly balanced and blind communicating vessels. The fact that there are two identical towers signifies the end of all competition, the end of every original reference ... The two towers of the WTC are the visible sign of the closure of a system in the vertigo of doubling while the other skyscrapers are each the original moment of a system continually surpassing itself in the crisis and the challenge.[27]

It is within the realm of the hyperreal that Baudrillard offers his reading of the War on Terror.

The Spirit of Terrorism

In *The Spirit of Terrorism*, Baudrillard addresses the War on Terror directly, or more specifically, he addresses the attacks of September 11, 2001. This short text is both a rethinking and a reassertion of much of his prior work. In his previous books, notably in *The Illusion of the End*, Baudrillard makes reference to "the event strike." This is the condition of prevalent hyperreality where nothing happens that does not already conform to a prior understanding of how it ought to happen. He uses the Timisoara massacre during the Romanian revolution as his example. In this case, television images of the aftermath of a clash between protestors and government forces were broadcast that included numerous faked corpses. The "corpses" were there for the sake of the television audience so as to give the event a certain sense of credibility, to make it a "real" revolution in the eyes of the world:

> The actors and the media sensed obscurely that the events in Eastern Europe had to be given credibility, that the revolution had to be lent credibility by an extra dose of dead bodies. And the media themselves had to be lent credibility by the reference to the people. Leading to a vicious circle of credibility, the result of which is the decredibilizing of the revolution and the events themselves.[28]

Events become bracketed by their expectation, and nothing can open up the horizon of the possible as it has collapsed into is preset model.

Nothing is ever anything other than what it is expected to be. Events are "on strike." They cease to be experiences, or for that matter, events at all. The hyperreal is therefore the realm of the (non)event, encapsulated in the concept of deterrence.

> Events are not on strike any more. With the attacks on the World Trade Centre in New York, we might even be said to have before us the absolute event, the 'mother' of all events, the pure event uniting within itself all the events that have never taken place.[29]

The return of events is not accomplished through the destruction of lives or property, (plenty of this had gone on throughout the "event strike"), but through the destruction of the symbolic center of an entire global system of the (hyper)real.

The symbolic challenge of September 11 is the one challenge the system of global capital—and the code of the hyperreal that underwrites it—cannot respond to. The inability to respond is based on the inability of the hyperreal to allow a distinction between surface and depth. Nothing can stand for anything else because everything is always already a perfect equivalent of everything else. The logic of the hyperreal, *hyperlogic*, denies the very possibility of the symbol, as it is by way of the symbol that the system can be challenged. In a way, this effacement of the symbol is something like the third phase of the image that operates to conceal an absence. The hyperreal reasserts its hegemony by denying the very possibility of its being challenged. It is, because the hyperreal is vulnerable to symbolic challenge, that works to eradicate the very possibility of the symbol. The question then becomes "how is the hyperreal vulnerable to symbolic challenge?" An answer to this question is to be found in Baudrillard's discussion of gift giving.

> This is the spirit of terrorism.
> Never attack the system in terms of relations of force. That is the (revolutionary) imagination the system itself forces upon you—the system which survives only be constantly drawing those attacking it into fighting on the ground of reality, which is always its own. But shift the struggle into the symbolic sphere, where the rule is that of challenge, reversion and outbidding. So that death can be met only by equal or greater death. Defy the system by a gift to which it cannot respond except by its own death and its own collapse.[30]

The symbolic challenge of September 11 can be understood using the model of the potlatch, a concept Baudrillard takes from Mauss.[31] The entire social institution of the potlatch is predicated on the giving of gifts. The more resplendent the gifts given, the greater the status of the gift-giver. Each gift is therefore a challenge. The receiver is challenged to outdo the gifts he has received, and thereby outdo the prestige of the one from whom he has received. The potlatch is therefore based on an economy of escalation, prestige building on prestige. Each party in the exchange is under the perpetual imperative to outdo both the other and themselves. This is a far cry from the "zero degree"[32] of the hyperreal (non)exchange in which deterrence and not escalation is the aim. The "prestige" of the parties in the latter (non)exchange is not even considered, as it is always already equal. Prestige is not even possible within the ubiquitous non-differentiation of the hyperreal. In the symbolic exchange of the potlatch, there comes a point where a gift is given that is not returnable. This is the gift of death, the death-gift, in which one party gives his own life to the other. The power of this gift is readily discernable in the figure of the martyr.[33] The only appropriate response to the death-gift is the self-sacrificial death of the receiver in return. On September 11, 2001, the World Trade Centre along with the entire code of which it was the primary symbol was given the death-gift. The towers themselves responded to this gift according to the economy of exchange in which it was given. "When the two towers collapsed, you had the impression that they were responding to the suicide of the suicide-planes with their own suicides."[34]

The system of which the towers were the symbol has responded, to be sure, but not within the same economy of exchange. The "appropriate" response would have been for the system itself to implode, like the towers did. However, the response has been to reject this gift. The system has reasserted itself "in the position of God (divine omnipotence and absolute moral legitimacy)."[35] As seen from within the logic of the potlatch, this is to unilaterally declare the game to be completed with the giving of the penultimate gift. It is to declare victory before the game has concluded. It is a declaration of victory which is at the same time an admission of defeat. The events of September 11—and it is important to note that they were events[36]—expose the vulnerability of the system and its hyperlogic. The system rests on its perfection in accord with its own models. Its "reality" is expressed in the form of the universal law. The "rule of law" and the rule of the code are indistinguishable. Yet the basic tenets of law—that crime is punished, and the state is the locus of executive power (literally the power to execute)—are exposed to an unanswerable challenge. The ritual, crucial in the continual reestablishment of the state monopoly on force, wherein crime is followed by state sanctioned (and executed) punishment, is interrupted when the crime and the punishment are condensed into a single moment.

> A transcendent, "objective" agency requires a delegation of justice, death and vengeance. Death and expiation must be wrested from the circuit, monopolized at the summit and redistributed. A bureaucracy of death and punishment is necessary, in the same way as there must be an abstraction of economic, political and sexual exchanges: if not, the entire structure of social control collapses.[37]

On September 11, the crime (the murder of innocents) and the punishment (the death of the perpetrators) are one and the same. The state is entirely excluded from the exchange. It can only retroactively reassert its power monopoly, adding it on artificially to the fait accompli.

The other response remaining for the state is to invert the situation; to reabsorb the event into the simulation. The system feverishly reproduces the spectacularity of the event so that it becomes lost in its own spectacle. It is not the omnipotence of the system that is added to the event, but the event that is added to the omnipotence of the system.

> The fascination with the attack is primarily a fascination with the image (both its exultatory and its catastrophic consequences are themselves largely imaginary).
>
> In this case, then, the real is superadded to the image like a bonus of terror, like an additional *frisson*: not only is it terrifying, but, what is more, it is real. Rather than the violence of the real being there first, and the *frisson* of the image being added to it, the image is there first, and the *frisson* of the real is added.[38]

In a move reminiscent of the third phase of the image, the system itself operates to conceal the cracks made visible in its claims to omnipotence.[39] Thus the "shock and awe" strategy is not primarily that which marked the opening days of the war in Iraq, but that which the entire system undertook from the moment the second plane hit the South tower of the World Trade Centre. It is the immediate call to arms that reinstates the power of the state. It is "Operation Infinite Justice" that repositions the state in the position of God. Its intended audience was not so much the Iraqi military forces as the citizenry of the "civilized" West. If the (counter)attacks of September 11 challenged the system on the symbolic level, the subsequent (non)response of the system has worked to efface and deny that challenge.[40] The system that is already dead "proves" its vitality by spreading death, by making its condition universal.

"Hyperrealist Abjection" or the Shield of Baudrillard

The critique offered by Baudrillard, like that offered by Plato, promises to provide a sense of critical distance from the image of the shield by exposing it as an image. Speaking of the 1991 Gulf War, he says,

> The question is not whether one is for or against war, but whether one is for or against the reality of war. Analysis must not be sacrificed to the expression of anger. It has to be directed in its entirety against reality, against manifestness—here against the manifest reality of this war. The Stoics contest the very self-evidence of pain, when the body's confusion is at its height. Here, we must contest the very self-evidence of war, when the confusion of the real is at its height. We must hit out at the weak point of reality. It's too late afterwards: you're stuck with the "acts of violence", stuck in realist abjection.[41]

His comments are easily applicable to the current War on Terror, especially as it is played out in the ongoing conflict in Iraq. He is right to suggest that war should be challenged in its "manifest reality"—as something that "must be done." He is also right in noting the many parallels between the (Second) Gulf War and the Trojan War, thereby "giv[ing] force to the illusion of war, rather than becom[ing] an accessory to its false reality."[42] However, he cannot escape the flip side of the "realist abjection" he so vociferously opposes. In his many comments including, "we no longer have the choice of advancing, of preserving in the present destruction, or of retreating—but only of facing up to this radical illusion,"[43] and "there is no remedy for this extreme situation, and war is certainly not a solution"[44] Baudrillard remains deeply abject. The only difference is that his is a *hyperrealist* abjection.

Like Plato before him, Baudrillard is incapable of following through on his promise to provide critical distance. Indeed, he ends up doing the opposite and collapsing all possible distance in an incessant onslaught of images that no longer fade away into the past. Nor do they offer any promise for the future, but are always recycled and recirculated in the now.

Baudrillard, like Plato before him, ends up bearing the shield himself. Phrased in terms of the dual claim of the shield, Baudrillard gets as far as "this is the way it isn't", (or specifically "all is simulated"), which in the end is a thinly veiled version of the "this is the way it is" claim. All the same, he arrives at the same ethos; "nothing (else) to be done."

Baudrillard is quite explicit about this, and yet, interestingly, he is ambivalent in his explicitness. As already discussed, he tends to leave his readers stranded in a deep melancholia from which there is no escape. On the other hand, in his essay "The Masses: The Implosion of the Social in the Media," Baudrillard notes the "forced silence of the masses in the media" as not "a sign of passivity and of alienation, but on the contrary an original strategy, an original response in the form of a challenge."[45] Baudrillard's point is that if the images produced by the mass media are intended to ensnare the will of the masses, the masses have learned to resist by a wholesale abdication of rational choice, will, knowledge and liberty.

> The deepest desire is perhaps to give the responsibility for one's desire to someone else. A strategy of ironic investment in the other, in the others; a strategy toward others not of appropriation but, on the contrary, of expulsion, of philosophers and people in power, an expulsion of the obligation of being responsible, of enduring philosophical, moral, and political categories.[46]

Baudrillard is saying that once the masses are completely devoid of will, desire, even the capacity to act independently, they are immune to manipulation by the media, much the same way the soldier, allowing himself to be killed by Achilles' spear, is immune to the stunning effects of the shield.[47]

Christopher Norris, noting the desperation of this position also notes its central logical flaw. Baudrillard's position, while propounding the wholesale rejection of appeals to truth must simultaneously sustain them:

> Baudrillard in effect contrives to have it both ways by playing on these distinctions—without which he could not even begin to articu-late his case—while rhetorically denying that they possess any kind of operative force. So long as we do not read too carefully he can thus carry off the performative trick of conjuring away with one hand those same criteria (truth, reality, history, etc.) which he then summons up with the other for purposes of contrastive definition.[48]

If Plato's position suffers from what can be understood as an overabundance of the real, Baudrillard suffers from the opposite malady. Baudrillard's near total effacement of the real leaves him no grounds upon which to articulate a system of justice. He cannot, if he is to be consistent, mark any policy as favorable over any other. It does not matter if one is opposed to the reality of war or not because there is no reality of war, and this is so because there is no *reality* at all.

Baudrillard's position may be even more tenuous than this because if he is to insist on the radical illusion of the world, he must preserve the real that he says is irretrievably lost. The real is *not* lost, for if it were truly lost, Baudrillard would have nothing upon which to rest his overwhelming melancholia. Indeed, through Baudrillard's work the real is *decidedly* not lost, but sealed away, cryogenically suspended and permanently inaccessible, yet always locatable in its absence. In denying the real, Baudrillard must simultaneously confirm it. The confirmation through cryogenization of the real resuscitates the possibility of critical distance in spite of Baudrillard's effacement of it. It highlights his failure to follow through on his promise to provide a perspective of critical distance. Like Perseus, Baudrillard is successful in his decapitation of Medusa. So too is he successful in recognizing the extreme hazard of his prize. But unlike Perseus, he is not ultimately victorious, as for him there is no overriding locus of responsibility, nor is there anything beyond the instantaneously transmitted image to which one could be responsible. There is no Athena to whom he might return the Gorgon's head, and the (borrowed) shield.

Perseus, Plato, Baudrillard

Plato's critique of Homer using mimesis as a critical tool adopts the strategic approach of Perseus, as does Baudrillard's hyperreal. Like Perseus, they approach the offending problem by way of a representation. They attempt to diffuse the offending power—Medusa's gaze; Homer's "thus it is;" the predominance of global capitalism—by recreating a likeness of it. Like Perseus, They hope to better approach and (en)counter the threat in this way. The logic of such an approach is that if one cannot resist the gaze of Medusa, or the overwhelming "this is the way it is" of the shield, then if one is to resist, it must be attempted on different grounds. The likeness and the simulation can potentially offer such grounds.

This strategy is effective, but ambivalently so. First, there is the question of "the strategy" itself, for indeed there appears to be more than one.

Perseus either kills Medusa by turning her own gaze back on her, or renders his proximity and deadly aim possible by recreating an image of her gaze in the mirrored shield, thereby diffusing its power. This matter is far from settled in the ancient texts. The second strategy (that is the second interpretation of Perseus' strategy) recognizes that the offending power is an effect overcome by distance. The image in the mirrored shield, just like the mimetic image or the simulation, acts as a buffer between the threat and the threatened, the claim and the audience, the sender and the receiver. The buffer provides a kind of distance at which critical reflection becomes possible. Here is the standpoint of the detached, rational observer.

The first strategy overcomes the threat by turning its power against itself. A good example of this is Plato's use of mimetic poetry to undo what he sees as the untoward power of mimetic poets. It is important to note that this turning of the threat, (the paralyzing double claim of the shield; Medusa's gaze), against itself does not nullify its power. Perseus does not so much eradicate as relocate the power of Medusa's gaze. Neither does Plato nullify the power of mimetic poetry and image making. Nor does Baudrillard nullify the power of the simulated non-event by turning the tools of its construction against it.[49]

In either case Perseus' encounter with Andromeda's father, (the king of Ethiopia), and his army clearly demonstrates that the power of Medusa's gaze remains perfectly intact, even if her body does not. Perseus' strategy does not result in victory over Medusa, or rather over the problem and threat of her gaze, so much as it results in a postponement of that problem. Indeed, the threat posed by her gaze may even be magnified after the death of Medusa who, after all, was quite content to remain hidden away on her remote Hyperborean rock along with her sisters. In the hands of the adventurous Perseus (winged sandals and all) the gaze becomes much more mobile, less contained. A much larger demographic is now subject to exposure to its fatal power, as the soldiers of Ethiopia would (mutely) attest. Plato's reliance on the Forms, at least in the *Republic*, leads him into this same trap. Baudrillard's cryogenization of the real and insistence on the ubiquity of simulacra does the same in his case. Put in the terms of Perseus' tale, Plato and Baudrillard alike remain on the shores of Ethiopia. Their newly acquired power may permit them to defeat all comers, and to render resistance an exercise in futility, but their quest to rid the world of just this power remains incomplete.

Notes

1 Plato, *Cratylus*, in *Plato: Complete Works*, ed. John M. Cooper (Indianapolis: Hackett Publishing Company, 1997), 387c–7d.
2 And of course "language" here means ancient Greek.
3 Ibid., 440a–0d.
4 The power of this premise is such that it is most often accepted as common sense. The sense of human history (or rather History) as found in Hegel and Marx stand out as two particularly influential and important examples.
5 Of particular note on this point is the work of Ferdinand de Saussure. He takes up the argument of the *Cratylus* where it leaves off:

> Some people regard language, when reduced to its elements, as a naming process only—a list of words, each corresponding to the thing that it names ... This conception is open to criticism at several points. It assumes that ready-made ideas exist before words; it does not tell us whether a name is vocal or psychological in nature (arbor, for instance, can be considered from either viewpoint); finally, it lets us assume that the linking of a name and a thing is a very simple operation—an assumption that is anything but true. But this rather naïve approach can bring us near the truth by showing us that the linguistic unit is a double entity, one formed by the associating of two terms. (Ferdinand de Saussure, *Course in General Linguistics*, trans. Wade Baskin (New York: Fontana/Collins, 1974), 67.)

The two terms he classifies as the concept or signified and a sound-image or signifier. Both terms are entirely psychological and the relationship between them is arbitrary, hence "the linguistic sign is arbitrary." If the sign is arbitrary, then it cannot provide any direct access to an underlying reality. Baudrillard takes this point and pursues it to an extreme.
6 Christopher Norris, *What's Wrong With Postmodernism: Critical Theory and the Ends of Philosophy* (Baltimore: Johns Hopkins University Press, 1990), 156–66.
7 Mark Poster, ed. *Jean Baudrillard: Selected Writings* (Stanford: Stanford University Press, 1988), 170.
8 Ibid., 170.
9 Plato, "Cratylus," 428d.
10 David Frum, and Richard Perle, *An End to Evil: How to Win the War on Terror* (New York: Random House, 2003).
11 Plato, "Cratylus," 425d.
12 Ibid., 425d.
13 Ibid., 425d.
14 Ibid., 426a–6b.
15 Julia Annas, *An Introduction to Plato's Republic* (Oxford: Clarendon Press, 1981).

[16] Mark Poster, *Jean Baudrillard: Selected Writings*, 172.

[17] The term "relativism" is placed in quotes because it is not relativism that is on the rise, but rather something that operates outside of the absolutism versus relativism binary. For those stuck in that matrix, any challenge to the absolute can only be understood as relativism, even if that is not what it is. As such, those whose absolutes are challenged will take extreme measures to preserve it, even if it is irretrievably gone. Neoptolemus as portrayed in Sophocles' *Philoctetes* finds himself in just this position. His (re)turn at the end of the play to a demonstrable honorability and transparency serves to mask his irredeemable status as an accomplished deceiver and dissimulator. For a more thorough discussion, see Chapter 3.

[18] The idea here is that for two things to be "the same," in this case reality and its representation, they must first and foremost be two things. As such, they must be different. In the current example, the real is perfectly duplicated in its image. The real, because it is perfectly duplicated, has ceased to be real. The image, which is perfect, ceases to be an image for that very reason. It is only an image of itself, and thus not an image at all.

[19] Ibid., 170.

[20] Jean Baudrillard, *The Illusion of the End*, trans. Chris Turner (Cambridge: Polity Press, 1994), 5–6.

[21] Baudrillard's genealogical account is useful a guideline, but as is already evident, the hallmarks of the various orders of simulation can be found outside of the timeline he provides. A recognition of this on Baudrillard's part will lead him to the conclusion that not only is our current situation one in which there is no recourse to an underlying truth, but that it has always been so.

[22] Jean Baudrillard, *Symbolic Exchange and Death*, trans. Iain Hamilton Grant, Theory, Culture & Society (London: Sage Publications, 1993), 50.

[23] Ibid., 51.

[24] Ibid., 56.

[25] Ibid., 56.

[26] Ibid., 56.

[27] Ibid., 69–70.

[28] Jean Baudrillard, *The Illusion of the End*, 58.

[29] Jean Baudrillard, *The Spirit of Terrorism and Requiem for the Twin Towers*, trans. Chris Turner (London: Verso, 2002), 3–4.

[30] Ibid., 17.

[31] See Mike Gane's introduction to Jean Baudrillard, *Symbolic Exchange and Death*.

[32] Jean Baudrillard, *The Illusion of the End*, 63.

[33] A recognition of and response to this power can be seen in the efforts made in the Western press to downplay and deny the status of the September 11 hijackers as martyrs, branding them instead as "cowards."

[34] Jean Baudrillard, *The Spirit of Terrorism and Requiem for the Twin Towers*, 7.

[35] Ibid., 7. Consider "Operation Infinite Justice," the original code name for the American assault in Afghanistan. This name was changed only after an objection was raised that infinite justice was the prerogative of God/Allah alone. Despite the name change, Baudrillard's assertion bears considerable weight. Consider also President Bush's claim that "freedom and fear, justice and cruelty, have always been at war, and God is not neutral between them." George W. Bush, "Address to a Joint Session of Congress and the American People, 20 September, 2001," (2001).

[36] This is to say that they were not reducible to their representation. They did extend a range of possibilities beyond those that might be expected given the predominant frameworks of the time.

[37] Jean Baudrillard, *Symbolic Exchange and Death*, 175.

[38] Jean Baudrillard, *The Spirit of Terrorism and Requiem for the Twin Towers*, 29.

[39] The attacks on the World Trade Center and the Pentagon were attacks on the pillars of American power—globalised capital and military might. Much of the speculation regarding the intended target of the fourth plane that went down in rural Pennsylvania has claimed that it was headed to the White House. But what if, like the two planes that crashed in New York, it was headed to the Pentagon as well? The question becomes "what need is served by making the statement that it was intending to target the White House?" Were the White House to have been hit, it would have been identified in no uncertain terms as one of the central pillars of the American global hegemony. It is possible that the insistence that the White House (or perhaps Congress) was a target does the same thing. This claim is the reinstitution of a belief that power resides in the elected leadership and therefore in the electorate (the voting public). To say that the White House was the target is to say "your vote counts!" in an oblique, yet discernable way, despite the evidence to the contrary to be found in the 2000 election.

[40] I use the term (counter)attack to indicate that the events of September 11 were already embedded in an ongoing exchange, and did not occur entirely ex nihilo. An earlier attack on the World Trade Center had occurred in 1993, indicating that the grievances were not new.

[41] Jean Baudrillard, *The Illusion of the End*, 63–64.

[42] Ibid., 64. Drawing on the version of events dramatized in Euripides' *Helen*, Baudrillard says: "If the Helen of the Trojan War was a simulacrum, what was the Gulf War's Helen? Where was there a simulacrum here, except in the simulacrum of war itself?" Ibid., 65. It seems to me at least that he too hastily jumps to this conclusion. Helen is a *causus bellum*, a role filled in the Gulf War by Iraq's invasion of Kuwait. In the current conflict in Iraq, (the Second Gulf War), the simulacrum of Weapons of Mass Destruction looms large. Following Baudrillard's logic, the current conflict is even less real (or rather more hyperreal) than its predecessor. A simulated war waged on a simulated premise. A reproduction of the original as it ought to have been (e.g. the overthrow of Saddam Hussein and the institution of a friendly democratic state in

the Middle East). Current conditions, expressed in an increasing death toll and instability in Iraq years after the American invasion are evidence of a reality that refuses to be contained in its model.

43 Ibid., 123.

44 Jean Baudrillard, *The Spirit of Terrorism and Requiem for the Twin Towers*, 34.

45 Mark Poster, *Jean Baudrillard: Selected Writings*, 208. It is clear that Baudrillard sees in the mass media another iteration of the bearing of the shield. For him, the media operate in the realm of simulacra, but present their images against a traditional system of values.

> It is a lack of relationship between the two systems which today plunges us into a state of stupor. That is what I said: stupor. To be more objective on would have to say: a radical uncertainty as to our own desire, our own choice, our own opinion, our own will. Ibid., 209.

Here is exactly the paralysis engendered by the shield, even if Baudrillard is correct in saying that this is "a completely new species of uncertainty, which results not from a lack of information but from information itself and even from an excess of information." Ibid., 210.

46 Ibid., 215.

47 It does seem odd to declare this a form of resistance, but it does, ultimately, put an end to the manipulative power of the mass media, or to the "all is war" of Achilles' shield. In the first case, it renders such manipulation entirely unnecessary, as its aim is already accomplished. In the second, war will eventually stop if only because there is no one left to kill. Put differently, Medusa's gaze loses it power in a world of stone. In any case the "success" of this resistance—one dare not call it a "strategy" for this implies a deliberate course of action—does not leave the possibility of any action whatsoever beyond its successful implementation. It is a "success" only in the way Ajax's suicide was a "successful" resolution to his conflict with Odysseus—and Homer brings even this into question. His portrayal of Ajax as unwilling to speak to Odysseus when he visits the land of the dead demonstrates the conflict to be perpetually unresolved, even unresolvable.

48 Christopher Norris, *What's Wrong With Postmodernism: Critical Theory and the Ends of Philosophy*, 182.

49 Baudrillard seems to recognize this, especially in his discussion of the Stealth Agency whose role it is to utilize the mass media to undo the images produced by the mass media. See Jean Baudrillard, *The Illusion of the End*.

6

Life as Literature: Politics as Poetics

Sing to me of the man, Muse, the man of twists and turns [polytropoi]

driven time and again off course, once he had plundered

the hallowed heights of Troy.[1]

For you only have to ask yourself carefully, "Why do you not want to deceive?" especially if it should seem—and it does seem!—as if life aimed at semblance, meaning error, deception, simulation, delusion, self-delusion, and when the great sweep of life has actually always shown itself to be on the side of the most unscrupulous polytropoi.[2]

Both Plato and Baudrillard, while extending important promises, do not deliver. Both end up bearing the shield they hope to resist. Plato's critique begins with his accusation of Homer as a bearer of the shield. What Plato means by this has already been detailed. However, it remains to be asked whether or not this is a fair accusation. In order to provide an answer to this question, the argument must return to the events following the death of Achilles.

Odysseus: Artfulness above All Else

It is true that after the death of Achilles, Odysseus wins his armor and the right to bear the shield. It is also true that he never does bear the shield in a literal way. It should now be asked—what does it mean that Odysseus wins the right to bear the shield, but does not bear it. First, an observation from the tale of Perseus: The victory over Medusa (over the fatal power of her gaze) is achieved only when Perseus relinquishes the severed head of the Gorgon over to Athena. Perseus is successful, which in this instance means heroic rather than tyrannical, when he abdicates the power that has rightfully become his to wield.[3] By not bearing the shield, Odysseus does much the same thing. He recognizes the shield as a tool that for him is redundant. It is a bit of technological trickery that can permit a decidedly "honest" or "truthful" character, like Achilles or Neoptolemus, to accomplish a stunningly powerful ruse.[4] Given his innate ability to execute such ruses, such a tool would be all but useless in the hands of Odysseus. Better yet to say that it would be redundant, but dangerously so.

Odysseus recognizes in the shield the externalization of a power of manipulation—of what amounts to mimetic *poiesis* on a grand scale—that threatens to be uncontrollable so long as it is externalized. Placed outside of the actor, the externalization of the power to create is all too easily surrendered. The presence of the external creation (the object in a material sense; the shield; the book) renders it all too easy to abdicate one's powers of creation to the reified creation. Odysseus' ruses, the representations and images of himself he puts forward for others remain largely under his control because they remain within himself. This is to say that operating in an oral tradition, rather than in a culture that relies on written documentation, he can shape and twist his stories of himself at will. Were any of his tales to be written in stone, or rather in gold, silver, tin and bronze, he would lose that control. He would become subject to his own creations.[5] As it is, Odysseus nearly loses himself in his own artifice, as is seen in his encounter with his aging father, Laertes.

Throughout his travels Odysseus tells many tales about himself, each designed to both conceal himself and to hasten his homecoming. It is not difficult to see how his concealment of himself as "Udeis" (Nobody) before Polyphemus is prudent. Likewise, when he disguises himself as a beggar before the suitors. These fabrications are easy to explain against the greater backdrop of his desired homecoming. The episode involving Laertes is intriguing because it strips away much of the backdrop against which Odysseus' other fabrications of his identity can be seen as legitimate or justifiable. He has achieved his goal. His enemies are defeated. He has returned and reclaimed his kingdom. It would seem that he has nothing left to fear, no agenda to advance. All the same he introduces himself to his grieving father under the guise of yet another false identity. This scene has been read in a number of different ways, summarized nicely by Barbara Clayton.[6] The reading here has a certain affinity with Pratt's commentary:

The poem insists that we once more appreciate Odysseus' ability to invent and deceive, even though the results are hurtful. In asking us to accept such a gratuitous falsehood, one that brings temporary but real pain to its hearer without advancing the plot, the Odyssey seems to favour artfulness above all else.[7]

Yet however much of an "appreciation" this is, it is also a warning. The emphasis on "artfulness above all else" can indeed be found in *The Odyssey* and especially in its eponymous hero. This same "artfulness" is to be found in the operation of the Shield of Achilles. It is with this artfulness that Plato takes issue.

To be sure, Plato does not mistake the threat of "artfulness above all else" but he does appear to miss the fact that Homer himself recognizes the danger. Plato's treatment of Homer in the *Republic* as a "bearer of the shield" tends to flatten out Homer's perspective, to condense his message into a single, if contradictory, viewpoint. The warning contained within the encounter between Odysseus and Laertes, and which Plato misses in the *Republic*, is that this same "artfulness" can become too much "above all else."[8] The creator can too easily be taken in by his or her creation. The hazard then resides in the artful obfuscation of artfulness itself. If art works to conceal art, creativity to conceal creativity, *poiesis* to conceal *poiesis*, then one can fall into a place where the ethos of "there is nothing (else) to be done" can more easily hold command.[9] To fall into such a state of belief (which will conceal itself under the guise of a state of knowledge) has disastrous results. The hazard of bearing the shield is that one all too easily becomes enthralled by its claim to invulnerability. One becomes increasingly less sensitive to changes in context and one is therefore increasingly less prepared for the inevitable collapse of that façade. Machiavelli makes a strikingly similar point when he discusses fortresses in *The Prince*.[10] The one who bears the shield runs the risk of trusting in its claim of invulnerability, just as a prince runs the risk of trusting too much in fortresses to secure his kingdom in all circumstances.

Homer does not so simply provide a readily identifiable "thus it is" despite Plato's treatment of him in the *Republic*.[11] Once again, it is Odysseus who helps us see this. Upon his return to Ithaca after numerous forestallings and postponements, Odysseus weaves a series of stories about himself that have come to be called the Cretan tales. These stories are intertwined in that in each of them Odysseus presents himself as being from Crete. Barbara Clayton offers a telling and detailed account of these tales, but the current argument will focus on a few salient points. First, as noted by W. B. Stanford the ancient world held a stereotypical view of Cretans as liars.[12] Second, each of these tales is careful to avoid any reference to the more fantastical (and in this sense "mythological") episodes of his travels. Absent are references to cyclopses, monsters, concubinage with goddesses, mystical conversations with the spirits of the dead. Instead there is reference to pirates, ill-fated military campaigns, foul weather and general bad luck of an everyday sort, albeit to a heightened degree. In these ways the Cretan tales are, at least to the modern reader, more believable than the "real" encounters the hero endures in the epic. The sheer believability of these tales (which are self-avowed falsehoods) has an unsettling effect. The Cretan tales can only be deemed falsehoods against the backdrop of the (far less believable) retelling of Odysseus' other experiences. The only assurance we have of the "truth" of these other experiences is the assurance of Homer that the latter Cretan tales are lies. The illogical trumps the logical, the true/false pairing is inverted, or rather suspended.[13]

The suspension of the true/false pairing works to profoundly shake the reader's certainty in the "true identity" of Odysseus. The reader suspects, in other words, that perhaps the entire epic is a grand and complex Cretan tale. Consider that each of the episodes retold in the Odyssey revolves around the question "Who is Odysseus?" Furthermore, each episode provides a different answer, and often more than one. The epic poses a question that can only be answered by means of the very events, or non-events as the case may be, that pose the question in the first place. It is quite possible that given Odysseus' reputation as a master of deception, it is the Cretan tales of the second half of the epic, and not the fanciful ("mythological") ones of the first half that reveal the bulk of what "really" happened to him. There is simply no standpoint from which to conclusively tell. With the Cretan tales the reader is faced with Odysseus's statement "I hail from Crete's broad land, I am proud to say" (13:228). The audience (which includes the reader) is in effect faced with a known liar making the statement "I am a liar." Hence a paradox. Is Odysseus' statement true or false? The problem is entirely self-referential, and therefore perpetually unsettled.[14]

Given that Odysseus is renowned as a shrewd tactician, a crafty opportunist, and an accomplished liar it is easy to see how he would garner considerable disdain from the perspective of the avowedly philo-sophic Plato. Yet Odysseus is a much more complex and problematic figure than this simplistic portrayal of him. Plato struggles with this in the *Lesser Hippias*. In that dialogue, Socrates questions Hippias's portrayal of Achilles as the "best and bravest"[15] as well as the most "truthful and simple"[16] of the Greeks, where Odysseus is "wily and a liar."[17] Socrates does not dispute

Odysseus' status as a liar, but argues that because he lies voluntarily, he has the better soul than Achilles who does so involuntarily. Socrates argues that Odysseus must know the truth if he is to voluntarily distort it. Achilles on the other hand has a worthless soul as he has no knowledge about the truth whatsoever, much like the bad runner who runs slowly not because he chooses to but because he is incapable of doing otherwise.[18] The character of Odysseus tends to disturb easy categorization as true or false, good or bad. Simple logocentrisms such as these are revealed as highly inadequate in his case.

The Homeric Question

One consequence of the instability of the identity of Odysseus is a corresponding instability in any answer to the question "Where does Odysseus stand?" "What is Odysseus' position?" Or even "What does Odysseus mean?" Authors such as Clayton, Casey, Lampert and Nagy, even Plato himself, have tended to equate Homer and Odysseus.[19] Evidence for this conclusion is drawn from the clear favoritism granted Odysseus by the bard. The connection between the two is not only drawn from this favoritism, but from their shared polymetic and polytropic qualities.[20] Indeed, the connection between the two is made by Homer himself when, for example, in Book 11 of the *Odyssey*, Alcionus clearly identifies Odysseus as a bard:

What grace you give your words, and what good sense within!
You have told your story with all a singer's skill.[21]

The question of Homer's identity is not a new one. It was vexing even to the ancients.[22] Yet Plato's dismissal of Homer in the *Republic* is notably unconcerned with this question. Plato is dismissive of Homer because Homer is logically inconsistent. According to Plato, at least as his arguments play out in the *Republic*, the messages of the works attributed to Homer do not coincide with that which reason tells us must be true. Plato's dismissal of Homer is based on the premise that the Socratic, dialectical logic Plato himself champions always already applied, even in the world of heroes described by Homer. Homer is thus open to criticism and dismissal because he has failed to meet the stringent demands of this logic. Plato can therefore say that the content of Homer's "this is the way it is" is flawed. It does not even come across as a possibility that Homer might be doing something other than making a "this is the way it is" claim.

This latter possibility is taken up in the work of Friedrich Nietzsche. In his 1869 Inaugural Address at Basle University, Nietzsche addresses the "Homeric question" in an explicit, forthright manner. The gist of Nietzsche's approach is that Homer cannot be unproblematically identified as a person to whom one might ascribe a certain and fathomable standpoint. Nietzsche sees Homer as problematic not because his contradictions indicate an untenable standpoint—a fatally flawed "this is the way it is"— but because his contradictions render it exceedingly difficult, and perhaps impossible, to attribute any standpoint to him, once and for all. For Nietzsche, the Homeric question indicates a problem with the making of "this is the way it is" type claims.

Nietzsche traces the history of the Homeric question back through Friedrich A. Wolf[23] to the "Alexandrian Grammarians" who "conceived the *Iliad* and the *Odyssey* as the creations of one single Homer,"[24] then to Aristotle who "considered Homer as the author of the original of all comic epics, the *Margites*."[25]

> If we go still further backwards from Aristotle, the inability to create a personality is seen to increase; more and more poems are attributed to Homer; and every period lets us see its degree of criticism by how much and what it considers as Homeric. In this backward examination, we instinctively feel that away beyond Herodotus there lies a period in which an immense flood of great epics has been identified with the name of Homer.[26]

Based on this early and rudimentary genealogy, and given the centralizing force exerted by Homer within the conglomeration of Greek identity, Nietzsche raises the question, "Was the person created out of a conception, or the conception out of a person? This is the real 'Homeric question,' the central problem of the personality."[27] This problem cannot be easily resolved "from the standpoint of the poems themselves which have come down to us."[28] Nietzsche says that it "costs us some trouble to obtain a clear impression of that wonderful problem which, like a coin long passed from hand to hand, has lost its original and highly conspicuous stamp."[29] The wide diffusion (and dissolution) of the available evidence and the absence of any unimpeachable vantage point from which to sift through it leads Nietzsche to say that "Homer as the composer of *The Iliad* and *The Odyssey* is not a historical tradition, but an aesthetic judgment."[30]

It is not that Nietzsche sees Homer alone as an aesthetic judgment but, as is detailed in much of his later work, he sees all of existence, life itself this way. Nietzsche does see in Homer an emphasis on "artfulness above all else," but rather than rejecting this as somehow removed from the truth, he celebrates it. For Nietzsche,

> [one] feels ashamed and fearful before the Greeks; unless one respects truth in all things and so also dares to admit to oneself that the Greeks as charioteers hold the reins of our and every other culture in their hands, but that almost always the chariot and horses are too slight and frail to live up to the glory of their drivers, who then consider it a jest to spur such a team into the abyss: while they themselves jump to safety with a leap of Achilles.[31]

There is no question that the Greek ways of understanding the world have had a profound impact on the development of all subsequent cultures. "Almost every period and stage of cultural development has at one time or another with profound moroseness sought to free itself from the Greeks."[32] In Plato's case, this would seem to apply to the Greeks themselves. The Socratic dialectics he champions as a reaction to the influence of the "imitative poets" is such an attempt, albeit a tremendously powerful one. It has already been shown that Plato works to uncover all that is hidden, to know all that is to be known, to contemplate the Good. For in his framework, "knowledge is virtue." This has come over time to be intimately linked with the project of the Enlightenment and in the influential works of the likes of Kant, Hegel and Marx, not to mention its centrality in the development of the tools of scientific inquiry. It is not difficult to see how many "advances" have been made possible by the operation of this framework and the ever expanding spheres of knowledge it makes possible. This is the logic of the shield and its claim "thus it is" which must presuppose the fathomability of life in order to present its depths. But Nietzsche sees a problem.

By attacking the poets in the *Republic*, Plato is reacting to what he sees as the ill effects of "artfulness above all else." His dialectical methods are intended to dispel the representation, to uncover that which is behind them. However, in the quest for perfect knowledge, there comes a point where,

> science, spurred on by its powerful delusion, hurtles inexorably towards its limits where the optimism hidden in the essence of logic founders. For the periphery of the circle of science has an infinite number of points and while there is no telling yet how the circle

could ever be fully surveyed, the noble and gifted man, before he has reached the middle of his life, still inevitably encounters such peripheral limit points and finds himself staring into an impenetrable darkness. If he at that moment sees to his horror how in these limits logic coils around itself and finally bites its own tail—then this new form of knowledge breaks through, tragic knowledge, which in order to be tolerated, needs art as a protection and remedy.[33]

What Nietzsche points out is that the unfathomability of art, its illusion and mystery, are required, even by science that self-avowedly seeks to dispel such things. The whole of human cultural development, he tells us, is best understood not as a dialectical operation in which a thesis and its antithesis are both overcome in a linearly progressive synthesis, but in terms of the interminable tensions between what he calls the Apollonian and Dionysian drives.

Apollo, god of the sun and reason, is "the apotheosis of the *principium individuationis*" and its central imperatives "know thyself" and "nothing in excess."[34] He is the god of dreams.

He shows us with sublime gestures how the whole world of torment is necessary in order to force the individual to produce the vision and then to sit in calm contemplation of it as his small boat is tossed by the surrounding sea.[35]

His counterpart is Dionysus, the god of intoxication. Where Apollo demands moderation, Dionysus is celebrated in the excess. Apollo's linearity, his orderliness, is met with the unrestrained exuberance and cyclical nature of the god whose ritualistic celebrations end in his being torn asunder by his celebrants before he is reborn again. The *principium individuationis* is met with the complete loss of the self, in the becoming animal of the Dionysian celebration. Dionysus embraces both the torment and joy of life. In the words of his companion Silenus, Dionysus teaches us that "the very best of all things is completely beyond your reach: not to have been born, not to be, to be nothing. But the second best thing for you is—to meet an early death."[36] In the face of this terrible knowledge, Apollo weaves his veil of dreams, that which makes life tolerable. Apollo and Dionysus are above all not opposites. Rather they rely on each other. To favor one over the other in a logocentric pairing is to invite disaster. This is the error of Socrates, the anti-Dionysian.[37]

In framing not only art, but also life itself as developing through "the duality of the Apollonian and the Dionysian"[38] Nietzsche is subtly reminding his reader that all of the products of this developmental dynamic are to be held suspect. Apollo and Dionysus alike are closely associated with musical instruments, the lyre and the pipes, respectively. Yet both of these instruments are inventions of Hermes, the trickster, ancestor of Odysseus.[39] Hermes was the messenger of the gods who swore upon being granted this office by his father Zeus to "never tell lies, though I cannot promise always to tell the whole truth."[40] Thus in both the ordered representations of the Apollonian dream and the frenzied chaos of the Dionysian intoxication there is an element of polytropism, of craftiness and deceit, of trickery. Both the *principium individuationis* and its dissolution are something less than the "whole truths" they appear to be. Both Apollo and Dionysus, as Nietzsche makes abundantly clear, require the other in a constant making and unmaking of claims to show the world "as it is." The error of the anti-Dionysian Socrates, as Nietzsche sees it, is that he has bought fully into what can only be, at best, a partial truth. Socrates, as portrayed by Nietzsche, has rescinded his ability to see this partial truth exposed in its partiality. What is worse is that through the writings of Plato, he has worked to make his rescission universal. This is why the question "what is Dionysian?" is so important for Nietzsche.

Nietzsche's emphasis on aesthetics reorients the framework employed by Plato. Where Plato judges Homer severely against the backdrop of dialectical logic and the transcendent Forms, in short against an ontological screen of Being, Nietzsche can say that Plato, under the tutelage of the anti-Dionysian Socrates,

> was obliged by full artistic necessity to create an art-form essentially related to the existing art-forms which he had rejected. The main reproach which Plato addressed to the older art—that it is the imitation of an apparent image, and so belongs to an even lower sphere [of knowledge] than the empirical world—certainly could not be directed against the new work of art: and so we see Plato's efforts to go beyond reality and to represent the idea which lies at the basis of that pseudo-reality. But in this way Plato the thinker arrived by a circuitous route at the place which had always been his home as an artist.[41]

This can be understood as a criticism of Plato if one abides by Plato's terms, but within Nietzsche's framework this is high praise indeed.

It elevates Plato above the status of "philosophical labourers after the noble exemplar of Kant and Hegel" to that of an "actual philosopher."

> Actual philosophers . . . are commanders and law givers: they say "thus it shall be!", it is they who determine the Wherefore and the Whither of mankind . . . they reach for the future with creative hand, and everything that is or has been becomes for them a means, an instrument, a hammer. Their "knowing" is creating, their creating is law giving, their will to truth is—will to power.[42]

Platonic thought is thus both a scourge and a blessing. It is a scourge in so far as it has become utterly convincing and therefore (apparently) unchallengeable, leading to a stagnation in human self-overcoming. In this guise it is hostile to life itself, which is overcoming. But it is also a blessing in that it forms a solid backdrop against which the "new philosopher" emerges, and against which Nietzsche emerges.

Nietzsche's Language

Language is Nietzsche's bugbear. In it he sees the embodiment and perpetuation of "a tremendous error."[43] "Belief in . . . identical facts and in isolated facts—has in language its constant evangelist and advocate."[44] Language, as with the perception of the historical philosopher, is situated within a specific history from which it draws its meaning. The specific history of the European languages is the same history of metaphysical thought already addressed.[45] The words of the European languages are thus steeped in presumptions of Being.

> To the extent that man has for long ages believed in the concepts and names of things as in æternae veritates he has appropriated to himself that pride by which he raised himself above the animal: he really thought that in language he possessed knowledge of the world. The sculptor of language was not so modest as to believe that he was only giving things designations, he conceived rather that with the words he was expressing supreme knowledge of things.[46]

Nietzsche sees a direct tension between the world and the word. Names presuppose fixity and self-identity. As such they deny the constant flux of becoming. "The word killeth, everything fixed killeth."[47]

Change, mutation, becoming in general were formerly taken as proof of appearance, as the sign of something which led us astray. Today, on the contrary, we see ourselves as it were entangled in error, necessitated to error, to precisely the extent that our prejudice in favor of reason compels us to posit unity, identity, duration, substance, cause, materiality, being; however sure we may be, on the basis of a strict reckoning, that error is to be found here. The situation is the same as with the motions of the sun: in that case error has our eyes, in the present case our language as a perpetual advocate [...] I fear we are not getting rid of God because we still believe in grammar ... [48]

Words in themselves presuppose the kind of self-identity of concepts Nietzsche rejects. To speak of life, of becoming, is to fix it as a concept. In doing so, one simultaneously denies it. The goal of the metaphysician is to uncover Being at which time no further questions or answers are necessary. The aim of the metaphysician then is to have done once and for all with the need to communicate. This may be related to the conceit of the metaphysician that in uncovering Being, he also uncovers the proper means for living in accord with it. [49]

Nietzsche is a metaphysician of sorts. But of what sorts? It seems contradictory to say he is a metaphysician when he describes himself as a "godless anti-metaphysician." The key to this apparent contradiction lies in the etymological origins of the word. "Metaphysics" is derived from the philosophical works of Aristotle. It literally translates as "the (works) after the physical (works)" and is a reference to those works of Aristotle which follow his text entitled *Physics*. [50] Etymologically the word is made up of two components; the prefix "meta-", meaning after, behind, or beyond, and "physika" or the physical. From this it has been traditionally employed as "beyond-"or "behind- the physical." It is this notion of metaphysics with its quest for categorical knowledge, transcendental truths and eternal verities that Nietzsche has in mind when he describes himself as "anti-metaphysician."

However, the etymological roots of the term contain an ambiguity, which justifies the claim that Nietzsche is a metaphysician of sorts. [51] The prefix "meta-" while meaning after, behind, beyond, can also be used to denote transformation, as in "metamorphosis." There is thus a possible literal translation of "metaphysics" as "the transformation of the physical." Furthermore "physika" meaning the body, is also the root of "physician" (doctor) and "physic" (prescribed remedy, cathartic). The implication here is that Nietzsche as meta-physician prescribes the embracing and celebration of change as a treatment for the sickness of traditional meta-physics. This variation on the traditional word emphasizes both Nietzsche's departure from that which precedes him and his proximity to it. In calling Nietzsche a meta-physician his work is placed within, or rather beyond, and built upon a specific avenue of philosophical inquiry.[52]

The aim of the meta-physician is to somehow come to terms with becoming, knowing the impossibility of this task. Nietzsche implies that question marks and "perhapses" are unending.[53] As a philologist, Nietzsche is well aware of the change in the usage of words over time. Thus even if a spoken word can never capture becoming, perhaps the speaking and re-speaking of a word over long periods of time can offer insight into becoming.

> It is good to repeat oneself and thus bestow on a thing a right and a left foot. Truth may be able to stand on one leg; but with two it can walk and get around.[54]

This last aphorism is key, and even more so when read in conjunction with one almost immediately preceding it:

> Thought in poetry.—The poet conducts his thoughts along festively, in the carriage of rhythm: usually because they are incapable of walking on foot.[55]

This implies that the poet is capable of doing something the metaphysician can not. The poet can name without fixing the named as a concept in the same way. For Nietzsche, naming is clearly an art. Any act of naming is also, in so far as it is an inscription of the speaker onto the world, an artistic expression:

> Even when we are involved in the most uncommon experiences we still do the same thing: we fabricate the greater part of the experience and can hardly be compelled not to contemplate some event as its "inventor." All this means: we are from the very heart and from the very first—accustomed to lying. Or, to express it more virtuously and hypocritically, in short more pleasantly: one is much more of an artist than one realises.[56]

As with all artists, metaphysicians and meta-physicians alike are dreamers.[57] The differences between them are subtle, but Nietzsche has forewarned the reader of his subtlety.[58] He says of himself: "I suddenly woke up in the midst of this dream, but only to the consciousness that I am dreaming and that I must go on dreaming lest I perish—as a somnambulist must go on dreaming lest he fall."[59] The difference is that the meta-physician is aware of his own dreaming. He becomes a "somnambulist of the day."[60] The names this artist/philosopher/somnambulist gives emerge from his dream.[61]

To start from the dream: on to a certain sensation, the result for example of a distant cannon-shot, a cause is subsequently foisted (often a whole little novel in which precisely the dreamer is the chief character). The sensation, meanwhile continues to persist, as a kind of resonance: it waits, as it were, until the cause-creating drive permits it to step into the foreground—now no longer as a chance occurrence but as "meaning."[62]

If this is the process by which words acquire meaning, then all words are inherently deceptions. Given that the metaphysician and the meta-physician alike deal in deceptions, how can the standards of life affirming and life denying be decided? How can Nietzsche give preference to one over the other?

The meta-physician, who speaks in terms of "life affirming" and "life denying" instead of "true" and "false", perpetuates an error in speaking at all. Even called "becoming" or "will to power" life is rendered a "thing", ("and there is no 'thing'").[63] The metaphysician however commits a double error. Not only does he render life a "thing," but also he convinces himself of its thing-ness. He has convinced himself that the claim he makes, his "this it is," refers to something outside of himself. Furthermore, he has convinced himself that it is something to which he (and everybody else) is beholden.

A metaphysician's ambition to maintain a forlorn position, may actually play a part and [he may] finally prefer a handful of "certainty" to a whole cartful of beautiful possibilities; there may even exist puritanical fanatics of conscience who would rather lie down and die on a sure nothing than on an uncertain something. But this is nihilism and the sign of a despairing, mortally weary soul, however brave the bearing of such a virtue may appear.[64]

Although Nietzsche continually attacks morality, he produces one himself. This is indicated in his reproval of those who would "deny life." Yet Nietzsche's moral language (his "immorality" to use his words) is structurally different than those he understands it to be supplanting. Nietzsche's (im)morality must be pronounced a "thing", but—here is the crucial difference—not a thing, so that further steps beyond it may be taken. It must however be taken very seriously if it is to solidify into useful material from which the future may be built. For this to happen, its originator must be convinced of its truthfulness. The meta-physician thus plays "*the dangerous game*"[65] of having to believe in the truth of his convictions while at the same time having to be able to free himself from both truth and conviction.

Nietzsche's View: From High Mountains

"From High Mountains: Epode" concludes *Beyond Good and Evil* by way of an aesthetic summarization of Nietzsche's ontological project.[66] In 15 short verses the rough parameters of the shift from a metaphysical history concerned with an ontology of being, to a future history which recognizes an ontology of becoming, a meta-physics, if you will, may be ascertained. It may be read as tracing the development, the becoming of Nietzsche's own thoughts and relationship to those thoughts on the ontology of becoming. As a specific mask on Nietzsche's thought.[67]

The opening stanza/aphorism is optimistic, celebratory in tone. The passage abounds with sensory information. "Oh life's midday! Oh festival! Oh garden of summer!" These evocations bring forth images highlighted by a noon time sun, the surging notes of a musical score, the pounding heart of a joyful dance in celebration of youth, the smell and taste of the celebratory feast, the orgiastic sensory deluge of exotic flowers in full bloom tended and extended (produced and reproduced) by a menagerie of birds and insects. This scene is not possible within the bounds of reason alone. To touch, to smell, to see, to hear, to taste, to dance, all require a body. Life's midday is lived, not rationalized. Here then is a hint of Nietzsche's break with the metaphysicians of old.

The evocation is simultaneously a convocation. Importantly, "life's midday, festival, garden of summer" are not present. They have no body but rather remain distant. The convocation, the call, "Come now!" is to precisely this body. "Here" is "I." "I" is a fixed point and certain in that fixity. There is no hint of doubt on the part of the speaker as to where "here" is, as to who "I" is, nor as to whom the speaker awaits. For the reader on the other hand, there may be a subtle hint of doubt in that the "whom" the speaker awaits is more likely thought of as a "what." Furthermore, the "here", normally a "where", is a "who", perhaps a "what" by virtue of its being "I." The apparently distinct categories of who, what, when, and where begin to slip and to blend into one another.[68]

The subtle doubts of the first stanza are brought into greater relief in the second and third stanzas, which render the "certain" identity of the speaker problematic indeed. The stanzas contain three figures; three "subjects" which stand in the place of "I." Glacier, brook and clouds all take the role of sentries, waiting "in restless ecstasy." "Here" is "I," is "glacier, brook, clouds." All are water. The slippage of categorical knowledge implied in the first stanza is recast as the fluidity of water. "Who lives so near the stars as I, or who so near the depths of the abyss?" The certain "I" is unveiled as mutable.[69] It is with this realization that the "friends" first arrive.

The "arrival" of the friends, which is more accurately a hesitation on the brink of arrival, marks the beginning of a rapid transformation, a melting of the solidity and certainty of "I." There is a manifold irony in the situation. The first irony brings attention to an epistemological difficulty which is insurmountable, and necessarily so. This difficulty has to do with the relationship between language and life, word and world. The "arrival" of "life's midday, festival, garden of summer" only takes place at the command of the speaker, the namer. These "friends" are summoned by the pronunciation of the name given them. Yet it is precisely this pronunciation which causes them to hesitate on the brink of arrival, to draw back in anger. Thus the evocation/convocation is also a provocation. In the very act of naming the namer and the named are kept apart. They are kept apart by the name itself. An indication of the contours of this provocation is given in a second irony.

The hesitation is that which provokes the melting of the solidity of "I." The certainty apparent in the first stanza gives way to a rapid series of questions. "Is it no longer—I? Are hand, step, face transformed? And what I am to you friends—I am not?" What these questions unveil is that the locus of convocation, the body to which "life's midday, festival, garden of summer" have been called no longer exists. The speaker, the certain "I" who was both sentry and commander is no longer. The irony of this melting is that it is expressed as a freezing. The imagery of stanzas six and seven expose the speaker as having become glaciated "by means of pale, cold, grey conceptual nets thrown over the motley whirl of the senses— the mob of the senses, as Plato called them."[70] The celebratory speaker of the first stanza, certain in its own movement, has relinquished dancing in favor of "wrestling." The free spirited movement of the dance has trans-formed into a confrontational, disciplined combativeness within the restrictive boundaries of the ring. Nietzsche, having "turned his own strength against himself too often, checked and wounded by his own victory", has come to recognize his own scholastic asceticism. He has changed in that he has come to believe in the truth of "life's midday, festi-val, garden of summer." He has come to expect them to arrive as things, having forgotten for the moment that "there is no 'thing.'"[71]

Here then is the key to understanding the provocative relationship of word and world. In the pronunciation of the name, the namer fixes the named. The name calls down the named to "this far domain of ice and rocks" where it is frozen, glaciated. Given an ontology of becoming, the named is never fixable by the name, but must (at least) retain the activity of the "huntsman" and "the Alpine goat." The danger in this glacial, metaphysical place is that one will (perhaps due to the effects of reason, a kind of hypothermia) forget the unfixability of the named.

"In the question of style there is always the weight or examen of some pointed object. At times this object might be only a quill or a stylus. But it could just as easily be a stiletto, or even a rapier."[72] Or perhaps an arrow. The purpose of the arrow is to bring down its target, to pierce the fleshy covering, even the very heart of life itself. The bow of metaphysical inquiry that lets fly the name/arrow thus runs the risk of deceiving the huntsman that he has brought down his prey. Here is the victory of the dogmatic philosopher, the herd animal that ceases to hunt and becomes hunted. But this too is a transformation of both hunted and hunter, namer and named. Here too, from a different perspective (looking down), is an affir-mation of becoming. The arrow/spur "might also be used as protection against the threat of such an attack, in order to keep it at a distance, to repel it."[73] The true philosopher, the "lover of the 'big-game hunt,'"[74] aims along with all philosophers to define life, to know life. Yet at the same time there is an awareness that even if the word/arrow should hit its mark, the result can only be the negation of life, that is death, and the negation of the huntsman himself. With no prey, there can be no hunt. Each name/arrow then turns back on itself, piercing the namer/huntsman. Herein lies the tragedy of Nietzsche's philosophy.

The will to knowledge and drive to not be deceived, both expressions of philosophy as "the most spiritual will to power, to 'creation of the world,' to *causa prima*,"[75] are capable only of perpetuating deception in that they claim to fix the unfixable with names. This is the concealed irony of Nietzsche's words "one no longer loves one's knowledge enough when one has communicated it."[76] The narrator has begun to realize that in naming there is a denial of the named. The "I" has moved to a stage where it is beginning to risk venturing into "such dangerous perhapses"[77] as those expressed in aphorisms such as 175,[78] 177,[79] 180,[80] and 183[81] of *Beyond Good and Evil* which conclude the chapter "Maxims and Interludes." The speaker's cries of "away! be gone!" attempt to revoke the evocation/convocation of "life's midday, festival, garden of summer" "for [their] own preservation." The cries are affirmations.

Where the evocation/convocation kept the namer and the named distant from each other, the revocation/affirmation allows for a reduction of that distance. The speaker has become aware of the difficulties of speaking and hesitates. The very uncertainty expressed in this hesitation—"what shall I call them"—allows for the named to move closer. Where the "I" of the first stanza waited for "the friends" to appear over the horizon, the revocated/affirmed, not-named "friends," "the ghosts of friends," are just outside the narrator's window, just outside the narrator's heart. That which had formerly been named "life's midday, festival, garden of summer" can be close so long as one does not believe in ghosts. The not-naming is thus a stylistic move which renders the tragic bearable.

> So, it seems, style also uses its spur (*éperon*) as a means of protection against the terrifying, blinding, mortal threat (of that) which presents itself, which obstinately thrusts itself into view. And style thereby protects the presence, the content, the thing itself, meaning, truth—on the condition that it should not already (*déjà*) be that gaping chasm which has been deflowered in the unveiling of the difference.[82]

Nor can the speaker believe in itself in the same confident way as did the youthful, ignorant "I." Stanza twelve sees a speaker, grown wiser from experience. It is not, however, any less youthful. It has not aged past its youth, but has become more youthful. What the speaker has come to know is its own mutability. It has come to know itself as water, which can not have confidence in its own shape. The most one can manage in the desire for such certainty is to become the glacier. But even the glacier expands and contracts. Even the glacier is not fixed in any absolute sense. "Only he who changes remains akin to me." Thus the speaker must be ever changing.

The next important shift in what has become the non-identity of the speaker takes place in a nearly identical recantation of the first stanza.[83] The parallel structures of the two stanzas beg comparison and highlight contrasts. Again there is an evocation: "Oh life's midday! Oh second youth! Oh garden of summer!" Yet this is not a convocation of the named. It is rather an invocation, a calling in the name of . . . . Where in the early stanzas of the song it is clear that "the friends," the convocated, are "life's midday, festival, garden of summer," in the later stanza the friends remain anonymous. They are simply "new friends," who-, what-, where-, when-ever that may be. They are not brought down by the name/arrow/spur nor thereby doomed to the decay of life-denial.

That the invocation drops the "festival" of the convocation affirms the reading of the speaker as wiser and more knowledgeable, while being no less youthful. The name "festival" conjures images of the free spirited dance. The speaker in the first stanza, who is also a dancer, dances without knowing why. The dancer is thus ignorant, and to some extent his enthusi-asm for the dance is not as complete as it could be. There remains the possibility that upon learning the purpose of the dance, the enthusiasm for it will cease. The dancer is in this sense dishonest. The "second youth" of the later stanza however has unveiled the purpose of the dance, has come to terms with the necessity of distance, "knows" that there is no "why?" behind it.[84] The dancer has faced the impossibility of dancing and because of that dances all the more enthusiastically. Here is a genuine, undeniable enthusiasm, the enthusiasm of a sagacious youth.

Stanza 13 is the final stanza to end with any definitive punctuating mark. The exclamation which ends the stanza (and which begins the spirit of the stanza) tells of the rebirth of the celebratory tone of the speaker. Again there is an expectation on the part of the speaker, but this expecta-tion is without any specific content. The expectation is no longer for the arrival of some thing. In the spirit of the lessons learned from the convo-cation of "life's midday, festival, garden of summer," the "I" (an "I") open endedly—expects. "I" (which has ceased to be certain and has become a question) is restlessly ecstatic to see what (if indeed it is a "what") comes through the open door. The narrator no longer postpones life until such time as it is complete. Rather the aim of the expectation has shifted away from the moment of arrival to expectation itself, the act of expecting.[85] "I" is complete as expect-er in the very lacuna, the call that is not a convocation, the not-naming that marks expectation as genuine.

The final two stanzas reiterate the word/world relationship which pre-cipitates the process of becoming from evocation/convocation through provocation and revocation to evocation/invocation. No longer is the focus on naming. Even the song becomes "this song" implying a multiplicity of other songs telling other stories. Naming has been foregone in favor of not-naming. The will to truth has been exposed as capable only of lying; "desire's sweet cry died on the lips." The name/arrows of the will to truth and drive to name have been turned aside by a not-name, by a name/ arrow/spur; "the timely friend, the midday friend—no! ask not who he is."

Nietzsche's phrase, (for it must be recalled that the speaker is Nietzsche and perhaps the reader which comes after him), "at midday it happened, at midday one became two ... " deserves a closer look. Midday is the time of day when the light is the brightest, when color is most vibrant. As used by Nietzsche it may be understood as something parallel to "the light of reason" of the dogmatic philosophers he criticises.[86]Here he is saying that with the shift from evocation/convocation to evocation/invocation a kind of knowledge or wisdom is gained. What then is this knowledge? What is the "one" which "became two?" This question is perhaps answered by turning to earlier stanzas which expose in their imagery the falsehood and impossibility of the will to truth. The one which becomes two is word and world, name and named. Here is an attack on the universalizing Stoic[87], the Liebnizian monad,[88] the Platonic form,[89] the Kantian categorical imperative.[90] All such metaphysical philosophies have come to believe in themselves too much. The dogmatic philosopher, (and Liebniz is most explicit in this), believes that the name/arrow brings down its prey. The name is believed to be one with the named. Furthermore, since the dogmatic philosopher has the answer, it is his by rights of discovery, by "the signature that appropriates it."[91] Thus history speaks of Kantianism, Platonism and so on. The namer and the named are thus understood as one.

Nietzsche's shift to not-naming, to open-ended invocation rather than definitive convocation makes him particularly resistant to becoming an "-ism" in the same way. Even Zarathustra insists that he does not want disciples. "The midday friend" does not claim to have the answer, but answers. Life has no set of permanent, substantive facts to which one individual may lay claim, which may be appropriated once and for all by a signature. If there is something like a natural law in the will to power, it exists only in spirit, not in letter. In this way the "one" of namer/named— wor(l)d—is unveiled as necessarily two, namer and named, word and world. The punctuation at the end of the phrase in question—the phrase which is a question—indicates not a conclusion, but a continuation. This is not a statement, but a prelude to statements, which are themselves, preludes to further statements ...

In the light of the midday sun, in the presence of Zarathustra, Nietzsche's ontological shift from being to becoming is completed. But as may be expected, this completion is not a completion at all, but a beginning. The antithetical pairings of light and darkness, truth and lies, sameness and difference have been wed. The punctuation which, again, does not punctuate, indicates another wedding. Being and becoming too are wed. The tragedy of the namer/name/named relationship becomes a triumph of sorts. The namer has no other option but to exist within the horizons of its own grammar which can never pin down the named. The shift to invocation in the presence of Zarathustra allows the namer to come to terms with this tragedy. The namer is triumphant in that through "dangerous perhapses" it is able to "rise above the belief in grammar."[92] In the imposition of new grammatical constraints, and the subsequent revocation of those laws, the namer becomes through a series of momentary points of being. That the namer is, is precisely that which allows the namer to become, thereby doing justice to the named. Evocation, convocation, revocation, invocation, forgetting.

> A joyful wisdom shows it well: there never has been the style, the simulacrum, the woman, [the friends, life's midday, festival, garden of summer].
> If the simulacrum is ever going to occur, its writing must be in the interval between several styles. And the insinuation of the woman (of) Nietzsche is that, if there is going to be style, there can only be more than one.[93]

The special contribution of Nietzsche's morality, his response to the life-affirming meta-physical challenge, is that his moral formula does not privilege a specific content. Rather it presents a privileged method. "The most valuable insights are the last to be discovered; but the most valuable insights are methods."[94] "Methods, one must repeat ten times, are the essential, as well as being the most difficult, as well as being that which has habit and laziness against it longest."[95] This method, which places an emphasis on artfulness above all else, is strikingly Odyssean. It does not dictate what is to be done, but it does create the conditions under which the doing itself becomes possible, and indeed imperative. If the insights afforded by Nietzsche's approach are to be applied to the double claim of the shield, then it can be shown that the claim "this is the way it is" must always amount to "Thus it shall be!" The corresponding "nothing (else) to be done about it" claim may hold sway, but in a far less compelling way. It is not that there is nothing to be done, but simply that there is no-thing to be done. This does not, however, preclude action or creative activity in the least. It is simply a reminder that whatever is done must not be reified as a natural "thing." It is a reminder that through a self-consciousness of our own roles as creators, we are better able to create.

Notes

[1] Homer, *The Odyssey,* trans. Robert Fagles (New York: Penguin Books, 1996), 1.1–3.

[2] Friedrich Wilhelm Nietzsche, *The Gay Science: With a Prelude in Rhymes and an Appendix of Songs,* trans. Walter Arnold Kaufmann, 1st ed. (New York: Random House, 1974), 282.

[3] Perseus' heroism in this sense is a dual victory both over the power of Medusa's gaze and the tyranny of Polydectes. It should be noted that this victory is not simply allegorical as Perseus' last action before returning his prize is to reveal it to Polydectes, petrifying him and ending his reign of terror over Perseus' mother, Danaë. See Robert Graves, *The Greek Myths* (New York: George Brazillier, Inc, 1955).

[4] The terms "honest" and "truthful" are placed in scare quotes here precisely because of the difficulty Odysseus reveals in their typical usage. See Plato, "Lesser Hippias," in *Plato: Complete Works,* ed. John M. Cooper (Indianapolis, IN: Hackett Publishing Company, 1997).

[5] This is not to say that he would necessarily lose all control, nor is it to say that *poiesis* in a material sense is ill-advised. It is to say that a different kind of control, of mastery over oneself, is required. Odysseus's self-mastery is one of the few redeeming qualities Plato recognizes in him. It also makes an appearance in Nietzsche's work, which will be discussed, below.

[6] Barbara Clayton, *A Penelopean Poetics: Reweaving the Feminine in Homer's Odyssey,* Greek Studies: Interdisciplinary Studies (Lanham, MD: Lexington Books, 2004), 78–9.

[7] L. Pratt, quoted in Ibid., 78 n59.

[8] The warning resides as much in the cruelty of Odysseus as in the fate of Neoptolemus, or even that of Achilles himself.

[9] Echoes of the seeming paradox of this position can be found in the existentialist observation that if you choose not to decide, you still have made a choice. *Poiesis* concealing itself does not nullify the power of *poiesis,* but rather confirms it.

[10] See the discussion of Chapter 3, above.

[11] Neither, for that matter, does Plato maintain as unshakable a "this is the way it is" claim in his later works as he does in the *Republic.* For example, in the *Laws,* imagining a situation in which tragedians are requesting admittance to the city, the Athenian states:

> Most honored guests, we're tragedians ourselves, and our tragedy is the finest and best we can create. At any rate, our entire state has been constructed so as to be a "representation" of the finest and noblest life—the

very thing we maintain is most genuinely a tragedy. So we are poets like yourselves, composing in the same genre. (Plato, *Laws*, in *Plato: Complete Works*, ed. John M. Cooper (Indianapolis, IN: Hackett Publishing Company, 1997), 817b.)

[12]   Stanford cites the Cretan poet Epimenides as well as Paul's letter to Titus 1.12–13 which reads "One of themselves, even a prophet of their own, said, the Cretans are always liars, evil beasts, slow bellies. This witness it true. Wherefore rebuke them sharply, that they may be sound in the faith." See W. B. Stanford, *The Odyssey of Homer* (London: Macmillan, 1959), 209.

[13]   A contemporary example of a text that has the same overall effect is Yann Martel's *Life of Pi*. Consider, in particular the closing scene where Pi having been rescued from his ordeal retells his story to the interviewing officer twice. The first tale is that with which the reader is already familiar. The second is completely different and entirely undoes the first, but is in many ways more believable. The reader, like the officer, is left with absolutely no definitive way of deciding which tale "really" happened. In the end his "official" version resides solely on the basis of an aesthetic (and possibly compassionate) choice. Yann Martel, *Life of Pi* (Orlando: Harcourt Books, 2001).

[14]   This paradox is classically formulated as the "*pseudomenon*" or "liars paradox." It is often credited to the pseudo-mythical Epimenides (see note 13 above) although it is more likely the doing of the philosopher Eubulides. The liar paradox has been the subject of considerable analytic scrutiny. For a brief outline of the problem and some suggested solutions, including a bibliography of a number of relevant sources, see Bradley Dowden, "Liar Paradox," *The Internet Encyclopedia of Philosophy*.

[15]   Plato, *Lesser Hippias*, 364c.

[16]   Ibid., 365b.

[17]   Ibid., 365b.

[18]   Ibid., 373d.

[19]   Gerard Casey, "The Shield of Achilles," *Studies In Comparative Religion* 10, no. 2 (1976); Barbara Clayton, *A Penelopean Poetics: Reweaving the Feminine in Homer's Odyssey*; Laurence Lampert, "Socrates' Defence of Polytropic Odysseus: Lying and Wrong-Doing in Plato's *Lesser Hippias*," *Review of Politics* 64, no. 2 (2002): 231–60; Gregory Nagy, *Homeric Questions* (Austin, TX: University of Texas Press, 1996).

[20]   Lampert is most forward about this:

Plato's *Lesser Hippias* suggests that insight into the imperial project on behalf of philosophy can be aided by indefatigably questioning Homer and reflecting on who is the better man in Homer, straight Achilles or polytropic Odysseus. Because Odysseus is better, because Odysseus's polytropism makes possible the fall of Ilium and his own homecoming, an inference suggests itself about Homer: the great success of the educator of Hellas derives from his own capacity and knowledge, his wise "injustice" and "wrong-doing" able to create the gods and heroes imitation of whom helped forge the singular Hellenic people. Homer's greatness peaks in his polytropic capacity to create the shared horizon of heroic contest and surpassing within which Greek achievement rose to unparalleled heights. The best man in Homer is Homer. (Laurence Lampert, "Socrates' Defense of Polytropic Odysseus: Lying and Wrong-Doing in Plato's *Lesser Hippias*.")

21 Homer, *The Odyssey*, 11.416–17.
22 James I. Porter, "Nietzsche, Homer, and the Classical Tradition," in *Nietzsche and Antiquity: His Reaction and Response to the Classical Tradition*, ed. Paul Bishop (Rochester: Camden House, 2004), 10–11.
23 Wolf argued that the Homeric epics were the end result of a long oral tradition of composition and compilation. See F. A. Wolf, *Prolegomena to Homer (1795)* (Princeton, NJ: Princeton University Press, 1985).
24 Friedrich Wilhelm Nietzsche, "Homer and Classical Philology," in *On the Future of Our Educational Institutions*, ed. Oscar Levy (London: George Allen & Unwin, Ltd., 1924), 152.
25 Ibid., 155.
26 Ibid., 155.
27 Nietzsche's choice of words indicates that the "Homeric question" is a problem of "the personality" in general, not just that of the bard.
28 Ibid., 155. His position is similar in this respect to those including Tarsky, who would deny that the so-called "liar sentence" is a legitimately declarative one. Bradley Dowden, "Liar Paradox."
29 Friedrich Wilhelm Nietzsche, "Homer and Classical Philology," 156.
30 Ibid., 163.
31 Friedrich Wilhelm Nietzsche, and Douglas Smith, *The Birth of Tragedy* (Oxford: Oxford University Press, 2000), 81.
32 Ibid., 80–1.
33 Ibid., 84.
34 Ibid., 31.
35 Ibid., 31. It is not surprising then to find a representation of the sun at the centre of the Shield of Achilles. Extrapolating, Nietzsche is arguing here that the entirety of the edifice in all its order and aesthetic magnificence is Apollonian, at least up to the outer rim which depicts the Ocean River surrounding all. One can easily see the shield itself as this "small boat tossed by the surrounding sea." This image also lends weight to the significance of the sea in the tale of Odysseus. *The Iliad* is a land-based epic. Landmarks are readily available. The lines of conflict are clear. It is a world that can quite readily sustain the "thus it is" claim of the shield. *The Odyssey*, on the other hand, is ocean based. There is

a conspicuous absence of landmarks, and safe harbors are few and far between. It does not describe a world where the simple "this is the way it is" of the shield can maintain itself as unquestionable.

[36]   Ibid., 27.

[37]   In the *Symposium*, Alcibiades says "Socrates will drink whatever you put in front of him, but no one has yet seen him drunk" (214a). He is apparently immune to intoxication (223c–d) as he is to fear or bloodlust in battle (221a–b). It is notable that in the same breath as he establishes Socrates as "anti-Dionysian," Alcibiades also compares him to Silenus, and calls him "quite a flute player"—the flute being the instrument most closely associated with Dionysus (215b). What appears to be happening here is that Socates is supplanting Dionysus, just as he supplants Achilles in the *Apology*. See Plato, *Symposium*, in *Plato: Complete Works*, ed. John M. Cooper (Indianapolis, IN: Hackett Publishing Company, 1997); Plato, *Apology*, in *Plato: Complete Works*, ed. John M. Cooper (Indianapolis, IN: Hackett Publishing Company, 1997).

[38]   Friedrich Wilhelm Nietzsche, and Douglas Smith, *The Birth of Tragedy*, 19.

[39]   Hermes was the father of Autolycus, whose daughter was Anticlea, wife of Laertes and mother of Odysseus.

[40]   Robert Graves, *The Greek Myths*, 65. The connection between the three gods is drawn closer when one takes into account that Hermes and Apollo were both associated with the art of divination, and that Hermes was the god of shepherds before that role was increasingly taken by Dionysus.Graves notes that "the Apollonian priesthood constantly trespassed on the territory of Hermes, an earlier patron of soothsaying, literature, and the arts; as did the Hermetic priesthood on that of Pan" (67). Pan is yet another god closely associated with Dionysus.

[41]   Friedrich Wilhelm Nietzsche, and Douglas Smith, *The Birth of Tragedy*, 77.

[42]   Friedrich Wilhelm Nietzsche, *Beyond Good and Evil*, trans. R. J. Hollingdale, Penguin Classics (London: Penguin Books, 1973), 142.

[43]   Friedrich Wilhelm Nietzsche, and R. J. Hollingdale, *Human, All Too Human*, Cambridge Texts in the History of Philosophy (Cambridge; New York: Cambridge University Press, 1996), 16.

[44]   Ibid., 306. See also Friedrich Wilhelm Nietzsche, *Beyond Good and Evil*, 50.

[45]   Here again is the difficulty of language in the use of the word "same." This word itself carries all the presuppositions of Being Nietzsche attempts to move beyond. See Friedrich Wilhelm Nietzsche, and R. J. Hollingdale, *Human, All Too Human*, 22.

[46]   Ibid., 16.

[47]   Friedrich Wilhelm Nietzsche, *Twilight of the Idols and the Anti-Christ*, trans. R. J. Hollingdale, Penguin Classics (Harmondsworth: Penguin, 1968), 156.

[48]   Ibid., 48. There is an implication in this passage that the necessity of which Nietzsche speaks can be avoided, but doing so requires an elimination of

"our prejudice in favor of reason." It is a questioning of just that prejudice that serves as a backdrop for the argument of this chapter.

[49] Some of the implications of this belief are to be found in Friedrich Wilhelm Nietzsche, and R. J. Hollingdale, *Human, All Too Human*, 216.

[50] Interestingly, the positional inference of this literal translation meshes quite nicely with the insistence on contextualization inherent to Nietzsche's "historical philosophy."

[51] The ambiguity is one Nietzsche as a philologist is no doubt aware. Philology is to be understood here in a very wide sense as the art of reading well—of being able to read off a fact without falsifying it by interpretation, without losing caution, patience, subtlety in the desire for understanding. Philology as *ephexis* in interpretation. Friedrich Wilhelm Nietzsche, *Twilight of the Idols and the Anti-Christ*, 181–2.

[52] In so far as he goes beyond the tradition of metaphysics, he may be called a "meta-metaphysician." To avoid excessive awkwardness I will continue with the use of the term "meta-physician" to encapsulate both this and his widespread usage of the medicalized analogy.

[53] Friedrich Wilhelm Nietzsche, *Beyond Good and Evil*, 32–3.

[54] Friedrich Wilhelm Nietzsche, and R. J. Hollingdale, *Human, All Too Human*, 307.

[55] Ibid., 93.

[56] Friedrich Wilhelm Nietzsche, *Beyond Good and Evil*, 115.

[57] Nietzsche has already referred to metaphysical thought as "dream thinking." Friedrich Wilhelm Nietzsche, and R. J. Hollingdale, *Human, All Too Human*, 18.

[58] Friedrich Wilhelm Nietzsche, *Beyond Good and Evil*, 59.

[59] Friedrich Wilhelm Nietzsche, *Gay Science*, 116.

[60] Ibid., 123.

[61] Nietzsche takes the skeptical position found in Descartes as a necessary and irreducible starting point. See Friedrich Wilhelm Nietzsche, *Twilight of the Idols and the Anti-Christ*, 184.

[62] Ibid., 128.

[63] Friedrich Wilhelm Nietzsche, and R. J. Hollingdale, *Human, All Too Human*, 22.

[64] Friedrich Wilhelm Nietzsche, *Beyond Good and Evil*, 40.

[65] Ibid., 132.

[66] Ibid., 178.

[67] Prior to proceeding further, an important qualification must be made. The argument is an attempt to speak the unspeakable, and as a text itself, is implicated in the problematic relationship between language and the world it attempts to speak. In an attempt to overcome this difficulty, or at least to come to terms with it, I adopt (and adapt) a kind of "spurring style" imperfectly and experimentally derived from that of Nietzsche and Derrida.

[68] The obvious exclusion—"why?"—applies because Nietzsche is attempting to outline an ontology which, as such, has no "why." It simply is, or rather, becomes.

[69] "Being remains absent in a singular way. It veils itself. It remains in a veiled concealment (*Verborgenheit*) which itself veils itself." Jacques Derrida, *Spurs: Nietzsche's Styles/Eperons: Les Styles De Nietzsche*, trans. Barbara Harlow (Chicago, IL: The University of Chicago Press, 1979), 141.

[70] Friedrich Wilhelm Nietzsche, *Beyond Good and Evil*, 45.

[71] Friedrich Wilhelm Nietzsche, and R. J. Hollingdale, *Human, All Too Human*, 22.

[72] Jacques Derrida, *Spurs: Nietzsche's Styles/Eperons: Les Styles De Nietzsche*, 37.

[73] Ibid., 37.

[74] Friedrich Wilhelm Nietzsche, *Beyond Good and Evil*, 74.

[75] Ibid., 39.

[76] Ibid., 104.

[77] Ibid., 34.

[78] "Ultimately one love's one's desires and not that which is desired." Ibid., 106.

[79] "Perhaps no one has ever been sufficiently truthful about what 'truthfulness' is." Ibid., 106.

[80] "There is an innocence in lying which is the sign of good faith in a cause." Ibid., 107.

[81] "'Not that you lied to me but that I no longer believe you—that is what has distressed me—.'" Ibid., 107.

[82] Jacques Derrida, *Spurs: Nietzsche's Styles/Eperons: Les Styles De Nietzsche*, 37.

[83] This same non-identity is granted by Derrida to Nietzsche's woman-as-truth. Perhaps the shift marks a becoming truthful on the part of the narrator? Certainly Derrida's words are aptly descriptive of the lessons precipitated by the convocation become provocation.
Perhaps woman [truth or, here, 'life's midday, festival, garden of summer'] is not some thing which announces itself from a distance, at a distance from some other thing. Perhaps woman—a non-identity, a non-figure, a simulacrum—is distance's very chasm, the out distancing of distance, the interval's cadence, distance itself, if we could still say such a thing, distance itself. Ibid., 49.

[84] And by extension, "no 'totality of Nietzsche's text,' not even a fragmentary or aphoristic one." Here then is the crux of this interpretation. What is important is not that there is no meaning, (which, were it the case, would render the name/arrow harmless), but that the possibility remains that there may be no meaning. "Because it [name/arrow/spur] is structurally liberated from any living meaning, it is always possible that it means nothing at all or that it has no decidable meaning." Ibid., 131–3.

[85] Even now the name/arrow is released, piercing the certainty of the author and protecting his prey . . .

[86] Of course "parallel to" is not "the same as."

[87] Friedrich Wilhelm Nietzsche, *Beyond Good and Evil*, 39.

88   Ibid., 43–4.

89   Ibid., 32.

90   Ibid. See in particular aphorisms #5, #11, #210. Kant often takes the role of prime target and foremost enemy. Given Nietzsche's comments on enmity from the perspective of the noble, one may well ask if in this high priest of asceticism Nietzsche does not see a fellow noble? See also Friedrich Wilhelm Nietzsche et al., *On the Genealogy of Morality*, Rev. student ed., Cambridge Texts in the History of Political Thought (Cambridge; New York: Cambridge University Press, 2007).

91   Jacques Derrida, *Spurs: Nietzsche's Styles/Eperons: Les Styles De Nietzsche*, 125.

92   Friedrich Wilhelm Nietzsche, *Beyond Good and Evil*, 66.

93   Jacques Derrida, *Spurs: Nietzsche's Styles/Eperons: Les Styles De Nietzsche*, 139.

94   Friedrich Wilhelm Nietzsche, *Twilight of the Idols and the Anti-Christ*, 135.

95   Ibid., 194.

7

Ekphrasis as Critique

Nietzsche blurs the divisions between reality and imagination, between the natural and the constructed, and allows for the broad scope of life to be understood as poetic. His emphasis on the centrality of the grammarians with their insistence on the hard and fast rules of language is important in that it reveals the literary nature of experience. Nietzsche leads his reader to the point where claims like the one made by Franz Bäuml are possible:

> I do contend that the tools with which one thinks affect one's thinking, that the way in which one thinks has its social consequences, and that therefore control of the tools of thought is of the utmost importance for the maintenance of power.[1]

But this is nothing new. It is from these same grounds that Plato launches his assault on the poets.[2] His use of mimesis as a critical tool adopts the strategy of Perseus as has already been said. Foremost among the shortcomings of this strategy is that it tends to leave the structural operation of the shield intact. Just as the decapitation of Medusa does nothing to diminish the power of her gaze, so too does Plato's "this is the way it really is" do nothing to counter the structural power of the shield's "this is the way it is." Likewise Baudrillard's "this is the way it is," even if expressed as "this is the way it isn't," leaves the problematic structure of a totalizing cosmos/ethos pairing intact. Mimesis, even if it is the mimesis of mimesis, remains mimesis and preserves the natural or ontological status of that which it purports to represent. It thus remains blind to the irreducibility of change. It keeps in place, and relies on "the natural sign."[3] The argument thus far suggests that no longer can mimesis be deployed as a means to evaluate claims against a fixed and fathomable backdrop of the Good, or the real, or, after Nietzsche, of Truth.[4]

So where does this leave us? The problem is not only the totalizing and paralyzing cosmological and ethical claim of the shield, which leaves its audience and its speaker alike paralyzed, devoid of responsibility (response-ability), but also its oft-unintentional perpetuation. This is not a purely abstract problem, reserved for theorists and philosophers. It shows up in multiple forms, including the branding of dissent against the War on Terror as unpatriotic. It appears in the spate of suicide bombings and the targeting of civilians by extremist groups of all stripes. "This is how it really is," we are told. "There is nothing to do but see the war through to its end," we are told. And the flood of messages to this effect sinks in. The messages become believable. And so the war goes on and on. In the mathematics of such thinking, 138 becomes 4,000 becomes 10,000.[5] So the question remains: how does one resist the power of the shield?

From Perseus to Paris

Perseus defeats Medusa by means of a mimetic approach. He uses the reflective surface of Athena's shield to distance himself from the Gorgon's gaze. His victory is completed—it congeals as a victory—in the abdication of his new power, Medusa's gaze. Recognizing its power as too great to be wielded by a mortal, he relinquishes it to Athena for safekeeping. But Nietzsche has told us "God is dead!"[6] Not only is Perseus' abdication of this power a truly heroic act, beyond the horizon of ordinary human beings, but there remains no divine locus of responsibility to which such a power might be abdicated. There is an irony then in the observation that it is exactly those groups who insist on the presence of such a divine centre, be they "Christian," or "Muslim," or "Jewish," who are the most incapable of relinquishing this power. The scare quotes are self-consciously employed, as there is some question as to the theological credentials of some of the groups currently bearing the shield. President Bush spoke of al Qaeda as promoting a form of Islam so distorted that it can hardly be called Islamic.[7] Yet the same kinds of arguments can be applied to President Bush's own form of Christianity. Heroism, as exemplified in the actions of Achilles, Odysseus, and Perseus involves a setting aside of the shield. It is ironic that those contemporary groups most prone to cloak themselves in the garb of heroism are often the most pronounced bearers of the shield. Clearly another tactical approach is required.

One can be found in Paris: Paris the archer, son of Priam and Prince of Troy: Paris who neither bears the shield nor is paralyzed by it.[8] Paris the archer is not stunned into inaction by the shield precisely because he never directly faces it. As an archer, his weapon only operates when he stands at the margins of the battle. Following the clues left by Plato's use of mimetic poetry against itself, by Nietzsche's linguistic turn, and by Derrida's deconstructive techniques of reading a text from its margins, it is advisable that one treat the Shield of Achilles as a literary construct, which, obviously, it is. By extension it is advisable that one treat every instance of the bearing of the shield as a literary construct, subject to textual criticism. For it is literary criticism that offers up a tool most useful for the critical theorist faced with an instance of the bearing of the shield.

Auerbach: The Insights of Comparative Mimesis

Erich Auerbach makes headway along this road in his use of mimesis as a comparative tool.[9] By setting multiple examples of life-like representation side by side, each quite different from the others, Auerbach calls into question not only the beliefs or capacities of the audience that accepts these representations, but also that which is being represented. If it is granted that each instance is life-like and an accurate and believable representation of the world, then not only is the comparison a comment on the developing ways of understanding the world, but it is also a comment on the world itself. What kind of a world is this that it can be represented in so many, sometimes incompatible ways? It is certainly not the kind of a world about which a simple "thus it is" statement can be made once and for all. Hence it is not the kind of world that can easily sustain a simple ethos of "nothing to be done about it." This is obviously not to say that such claims are not made, and enforced. Nor is it to say that such claims cannot be made. It is to say that if they are made (and they are), they cannot be as unchallengeable as they claim themselves to be. Mimesis can give these insights, but has difficulty maintaining this perspective unless deployed comparatively across a number of different cases. But what if only a single case is available? Is there a way to retain these insights? Indeed there is. This tool is not mimesis, but ekphrasis.

Krieger: The Still Mo(ve)ment of Ekphrasis

Ekphrasis has an original meaning of "to tell in full."[10] It has come to refer to the representation of art in poetry, and its archetypical example is Homer's description of the Shield of Achilles in Book 18 of *The Iliad*.

Although a relatively obscure and minor genre, ekphrasis has proven remarkably long-lived. In an attempt to unify the multitude of examples of ekphrasis from Homer and Virgil to Keats and Auden, James Heffernan defines ekphrasis as "the verbal representation of visual representation."[11] It is from a slight but important modification of this definition that the argument will proceed. W. J. T. Mitchell notes, "from the semantic point of view, from the standpoint of referring, expressing intensions and producing effects in a viewer/listener [/audience], there is no essential difference between texts and images."[12] If this is the case, then from a semantic point of view neither is there a difference between visual and tactile representation. Following this implication, I propose to expand the definition of ekphrasis by de-emphasizing "visual representation" in favor of "nonverbal representation." Hence the definition of ekphrasis is amended to be "the verbal representation of non-verbal representation." This would appear to be paradoxical, since by the logic of Mitchell's argument and its semantic point of view, there is no non-verbal representation. For the time being this problem will be postponed, but it will be taken up again in the discussion of the operation and destabilizing effects of ekphrasis.

Ekphrasis is a powerful disturber of what Murray Krieger calls "the natural-sign aesthetic."[13] The natural-sign is that in which there is a certain, direct, non-arbitrary relationship between the signifier and the signified. The natural-sign is the Holy Grail of Nietzsche's grammarians. It underlies the position of Cratylus in Plato's dialogue that bears his name. Krieger argues,

> Our semiotic desire for the natural-sign is a reflection of our ontological yearning: our anxiety to find an order or structure objectively, "naturally," "out there"—beyond society as well as ourselves—that would authorise the signs and forms that our subjectivity projects and that we then want—nay, require—others to respond to and acknowledge as being there. It is an anxiety exploited by all holders of power and bearers of doctrines that they seek to impose through a claim to a natural authority. This attempted imposition so often succeeds because it meets and satisfies our semiotic desire for the natural-sign, as it confers the special privilege of mature upon the conventional—and arbitrary—signs dictated by various motives, most of them politically suspect.[14]

As should now be obvious, the natural-sign aesthetic underlies the power of the shield. Its "this is the way it is" aspires to the status of the natural-sign, and it is in the garb of the natural-sign that it is presented by its bearer.

Ekphrasis disturbs the natural-sign aesthetic by imposing multiple layers of representation between the reader/audience and that which is represented. Where mimesis works both to represent and to conceal itself as a representation—to "tell it like it is"—ekphrasis constantly reminds the reader/audience of its status as a representation. What is more, it openly displays itself as a representation of a representation. This distance from the object being represented, if one can rightly call it that, leads Plato to the wholesale rejection of poetry—at least on an ostensible level. But if one does not place this doubly distant representation against the backdrop of a fixed object "out there" then ironically enough, the ekphrastic representation "corresponds" more closely to a reality which is not representable in its totality (or perhaps at all). The ekphrastic image is a natural-like-sign of an unrepresentable referent in that it is a reminder of the contingency and artificiality of the natural-sign.

Ekphrasis leaves us in very much the same situation as does Derrida's encounter with a fragment left by Nietzsche:

"I have forgotten my umbrella."[15]

Derrida notes in this short line of text a radical and irreducible inaccessibility. It may or may not have "some hidden secret,"[16] and what is more,

> To whatever lengths one might carry a conscientious interpretation, the hypothesis that the totality of Nietzsche's text, in some monstrous way, might well be of the type "I have forgotten my umbrella" cannot be denied.
>
> Which is tantamount to saying that there is no "totality to Nietzsche's text," not even a fragmentary or aphoristic one.[17]

This is not to say that because this possibility cannot be denied, that another possibility, namely that there is "some hidden secret" must be denied. For that would be an extreme form of relativism and nihilism. (This is the pitfall that claims Baudrillard.) It is just that one cannot tell. Both possibilities must remain, hence "the text remains closed, at once open and closed, or each in turn, folded/unfolded (ployé/déployé), it is just an umbrella that you couldn't use (dont vous n'auriez pas l'emploi)."[18]

Ekphrasis disturbs the natural-sign, but it does not eradicate it entirely. Rather it renders explicit the difficulties of making a "this is the way it is" (hence also a "nothing to be done") claim.

What we call "nature" thus comes more and more to be deconstructed into a mirror of our own historically conditioned selves, of our desires, and of our desire to validate those desires by grounding them in what we claim to be an objective nature out there . . .

Once nature is thus relativised, so that it loses its ontological grounding, it can of course serve no longer as the fixed referent for a natural sign. And the natural sign, no longer authorised, will be consigned to the realm of myth and will give way to the acknowledgement of the conventional character of all signs.[19]

The disruptive features of ekphrasis are self-reflexive as well. Ekphrasis by its very definition operates on the contested borderlines between "the Sister Arts" of poetry and plastic media such as painting or sculpture. It disrupts the clean provincialities of Gothold Lessing who insisted that the proper domain of art is space, while the proper domain of poetry is time.[20] It even appears to disturb any clear-cut and final delineation of its own purpose or intent. Krieger has pointed to the ekphrastic principle, which in the circular form of the poem "must convert the transparency of its verbal medium into the physical solidity of the medium of the spatial arts."[21] Thus ekphrasis effects a "total mastery of moving life, the capturing of it in a 'still' pattern."[22] But this is not "still life" as in *nature mort*. Krieger uses the term "still" in a very different way:

[He has] freely used it as an adjective, adverb and verb; as still movement, still moving, and more forcefully, the stilling of movement: so "still" movement as quiet, unmoving movement; "still" moving as a forever-now movement, an action that is at once the quieting of movement and the perpetuation of it, the making of it, like Eliot's wheel and Chinese jar, a movement that is still and that is still with us, that is—in his words—"forever still."[23]

Mitchell: Ekphrastic Hope

Krieger's "stilling" expresses a subtle and difficult feature of ekphrasis, namely its simultaneous freezing and perpetuation of motion. This point is difficult in that it is all too easy to ignore the latter half of its function. It is all too easy to read Krieger, as W. J. T. Mitchell does, as propagating an understanding of ekphrasis that is akin to Nietzsche's understanding of the name. Nietzsche held that the name worked to fix, and therefore to kill, that which it names. "The word killeth, everything fixed killeth."[24] Mitchell is critical of Krieger precisely because Mitchell takes the "stilling" of ekphrasis to refer to its "descriptive 'arresting of movement.'"[25] In the context of a discussion of Shelly's poem "On the Medusa of Leonardo Da Vinci in the Florentine Gallery" Mitchell states, "if the poet's ekphrastic hopes were fulfilled, the reader would be similarly transfixed, unable to read or hear."[26]

Mitchell sees ekphrasis as having "three phases or moments of realization. The first might be called 'ekphrastic indifference,' and it grows out of a commonsense perception that ekphrasis is impossible."[27] This is to say that if ekphrasis is "the verbal representation of a visual representation" then it can never fully complete its task. Language, no matter how detailed, cannot bring the visual presence of a visual representation before us.[28] Homer's description of the Shield of Achilles, for example, can never make it present for his audience in the same way it would be present for those on the battlefields of Troy. In the same way, a news report, however in-depth, cannot place its audience in the situation being reported in the same way as actually being there would. The description always remains a description, and not the object described.

The second phase of ekphrasis, called "ekphrastic hope" by Mitchell, comes "when the impossibility of ekphrasis is overcome in imagination or metaphor, when we discover a 'sense' in which language can do what so many writers have wanted it to do: 'to make us see.'"[29] This phase sees the dissolution of the obscurity of ekphrasis. It ceases to be something out of the ordinary and "begins to seem paradigmatic of a fundamental tendency in all linguistic expression."[30] The greatest hope of this phase is that a kind of dialectically synthetic closure will be obtained in the rise of the "verbal icon or imagetext."[31] Mitchell places Krieger at this stage that, although wrongly so, for reasons discussed below.

The third phase closely follows on the second. "This is the moment of resistance or counter desire that occurs when we sense that the difference between the verbal and visual representation might collapse and the figurative, imaginary desire of ekphrasis might be realized literally and actually."[32] This is "ekphrastic fear." According to Mitchell, ekphrastic fear highlights "the difference between verbal and visual mediation [as] a moral, aesthetic imperative rather than (as in the first 'indifferent' phase of ekphrasis) a natural fact that can be relied on."[33] Mitchell sees this phase as being quite widespread.

It would be easy to show its place in a wide range of literary theorizing, from the Marxist hostility to modernist experiments with literary space, to deconstructionist efforts to overcome "formalism" and "closure," to the anxieties of Protestant poetics with the temptations of "imagery," to the romantic tradition's obsession with a poetics of voice, invisibility, and blindness. All the goals of "ekphrastic hope," of achieving vision, iconicity, or a "still moment" of plastic presence through language become, from this point of view, sinister and dangerous.[34]

The main aim of ekphrastic fear is to undo the veiled threat of ekphrastic hope. It is to expose the notion of the imagetext as a "deceitful illusion, a magical technique that threatens to fixate the poet and the listener."[35]

These three phases centre on ekphrastic hope, which, as has been noted, rests on a misreading of Krieger's "still moment." This is not to say that Mitchell's architecture is to be disposed of entirely. He is quite correct to emphasize the destabilizing effects ekphrasis and its inherent ambiguity. This ambiguity is evident in the very phases of ekphrasis, even if there is an issue to be taken with Mitchell's nomenclature. It is not the case that each phase follows as a consequence of another, but rather that each phase is simultaneous with the others. It is part and parcel of ekphrasis to be impossible, hopeful and fearful all at once.

The problem is that Mitchell tends to equate Krieger's ekphrasis with what he calls ekphrastic hope. In doing this, he runs the risk of glossing over much of its unsettling operation, its ability to upset, to render the obvious difficult, and to make the simple problematic. Mitchell is quite right to place such an emphasis on ekphrasis as resistant to "placement," not only in regards to its object, but also in its own operation. That is, ekphrasis disturbs the naïve realist notion, the "natural sign aesthetic," by being doubly removed from its "object" as a representation of a representation.[36] At the same time ekphrasis is self-referentially disruptive. It disturbs its own operation as "a minor and relatively obscure literary genre" and "paradigmatic of a fundamental tendency in all linguistic expression."[37] Ekphrasis is simultaneously "an ornament to epic," (following Lessing's description), *and* epic is an ornament to ekphrasis.

If Lessing could have seen the subsequent development of Homeric criticism, he would have found his worst fears justified. Not only did ekphrasis establish itself firmly as a distinct poetic genre, but the great prototype of Achilles' shield seems, in the work of modern classical scholarship imbued with assumptions of formalism, to have established a kind of dominance over the epic of which it is supposed to be a mere ornament ... Indeed, the shield (and ekphrastic hope along with it) may have even more grandiose aspiration than this synech-dohcial representation of the whole in the part, for the shield presents much more of Homer's world than the *Iliad* does. The entire universe is depicted on the shield . . . the entire action of the *Iliad* becomes a fragment in the totalizing vision provided by Achilles' shield.[38]

Mitchell says "ekphrasis resists 'placement' as an ornamental feature of larger textual structures, or as a minor genre. It aims to be all of literature in miniature."[39] But this is only partly right. His misreading of Krieger leads him to gloss over the equally pronounced resistance of ekphrasis to being "all of literature in miniature." Krieger's "still moment" shows that it adopts and resists both roles at once, generating an irreducible and irresolvable tension.

Becker: Breaking the Illusion

The disruptive power of ekphrasis extends the same promise of critical distance that could not be followed through on by mimesis. It remains to be seen if ekphrasis can follow through on this promise. One hopeful sign is noted very early on in Andrew Sprague Becker's survey of the history of ekphrasis. He notes

a double movement of literary representation in ekphrasis: accep-tance of the illusion proposed by the ekphrasis is accompanied by a complementary breaking of that illusion. The phrase "breaking the illusion" carries, here, a rather mild sense; it indicates that a certain self-consciousness expressed in the description adds another dimen-sion, perhaps unsettling the illusion, or balancing it, or bracketing it. The illusion is still in play, but it is held a bit more lightly and with an acknowledgement of its irony.[40]

Becker not only delineates that ekphrasis accomplishes this feat, but also outlines the way in which it is accomplished. He details four levels of representation to which ekphrasis calls attention. These are,

Res Ipsae—Referent.
Opus Ipsum—A focus on the physical medium.
Artifex et Ars—a focus on the creator and the creation of the work of art and their relation to the medium and the referent.
Animadversor—A focus on the effect of or reaction to the work of visual art.[41]

It is through the interplay of these levels of representation that ekphrasis both sustains and disrupts the mimetic illusion. It is possible to utilize this "terministic screen"[42] to offer a critical perspective on a significant range of political pronouncements, in particular those that employ the logic of the Shield of Achilles. However, before reaching that end, the contours of this "terministic screen" should be more carefully laid out.

The *res ipsae* or referent is the mimetic level of representation and it is "based upon the recognition and elaboration of what is depicted by the image."[43] Under the rubric of the *res ipsae* "the subject matter is often turned into a small story."[44] As is the case with a mimetic representation, this phase sees an establishment of the object. That which lies behind any representation is brought to the fore. This phase has three subdivisions; naming, interpreting and dramatizing. The name fixes the object, interpretation endows it with meaning, and dramatization sets the object in motion. Working in conjunction, the three serve to create a mimetic illusion; a presentation of (the image of) the object before the mind's eye. The phrase "the image of" is bracketed here because although all that is presented is an image, part of the power of that image is to conceal itself as an image. Hence "the surface of the work becomes a transparent window to the scene evoked therein."[45] Thus in *The Iliad* the *res ipsae* is discernable in Homer's tendency to "forget that he is representing graphic art; he suppresses all reference to metal as he tells the gruesome story of the lions and the ox."[46] The hazards of this "forgetting," if left unchecked, have already been discussed in the terms of the tendency of mimesis to conceal itself and thus to perpetuate the bearing of the shield.

Fortunately, ekphrasis builds into itself several checks on this "forgetting." One of these is the *opus ipsum*. Here the focus is not the perpetuation of an illusion through its dramatization. Instead there is an emphasis on the physical medium, "the surface appearance." If the *res ipsae* offers a view of the referent through "a transparent window," then *opus ipsum* draws attention to the glass. "Attention is paid to color, shape, texture, arrangement, size, and, at times, material."[47] In its interaction with *res ipsae*, *opus ipsum* can be somewhat jarring. For example,

> and the earth churned black behind them, like earth churning
> solid gold as it was ... (18:637–8)

Here Homer focuses the attention of his audience on the "earth"—and notably not the representation of earth—but then says it "churned . . . like earth churning." This latter connection destabilizes the image that had formerly concealed itself. It is redundant to say "earth churns like earth," for how else could it churn? Thus the mere fact that Homer says it indicates something amiss about this "earth." This something is explained in the immediate shifting of the audience's attention to the medium in which the representation is created ("solid gold"). Thus "earth" (the image) is not earth (the referent). This difference is only made "visible" through the interplay of *res ipsae* and *opus ipsum*. *Opus ipsum* renders the viewpoint of the reader highly mobile, shifting as it does from an immersion in the illusion to a vantage point outside of it and back again. The mimetic illusion is placed within a context, not of faithful retelling ("telling it like it is") but of artificiality; of craftsmanship rather than correspondence. It therefore accomplishes what Becker calls a defamiliarization, which he takes to mean, "that the description is making the representation more representation-y."[48]

Opus ipsum works to defamiliarize and recontextualize *res ipsae*. *Artifex et ars* continues this process. Here, by means of a direct reference to the artist and the process of artistic creation, the audience is further distanced from the illusion. The audience is shown what that illusion is made of, who makes it, and how it is made. It is more and more the case that a solidly established sense of critical distance from the image is established for the audience. From such a distance the audience has the ability to render judgments on the illusion that are not possible from within it. In this third stage of ekphrasis, the natural sign aesthetic is no longer possible as the ontological grounds upon which such an aesthetic have been shaken. It is perhaps better to say that in this third level of representation (and even more so in the fourth) the natural sign for the first time appears as an aesthetic—rather than given—feature of the world.

The fourth level of representation, *animadversor* in Becker's terminology, supplies exactly the kind of judgment that is made possible by *artifex et ars*. Here the interlocutor, the author, exposes himself or herself as yet a further intermediary between the audience and the illusion. This is accomplished through the offering of a reaction to the work described. Returning to the previous example taken from Homer,

And the earth churned black behind them, like earth churning
Solid gold as it was—that was the wonder of Hephaestus' work.

Homer's awe at "the wonder of Hephaestus' work" is a reaction intended to guide that of his audience. This guidance does not take the commandeering form of an imperative. Nor is it the case that the reaction of the author is the only one permitted to the audience. If it were, the author would be guilty of making yet another "this is the way it is" claim of exactly the type ekphrasis works to undermine. Rather the author offers a guide to the audience who is then able to make up his or her own mind, and to form his or her own response. The reaction of the author is therefore an invitation for the reader to react. The mimetic illusion makes a double claim: "this is the way it is" attended by "nothing (else) to be done" (which can be voiced in the imperative "do nothing!"). Ekphrasis embraces the power of this representation in its focus on the referent—*res ipsae*—yet at the same time undermines it, admonishing the reader to "do something!"

Utilizing these four levels of representation, an ekphrastic tactical approach serves to wedge open an otherwise easily overlooked gap in any claim to certainty, absoultivity, or unimpeachabilty. This tactical approach is made possible once one comes to realize, following Nietzsche, that ideologies, institutions, customs and faiths are shaped by human action and are in this manner examples of *poiesis*. These are representations of what is thought to be right, good, appropriate, true. They are never themselves the right, the good, the appropriate, or the true despite any claims that they are—and such claims are both numerous and forceful. Although the interplay of the four levels of representation do open up an opportunity for critical distance, they can also draw the reader further into the illusion. The author offers the reader distance from the object described, but in so doing enhances the reader's trust in the author. It is as if the author, by revealing his or her own distance from the illusion puts his or her own "objectivity" on display. Ironically it is the "subjective" value judgments of the animadversor that bring this "objectivity" into relief.

Plato and Baudrillard alike have displayed the power of the mimetic image, "the illusion." To simply disregard this power is a mistake. The ability of ekphrasis to hold the illusion "a bit more lightly and with an acknowledgement of its irony" is of tremendous importance. This ironic stance can stave off what Baudrillard calls "realist abjection," as well as Baudrillard's own "hyperrealist abjection." If this is stated in the terms of the double claim of the shield, the exposure of the "this is the way it is" as illusory, as ironic, renders the "nothing (else) to be done" that rests upon it equally illusory, equally ironic. If "it" is an illusion, then the categorical dictates of "its" contents ("all is war," "to know the Good is to be good", "all is simulation," "you are with us or you are with the terrorists," *etc.*) do not carry categorical force. Rather, they carry the unsettled *illusion* of categorical force. Hence any ethical imperatives derived from the "this is the way it is"—specifically the "nothing (else) to be done" and its imperative "do nothing"—are illusions based on illusions.

There is a conscious effort here to avoid the language of "the real." Such language is highly charged and steeped in a long history of Platonist and Enlightenment thinking which presupposes that to call something illusory is to deny its reality. However, these are not mutually exclusive categories. It may well be that the Athenian embassy to Melos was enthralled by an illusory notion that "the strong do what they have the power to do and the weak accept what they have to accept,"[49] but this alone does not render their swords less sharp or the fate of the Melians any less bloody or cruel. That the arms of the Athenian soldiers were guided by an illusion does not render the suffering they inflicted any less real. Similarly, the presence of weapons of mass destruction in Iraq may have been an illusion, but that does not make the war or its economic and human costs any less real.

The disruptive, ironic power of ekphrasis renders any appeal to a self-evident reality problematic. Appeals of this sort underpin the "this is the way it is" of the shield and the "this is the way it *really* is" of the mimetic challenge. If mimesis renders the "this is the way it is" claim the equivalent of "this is the way it is *like*," ekphrasis adds another layer of distance: "this is something like the way it is like." This double distance does not eradicate the possibility of there being a reality behind the image, but it does remove the possibility of getting beyond the image to find out once and for all. The question of the real is suspended, which is to say it is maintained in suspense. This is different from Baudrillard's position because it is not that the real is no longer a question, or no longer relevant, but rather that the real is maintained as a perpetual question (always still a question). Hence any "this is the way it is" claim presenting itself as unquestionable is immediately suspect. Any attempt to bear the shield is an open admission that one is dealing in illusion. Ekphrasis marks the shift from "thus it is" to Nietzsche's "let it be thus!" By rendering the real (the "it is") a permanent question, ekphrasis also allows for a shift from "there is nothing to be done" to "what is to be done next?"

Case Study: Obama as Shield Bearer

This book opened with a comparison between the language of Homer's *Iliad* and a speech given by George W. Bush to a joint session of Congress in September of 2001. The comparison was made in order to demonstrate the applicability of the Shield of Achilles as a metaphor through which to understand a certain logic of fear. The shield in its metaphorical operation makes a double claim; "this is the way it is" and "there is nothing (else) you can do about it." Through a discussion of figures such as Plato, Baudrillard and Nietzsche, I have established grounds upon which one might gain some distance from the paralyzing logic of the shield, using ekphrasis as a critical tool. The argument has now come to the point where it should be possible to read any political speech that employs the logic of the shield as an example of ekphrasis. If these speeches can be read this way then, ironically, it can be demonstrated that the logic of the shield undoes itself simply by being spoken. What remains then is a test. In the pages to follow I will examine a speech that uses shield logic in order to determine whether or not Becker's four components of ekphrasis are present. If they are, then the certainties expressed in the language of the speech can be destabilized, and the political implications of this explored. By recognizing a speech as ekphrastic, the audience is far less likely to accept its claims at face value. In other words, *the politics of fear can be undone through an understanding of the poetics of fear.*

When choosing an example, one is struck by the vast range of issue areas and sources potentially available. Once recognized in the abstract, shield logic is not difficult to locate in the particular. One obvious choice would be to return to the very same speech that was used to identify the logic in the first place. President Bush's speech of September 20, 2001 came at a time of tremendous uncertainty. In the near term, there was still very little public knowledge about who or what was responsible for the events of September 11. Due to this uncertainty there was no clear path of response. A variety of possibilities remained open. Was it a criminal act, best met with a legal response? Was it an attack by another state? Was it a random act of violence? President Bush's speech attempted to answer these questions and to close down all avenues of response but one. The speech therefore offers an excellent example of shield logic, through its depiction of a particular understanding of the world as one at war.

This particular understanding of the world makes a good deal of sense when it is seen in the context of a longer term uncertainty that had been prevalent since the end of the Cold War. For much of the twentieth century the world had indeed been at war. The end of the Cold War which accompanied the collapse of the great other, the Soviet Union, had left the Western world, led by the United States, in a profound state of uncertainty. Its institutions and ideological orientations had been built on the premise of warding off a dangerous global enemy that was no longer there. Hence this speech aimed, in part, to redraw those lines between us and them, thereby putting the institutional structures of the West back on a more even keel.

In Book 18 of *The Iliad*, there are three distinct levels of reference.[50] There is the world, Hephaestus' depiction of the world as it appears on the shield, and Homer's representation of Hephaestus' work. In President Bush's speech of September 20, 2001 these levels are also present. There is the world, Bush's understanding of the world, and his depiction of that understanding to his audience. On a surface level, President Bush's speech differs from Homer's account of the shield in that Bush is describing his own creation. He is, in other words, both *artifex* and *animadversor*. And yet this difference begins to become less clear when one accepts the reasonably obvious argument that the shield was never a physical object, but a notional one, a poetic invention of Homer. Homer is thus both *artifex* and *animadversor*. He creates the object and tells his audience how to respond to it.

Over the years following the speech given by President Bush, it has become difficult to see how the ekphrasis of Bush's speech is itself purely notional. Since its initial delivery, more and more evidence has been produced to justify his understanding of the world as one at war. This is to say that his understanding of the world has subsequently shaped his actions in the world, which themselves reshaped the world. The world has become more and more the way it was imagined to be. This is the crux of Baudrillard's hyperreality. Where Baudrillard goes wrong is that he sees these representations as perfectible, thus revealing his overconfidence in the persuasive and coercive powers of the state or media, if not his over-confidence in the ontological fathomability of the world.[51] There is a tendency to naturalize the situation, to make it a mere fact about which nothing can be done and for which no responsibility can be borne (at the very least not on "our" part).[52]

The mimetic effect of the speech cannot be denied. Retrospectively, it is not difficult to be taken in by Bush's claim to tell it like it really is. His words do indeed look like an accurate representation of what is. But the undeniable presence of a potent mimetic image does not mean that it cannot be challenged. An ekphrastic reading of the speech focusing on the operation of Becker's four levels of representation is indeed possible. The insights gained thereby are of assistance in undoing this effect of mimesis concealing itself as mimesis.[53] And yet there is a problem. President Bush's speech is in fact so easy to analyze as an example of ekphrasis that it come across as almost a straw man. It is too easy a case.

While there is no doubt a certain aesthetic appeal to the symmetry of beginning and ending with the same speech, I am concerned with demonstrating the day-to-day applicability of employing ekphrasis in a critical manner. To draw on an example that is now nearly a decade old, and that was spoken by a public figure no longer in office seems, in a word, outdated. This is especially the case when the successor to President Bush, Barack Obama, came into office on a campaign platform of "hope, not fear." Given Obama's success, the question becomes whether or not the politics of fear is still relevant. "Isn't the time of fear over? Haven't we moved on?"[54] It is most tempting to simply say "yes," and to relegate the use of fear and the logic of the shield in the political arena to the past tense. One might take some comfort in the reassurance that a "that was then, this is now" attitude could bring. And yet to do so would be a dangerous mistake. Along with such complacency comes a greater likelihood that one will feel less inclined to maintain a critical stance. This is, admittedly, a difficult position to maintain at any time. However, one becomes far more vulnerable to a hazard if one merely assumes it has disappeared.

It is better to remain critical and questioning and to check to see if the threat has passed or not. To that end, I will look at a speech given by President Obama in March of 2009.[55] In it, he outlines "a new strategy for Afghanistan and Pakistan." The choice of this speech is based in part on its subject matter, and in particular in its presentation as a departure from what has come before. This provides ready-made grounds for comparison between it and President Bush's speech. If the time of the politics of fear has indeed passed, then one would expect its logic to also have passed. I will demonstrate that the politics of fear is still very much in play.

The first task to be undertaken is to establish whether or not the logic of the shield is at work in the speech. To do this, it is helpful to look for one or both of the central claims of the shield. Recall that the shield is a container that can hold a variety of contents. One must therefore remain attentive to both container and content. Most often the shape of the container is discernible through the layout of its contents. If the container is an indisputably knowable world about which one can say "this is the way it is" then it stands to reason that one should also pay attention to the "it is"—to what this world actually looks like. Its contents will determine the options available for action.

The logic of the shield with its two-part formula is without a doubt at work in President Obama's speech of 27 March, 2009. Recall that the Shield of Achilles, used as a metaphor, makes a double claim: "This is the way the world is" and "there is nothing (else) you can do about it." Both claims are readily identifiable in the speech, and in multiple instances. Obama establishes his shield logic almost immediately. After his opening greetings and acknowledgments of some of the notable audience members, he declares that he is going to unveil "a new strategy for Afghanistan and Pakistan." Shortly after this he says "I'd like to speak clearly and candidly to the American people. The situation is increasingly perilous." In this quote he quite explicitly states his intent to "tell it like it is," and provide a framework for understanding the world "as it is." The way things are is neatly summed up in the phrase "increasingly perilous." There can be no doubt that the first claim of the shield is to be found here.

To label the situation as "increasingly perilous" has a double effect. First, simply by calling the situation "perilous" Obama evokes a sense of urgency and danger. Peril implies a call for some kind of response intended to reduce or avoid that danger. One does not say "things are perilous, so let us leave them well enough alone." Moreover, the situation is not only perilous, but "increasingly" so. There is a call for action and that call is immediate. Something must be done, and it must be done now.

When shield logic is in operation it can be expected that there is some dire consequence to inaction or to taking the incorrect action. The incorrect action is, of course, anything other than that put forward by the speaker. What are the consequences of inaction or incorrect action in this case? Obama is quick to note that the great hazard of the moment is that Afghanistan might fall to the Taliban and that "terrorists" might continue to operate unchecked from a "safe haven in Pakistan." To bring this threat closer to home for his audience, Obama makes specific mention of "attacks on the United States homeland" and reminds his audience that the intent of al Qaeda is "to kill as many of our people as they possibly can."

There is a clear statement of the "this is the way the world is" claim, and it is equally clear that to make the wrong choice of action has severe and unacceptable consequences. Is there an equally clear expression of the second of the shield's central claims? Once again, the answer is an unequivocal "yes." This is demonstrable by asking the question "what is to be done about this situation?" The response Obama provides is this: "To disrupt, dismantle and defeat al Qaeda in Pakistan and Afghanistan, and to prevent their return to either country in the future. That is the goal that must be achieved." The force of this "must" resides in the consequences of inaction or improper action. Some of the parameters of what this might look like have already been discussed, but Obama provides much more detail. In the paragraphs that follow, he insists upon the connection between the futures of Afghanistan and Pakistan, arguing that the fight has moved across the border along with al Qaeda's leadership. He calls the border region between the two states "the most dangerous place in the world" for "the American people." In this comment, Obama offers a quiet yet powerful demonstration of how the threat posed by "al Qaeda and its extremist allies" has advanced, and hence is "increasingly perilous." Where they were once based in Afghanistan under the protection of the Taliban controlled state, they have now begun to threaten the sovereignty of Pakistan, all the while remaining a deadly threat to "the American people." It is interesting to note that Obama does not say that the American state is threatened, even though al Qaeda has already been presented as a threat to states (specifically Afghanistan and Pakistan). What Obama is doing is expanding the threat outwards, not only in a geographical sense through its movement across geopolitical borders, but also on a more abstract, theoretical plane through its movement across the levels of analysis often used to understand international politics.[56] This cross-cutting movement is completed when Obama says "this is not simply an American problem—far from it. It is instead, an international security challenge of the highest order." Not only is al Qaeda a threat to individuals and to states, but also to the system of states as a whole. The threat has become existential.[57] "The safety of people around the world is at stake." If the threat is existential, then the demand that it be met appropriately takes on an ethical imperative.

Within the first dozen paragraphs of Obama's speech there is a clearly presented shield claim: The situation is increasingly perilous. Al Qaeda and its extremist allies pose an existential threat to people, states and the international system as a whole. If this threat is not met appropriately, the results will inevitably be a world scarred by "brutal governance, international isolation, a paralyzed economy, and the denial of basic human rights . . . under the shadow of perpetual violence." There is no room left for argument about whether or not this threat must be stopped. What is more, it can only be stopped by adhering to a specific course of action. Not just any response will do. In the next few paragraphs Obama begins to outline what the right response will look like, and equally importantly, what it cannot look like.

The strategy he proposes is distinguished straight away as "stronger, smarter, and comprehensive." Even in this simple phrase he has rendered any other strategy than the one he has yet to set forth inherently "weaker, more stupid, and piecemeal." A good deal of the remainder of the speech provides more detail as to what his proposal involves, but it does not depart significantly from his initial call for an increase in "international support" and a close integration of "civilian and military efforts." Regarding the "military efforts," Obama places an emphasis on "tools, training and support" to strengthen both the Afghan and Pakistani security forces. "Civilian efforts" include a sizable influx of financial aid and investment ($1.5 billion per year over five years) to help build "schools, roads and hospitals" and to help create "opportunity zones" to foster continued economic growth. Both will proceed with increased involvement of other states and organizations such as the IMF and World Bank.

The logic of the shield is clearly at work here. It is presented early in the speech and repeated often throughout it. The audience is provided with an urgent call for action and given only two options from which to choose. As can be expected, one of the options is so horrific as to be a non-choice. One can follow Obama and rectify the situation, or one can do something else (indeed, anything else) with the inevitable outcome being a world of "perpetual violence." The duality of this choice is not presented in such stark terms as President Bush's "you are with us or you are with the terrorists," but its effect is the same. This can be seen not only in Obama's rejection of any option put forward by "al Qaeda and its extremist allies," but also in his rejection of the policies of the Bush administration. "The days of unaccountable spending, no-bid contracts, and wasteful reconstruction must end."

In fact, Obama places considerable stress on "accountability" and "clear metrics" throughout the speech. This addresses much of the criticism leveled against the policies of the Bush administration in the region. In a direct reflection of the rhetoric of the prior administration, Obama says "going forward, we will not blindly stay the course." A second effect of repeatedly stressing both accountability and clear metrics is that Obama establishes the problem as empirically identifiable and quantifiable. The threat posed by al Qaeda may be existential, but it is also readily discernible in the increasing tally of attacks and fatalities. Its presence is confirmed by the good science implicit in "multiple intelligence estimates" and by the numbers of dead.

> Al Qaeda and other extremists have killed several thousand Pakistanis since 9/11. They've killed many Pakistani soldiers and police. They've assassinated Benazir Bhutto. They've blown up buildings, derailed foreign investment, and threatened the stability of the state.

If the problem is factual, empirically testable, and quantifiably measurable then it is also subject to a technical and technological solution. It should come as no surprise that President Obama frames the issue in this manner as technology is what his country does best. That the problem is amenable to a technical solution is borne out in his call for the "deployment of 17,000 troops" to Afghanistan, along with "4,000 U.S. troops to train Afghan security forces." It can be seen in his insistence that "we will accelerate our efforts to build an Afghan army of 132,000 and a police force of 82,000 so that we can meet these goal by 2011." That it is amenable to a technological solution is evidenced by the ever increasing use of armed drones to carry out strikes against targets in the tribal areas of Pakistan.

Before moving on to a discussion of how one might respond to this instance of shield logic, there is one further component of it that should be discussed. The double claim of the shield is backed by "divine sanction" which can be taken literally, as is the case with the shield carried by Achilles himself, but can also refer to any "higher power" that fills the role of unimpeachable authority. This can include appeals to reason, nature or natural law, history or science.[58] The purpose of the divine sanction is to allow the bearer of the shield to deny his or her own agency in the creation of the situation he or she purports only to reflect or represent. In Obama's speech, the "divine sanction" is largely expressed in terms of empirical fact, hence it is an appeal to science. He reinforces this aspect of shield logic towards the end of the speech when he says,

> I remind everybody, the United States of America did not choose to fight a war in Afghanistan. Nearly 3,000 of our people were killed on September 11, 2001, for doing nothing more than going about their daily lives. Al Qaeda and its allies have since killed thousands of people in many countries.

The net effect of this statement and others like it is that the numbers alone dictate the need for a response. "I" (which has by this point in the speech been fused to "we") did not create the situation, but merely must respond to it.

The logic of the shield operates so as to shut down all avenues of response but one. It effectively paralyzes its audience into accepting its proposed solution as the only solution possible. It employs fear in that any other course of action inevitably brings with it an intolerable and unacceptable price. Obama, like Bush and many, many others before him makes no bones about this:

> The world cannot afford the price that will come due if Afghanistan slides back into chaos or al Qaeda operates unchecked. We have a shared responsibility to act—not because we seek to project power for its own sake, but because our own peace and security depends on it. And what's at stake this time is not just our own security—it's the

very idea that free nations can come together on behalf of our common security.

There is no room in this equation for debate about what action should be taken. Nor is there room for debate about whether action should be taken or not. At least, this is what the audience is led to believe.

I have argued that any example of shield logic is also identifiable as an example of ekphrasis. As ekphrasis, speeches such as the one under consideration here cannot provide the kind of certainty they claim to provide. If this is an example of ekphrasis, then it should be possible to identify the four components of ekphrasis within it. If it is possible to do this, then the paralysis induced by the shield logic within the speech is undoable. The argument can be understood as a representation of a representation rather than on its own terms as merely factual. The question is, then, are the four components of ekphrasis—*res ipsae, opus ipsum, artifex et ars,* and *animadversor*—present in Obama's speech? Yet again, the answer is an unqualified "yes." The exegesis to follow will proceed under the precautionary words of Becker who says,

> Some passages, phrases, and words can be pushed more than others; some offer more to unfold and consider: hence the commentary will be at times more extensive or repetitive and at others somewhat cursory.[59]

Perhaps the most straightforward place to begin is with the *res ipsae* or referent. Indeed, this component of ekphrasis is to be found precisely in what has already been discussed as the "this is the way it is" claim of the speech. In Homer's depiction of the shield, the *res ipsae* appears as the subject of his narration. It is the world depicted on the shield. In Obama's speech it appears in exactly the same guise. I have already discussed much of the content of Obama's version of "how things are," but specific examples of the res ipase can be found in statements such as "the situation is increasingly perilous," and "al Qaeda and its allies—the terrorists who planned and supported the 9/11 attacks—are in Pakistan and Afghanistan."

The *res ipsae*, according to Becker, can be broken down into three distinct sub-levels. These are naming, interpreting and dramatizing. Each of these sub-levels can be found in and around the passages just mentioned. It is not at all difficult to see naming at work in Obama's mention of "the Taliban" or "al Qaeda and its allies." Nor is it difficult to discern the blatant interpretive function of the phrase "the terrorists who planned and supported the 9/11 attacks." The dramatizing aspect of the *res ipsae* are implied in "planned and supported," but are clearly evident in the very next sentence which states in part "that al Qaeda *is actively planning attacks* on the United States homeland." [60] The function of these sub-levels of the *res ipsae* is to draw the audience further into the illusion of reality it presents. The audience is meant at this stage to take these linguistic representations of the world as the world itself.

Evidence of the *res ipsae* is to be found both early and often throughout the President's speech. Some of the multiple referents to be found depict negative aspects of the world, and some positive. Together the depictions form a cohesive picture of a world easily divided. This is all to say that just as Homer depicts a city at peace and a city at war on the shield of Achilles, so to does Obama portray a world of peace—one associated with "America," "the people of Pakistan," and the "Afghan people"—and a world of "perpetual violence" associated with "the Taliban" and "al Qaeda and its extremist allies." The two sides together form an overall referent; a complete picture of the world as it is. Yet on its own, the presence of the *res ipsae* is largely unremarkable. It is merely to point out that the speech has a referent; that it is *about* something. The speech can only rightly be said to be an example of ekphrasis if the other components are also to be found.

The *res ipsae* casts a powerful mimetic spell. Its language purports to be not a representation of its referent, but the thing itself. To remain trapped within this illusion is to accept unquestioningly the (non)options that are presented by the speaker. It is to remain paralyzed. If we want to gain any kind of critical distance from this image then we must be attuned to the other aspects of the language that would undo this spell in the very process of its incantation. This begin with the *opus ipsum*. The function of this aspect of ekphrasis is to render the representation put forward by the *res ipsae* "more representation-y." [61] It is to accomplish what Becker terms a "defamiliarization" of the image. [62] It does this through a focus on the physical medium including "color, shape, texture, arrangement, size, and sometimes material." [63]

Examples of the *opus ipsum* can be found by asking a question of the *res ipsae*: "What does it look like and what is it made of?" In Obama's speech, what it is is an "increasingly perilous" world in which "terrorists" threaten "us" and "our freedom." So what does this world look like? It looks like an ongoing war. It looks like "insurgents control[ling] parts of Afghanistan and Pakistan." It looks like increasing numbers of "attacks against our troops, our NATO allies, and the Afghan government." It looks like "the deadliest year of the war for American forces." Any of the multiple references in the speech to the geographical arrangement of either "us" or "them" fit into this category. For example, the sentence "in the nearly eight years since 9/11, al Qaeda and its extremist allies have moved across the border to the remote areas of the Pakistani frontier" provides not only an example of the naming, ("al Qaeda"), interpreting, (inherent in the reference to 9/11 and in the appellation "extremist"), and dramatizing, ("have moved"), aspects of the *res ipsae*, but also tells the audience how these forces are spatially arrayed ("across the border"). Furthermore, it offers an indication of the historical and temporal layout ("nearly eight years since 9/11"). By making reference to the ways in which the image provided by the *res ipsae* is arranged, an attentive audience can begin to see the referent as the result of a creative process rather than something merely given or "natural."

This process of creativity is explicitly highlighted by the *artifex et ars*. Where the *opus ipsum* speaks to the physical medium, the *artifex et ars* makes direct reference to the relationship between the medium and the referent. This is generally expressed in three primary ways. First, there is mention of the artist him or her self. Second, there is mention of the workmanship or material, and third, there is discussion of the process of manufacture. If the *res ipsae* can be spotted by asking "what is it?" and the *opus ipsum* by asking "what does it look like?" then the *artifex et ars* is found by asking "who makes it and how is it made?"

An excellent example, although by no means the only one, is to be found in the following passage:

> This almost certainly includes al Qaeda's leadership: Osama bin Laden and Ayman al-Zawahiri. They have used this mountainous terrain as a safe haven to hide, to train terrorists, to communicate with followers, to plot attacks, and to send fighters to support the insurgency in Afghanistan.

Here is the direct reference to the *ars* in the naming of both Osama bin Laden and Ayman al-Zawahiri. There is also straightforward mention of the "process of manufacture" by which they are creating the "increasingly perilous" world that is theirs. This "most dangerous" "city at war" is made by the "train[ing of] terrorists," the "communicat[ion] with followers," the "plot[ting of] attacks," and the "send[ing of] fighters to support the insurgency in Afghanistan." These are the artists and this is the process through which "the most dangerous place in the world for Americans" is created.

This last statement by President Obama is more than the declaration of fact it purports to be. There is a strong normative component to it. By using the phrase "most dangerous" he is providing his audience with a guideline as to how to feel about the situation. He is offering a built-in critique of the work intended to direct the response of his audience. Consider how this passage would read differently and how its effect would be altered had he said the word "wonderful" instead of "dangerous." In this sentence then we see the fourth component of ekphrasis, the *animadversor*. Thus all four components of ekphrasis can be identified in just the first few paragraphs of Obama's speech. The *res ipsae* is "defamiliarized" by the *opus ipsum*, which renders the given or "natural" aspects of the image "more representation-y." This distancing from the mimetic effect of the *res ipsae* is furthered in the *artifex et ars* which puts the image on display as an artistic creation. The *animadversor* completes the disruption of the illusion by passing judgment on it and in the process inviting the audience to do the same. It is clear that Obama's speech, as an example of ekphrasis, cannot be taken at face value. It cannot provide an unbiased portrayal of "the way it is" as it purports to do, and thus the course of action it proffers cannot be treated as so exclusive, necessary or obvious as it presents itself to be. It must be something other than what it claims to be.

The example provide so far has focused on what might be called a "terrorist's view of the world," or with a nod to Homer, the "city at war." As such, it is not necessarily surprising that such a view should be presented by Obama as illusory. If "their" world is a false one, there is a subtle implication, or rather a tacit assumption, that "ours" is not. Surely this should be put to the test. Is "our" world (the "city at peace") as portrayed by Obama also an example of ekphrasis?

The first question to ask will help to uncover the *res ipsae*. The question is, "what is it?" We know what "their" world is and that it is defined as one of "perpetual violence." It is to be expected that "our" world will likely be diametrically opposed to "their" world. The parameters of "our" world are discernible in statements such as "we are not in Afghanistan to control that country or to dictate its future. We are in Afghanistan to confront a common enemy that threatens the United State, our friends and our allies." "Our" world is "stronger, smarter" and is marked by "enhance[d] military, governance and economic capacity." It is a world in which "borders" and "laws of war" are heeded. It is a world whose people want "an end to terror, access to basic services, the opportunity to live their dreams, and the security that can only come with the rule of law." Where "al Qaeda offers the people of Pakistan nothing but destruction . . . We stand for something different." Although he does intend this to refer to "construction" as the obvious counterpart to "destruction, " the "something different" can be summed up in the following statement: "The United States of America stands for peace and security, justice and opportunity." This is "our" world. Where "al Qaeda and its allies" offer insecurity, violence and destruction, "we" offer a stable and secure Afghanistan and Pakistan, and by extension a greater degree of the same for the Unites States. Here is the contrapuntal *res ipsae* to that offered by al Qaeda. Together they form a greater whole about which Obama can say "the situation is increasingly perilous" and "these are challenging times" in which "resources are stretched." "We" are simultaneously in danger of losing a peaceful and secure world in which justice, law and opportunity prevail, and striving to achieve exactly that world.[64]

If "our" *res ipsae* is a peaceful, secure world, then what does it look like? How is it made? The answers to these questions aimed, respectively, at discovering the *opus ipsum* and the *artifex et ars*, take up the bulk of Obama's speech. Examples of each of the components of ekphrasis are to be found throughout the remainder of Obama's speech. Most are relatively straightforward. How could one miss the discussion of size and arrangement, indicative of the *opus ipsum*, in his recitation of "17,000 troops," "4,000 U. S. troops," and "an Afghan army of 134,000, and a police force of 82,000?" It is also quite easy to see *opus ipsum* in his reference to "schools, roads and hospitals" for these are the materials from which a stable and secure region is made. Additional examples of the *opus ipsum* can be seen in the references to "opportuniy zones" and in his call for an increase in the number of "agricultural specialists and educators, engineers and lawyers" present in Afghanistan.

Similarly, it is easy to spot the *artifex et ars* at work in Obama's mention of "a bipartisan bill co-sponsored by John Kerry and Richard Lugar that authorizes $1.5 billion in direct support" for the building of those same "schools, roads and hospitals." For what is the reference to the two senators but a reference to the "artists" (*artifex*) responsible for the creation of this particular aspect of the overall work? Obama makes this kind of specific mention in a number of locations in the speech, including reference to "Ambassador Richard Holbrooke," "General [David] Petreaus," "Maria Cantwell, Chris Van Hollen and Peter Hoekstra," "Secretary [Hilary] Clinton and Secretary [Robert] Gates," and "General [David] McKiernan." The majority of the instances of *artifex* in the speech come in Obama's use of the pronouns "I," "us" and "we." The preponderance of such references makes the overall project a collective one, and implicates the audience in the process of creation as its *artifex*. The responsibility for the triumph of the "city at peace" over the "city at war" rests squarely in "our" hands. It is also clear that the "us" extends not only to the specifically named members of the Obama administration, or to the specifically named Senators and Representatives, nor even to just the American people. As Obama makes abundantly clear, the "us" extends to "the United States, our friends and our allies, and the people of Afghanistan and Pakistan."

As for the *animadversor*, it is decidedly simple to detect in Obama's claims that "our troops have fought *bravely* against a *ruthless* enemy. Our civilians have made *great sacrifices*. Our allies have borne a *heavy burden*. Afghans have *suffered and sacrificed* for their future."[65] How could the audience of the speech not feel positively about the creation of "opportunity zones" in Pakistan that are intended to "bring hope to places plagued with violence." The words "opportunity" and "hope" bear the positive weight, while the term "plagued" carries the negative. It is also interesting to note that there is at times in the speech a decidedly medicalized tone to the *animadversor*, especially when he is speaking of "them." Obama's designation of "al Qaeda and its extremist allies" as "a cancer that risks killing Pakistan from within" not only places the threat within a framework that strikes very close to home for many of his audience members, but also fits nicely with his framing of the problem as technical and technological in nature. Just as cancer must be surgically removed, so too must the technologically enhanced military capability of the surgical strike be employed to remove al Qaeda.

It is helpful to parse the four components of ekphrasis out one at a time, but it is also important to note the considerable overlap between them. This is particularly true of the *opus ipsum* and the *ars*. This overlap is to be expected given Becker's admission that the *opus ipsum* sometimes refers to the material of which the image is made, and a that the *ars* speaks to the workmanship or material. If the *res ipsae* is a secure and stable Afghanistan and Pakistan, then some overlap between what it looks like and how it is made should not be surprising. Take the statement "to enhance the military, governance and economic capacity of Afghanistan and Pakistan, we have to marshall international support." In these few words there is an implication of the world as it is, where these capacities are wanting, (this is the negative *res ipsae* of al Qaeda). There is an invocation of the various components (*opus ipsum*), "military, governance and economic capacity" along with "international support" that make up the desired world. There is a reference to the process through which it is manufactured when Obama speaks of "marshaling international support," (*ars*), and even an indication of the responsible party, "we" (*artifex*). The overlap between the *opus ipsum* and the *ars* resides in the phrase "international support" which is simultaneously a material component and a process of creation.

Overlap between the components of ekphrasis is not strictly limited to the *opus ipsum* and the *ars*, although this is most common. For example, the words "we must focus our military assistance on the tools, training and support that Pakistan needs to root out the terrorists" contain multiple layers of ekphrastic componentry. In order of appearance, "we" is an instance of *artifex*. "Must" bears the weight of a strong normative claim which is a hallmark of the *animadversor*. "Focus" gives an indication of the process through which the image comes about (*ars*). "Our" is a return to the *artifex*. "Military assistance" is both *opus ipsum* and *ars* since it refers to both the material of which the *res ipsae* (a stable and secure Afghanistan and Pakistan) is made, and to the process through which it comes about. "Tools, training and support" displays far less of this overlap, and is instead a straightforward instance of *opus ipsum*. With the name "Pakistan" comes a second layer of ekphrasis, and hence more overlap. On the one hand, this is an obvious example of *artifex*, whose *ars* is to "root out the terrorists." The *res ipsae* in this case remains as before—a stable and secure Pakistan. On the other hand, "Pakistan" is also the very same stable and secure sovereign entity that is created by "us" (or rather by the "U.S.") as "our" *res ipsae*. Lest they be overlooked, there are also two potential examples of *animadversor* in the words "need" and "terrorists." "Need" is a clearer example. It is a judgment made on the part of the speaker intended to guide the response of the audience. It frames the parameters of the situation as necessary, not optional. This is not something merely desired, but urgently and emphatically required. The term "terrorists" is less obviously an example of *animadversor*. Its use as *artifex* has already been seen, and in so far as it names, it does have at least an element of the *res ipsae*. However, in this context, the word is intended to pass judgment on a specific target of justified state violence. A "terrorist," by the name alone, must bear the burden of thousands upon thousands of innocents killed. To highlight the judgmental effect of the *animadversor* here, imagine how the ethical tone of the sentence would change by substituting "freedom fighter" for "terrorist."

I have demonstrated how President Obama's speech is an example of the logic of the shield at work, and also an example of ekphrasis in both its positive and negative portrayals of the world. I have argued that "their" world is illusory, but so too is "our" world. Neither one can be taken at face value. Neither one can be understood as providing an unquestionable account of the facts "as they are." At best, the words of the speech are a likeness of a likeness that leaves the status of the original perpetually open to question. Any attempt to block or foreclose on such questioning must therefore be ruled as illegitimate.

By exposing the "thus it is" claim as a representation of a representation, ekphrasis as a critical tool opens the possibility for things to be otherwise. President Obama's worldview as presented in the speech does not offer unfettered access to the world as it is, but is rather a particular telling of one way of looking at it. Like the childhood "telephone game" the possibility— even the likelihood—that each subsequent telling will leave something out, or add something in, or alter things entirely remains irreducible. Thus any ethical imperative based on the "thus it is" is equally open to challenge. The "nothing else to be done" claim of the shield, and its imperative "do nothing else!" thus becomes the question "what else is to be done?

Notes

1 Franz H. Bauml, "Writing the Emperor's Clothes On: Literacy and the Production of Facts," in *Written Voices, Spokensigns: Tradition, Performance and the Epic Text*, ed. Egbert Bakker, and Ahuvia Kahane (Cambridge, MA: Harvard University Press, 1997). This same sentiment is to be found in the work of George Lakoff. See George Lakoff, "Simple Framing: An Introduction to Framing and Its Uses in Politics" (2004).

2 Plato too is Odyssean (Homeric) in his artistry, although he works to conceal that artistry in the *Republic*. Nietzsche helps to expose that which is concealed.

3 The term is taken from Murray Krieger, and will be discussed in some detail below. Murray Krieger, *Ekphrasis: The Illusion of the Natural Sign* (Baltimore, MD: Johns Hopkins University Press, 1992).

4 The capitalization of "Truth" here is intended to indicate its transcendent status as something beyond the reach of both spatial and temporal contextualization.

5 These numbers being in reference to the total American war dead in Iraq. 138 prior to President Bush's declaration of victory and a cessation of major combat operations, just over 4000 at the time of this writing. The figures say nothing of the tens of thousands of Iraqi citizens killed.

6 Friedrich Wilhelm Nietzsche, *Thus Spoke Zarathustra; a Book for All and None*, trans. Walter Arnold Kaufmann, vol. C196, Compass Books (New York: Viking Press, 1966), 12.

7 George W. Bush, "Address to a Joint Session of Congress and the American People, 20 September, 2001" (2001). For a similar assessment, see Barry Cooper, "Why the Koran Matters in Understanding Jihadist Terrorists," *Terrorism, Democracy and Empire* (2005). Cooper makes use of what he calls

"pneumopathology" (soul sickness) to describe the condition in which one justifies one's actions based on what one knows to be a lie. At first glance this position may seem indistinguishable from that of Odysseus, but there are very important differences. The concept of "pneumopathology" as deployed by Cooper marks a very clear distinction between the true and the false. As presented, the concept notes "their" sickness and "our" health. As such, it is radically non-Odyssean for the simple reason that it ignores the destabilization of the categories of true and false occasioned by the character of Odysseus.

[8] But also Paris the home of the *Ecole des Hautes Etudes en Science Sociales* and Jacques Derrida, not to mention Paris as the seat of government of the country foremost among those opposed to the war in Iraq, and hence a symbol of resistance.

[9] Erich Auerbach, *Mimesis: The Representation of Reality in Western Literature* (Princeton, NJ: Princeton University Press, 2003).

[10] Murray Krieger, *Ekphrasis: The Illusion of the Natural Sign*, 7.

[11] James A. W. Heffernan, *Museum of Words : The Poetics of Ekphrasis From Homer to Ashbery* (Chicago, IL: University of Chicago Press, 1993), 3.

[12] W. J. T. Mitchell, "Ekphrasis and the Other" (1994).

[13] Murray Krieger, *Ekphrasis: The Illusion of the Natural Sign*, 7.

[14] Ibid., 237.

[15] Nietzsche quoted in Jacques Derrida, *Spurs: Nietzsche's Styles/Eperons: Les Styles De Nietzsche*, trans. Barbara Harlow (Chicago, IL: The University of Chicago Press, 1979), 123.

[16] Ibid., 125.

[17] Ibid., 133–35.

[18] Ibid., 137. There is an intriguing connection between Derrida's observation, (immediately preceding the lines quoted), that "there is dissimulation only if one tells the truth, only if one tells that one is telling the truth," and the scene in which Homer tells of Odysseus' encounter with Athena upon his return to Ithaca. Notably, it is only after Athena drops her disguise and reveals herself to Odysseus that the hero doubts her:

> you're mocking me, I know it, telling me tales
> to make me lose my way. Tell me the truth now,
> have I really reached the land I love? (Homer, *The Odyssey*, trans. Robert Fagles (New York: Penguin Books, 1996), 13.371–73.)

Odysseus is in this way less dubious of the disguise than he is of the truth it supposes to conceal. For a detailed discussion of this scene, see Barbara Clayton, *A Penelopean Poetics: Reweaving the Feminine in Homer's Odyssey*, *Greek Studies: Interdisciplinary Studies* (Lanham, MD: Lexington Books, 2004).

[19] Murray Krieger, *Ekphrasis: The Illusion of the Natural Sign*, 251–52.

[20] G. E. Lessing, *Laocoon: An Essay on the Limits of Painting and Poetry*, trans. Edward Allen McCormick (Baltimore, MD: Johns Hopkins University Press, 1984).

21 Murray Krieger, *Ekphrasis: The Illusion of the Natural Sign*, 266.

22 Ibid., 267.

23 Ibid., 268.

24 Friedrich Wilhelm Nietzsche, *Twilight of the Idols and the Anti-Christ*, trans. R. J. Hollingdale, Penguin Classics (Harmondsworth: Penguin, 1968), 156.

25 W. J. T. Mitchell, "Ekphrasis and the Other."

26 Ibid.

27 Ibid.

28 One may suggest that typographical portraits are an exception. But in these cases it is more the shading and density of the physical medium of the text that is responsible for the image rather than the text itself. It serves my point—and Mitchell's for that matter—that such portraiture would not have the same effect if read aloud. For examples of such portraiture, see the typographical illustrations of Evan Roth. Evan Roth, "Evan Roth.Com,").

29 W. J. T. Mitchell, "Ekphrasis and the Other."

30 Ibid.

31 Ibid.

32 Ibid.

33 Ibid. Mitchell calls attention to Lessing who argued that poetry and the plastic arts (painting is his favored example) should operate in mutually exclusive spheres rather than allow poetry to "employ the same artistic machinery" as the painter, thereby "convert[ing] a superior being into a doll." See G. E. Lessing, *Laocoon: An Essay on the Limits of Painting and Poetry*.

34 W. J. T. Mitchell, "Ekphrasis and the Other."

35 Ibid.

36 There is not even a guarantee that this "object" even has an independent existence outside of its linguistic representation, as the Shield of Achilles so readily exemplifies.

37 Ibid.

38 Ibid.

39 Ibid.

40 Andrew Sprague Becker, *The Shield of Achilles and the Poetics of Ekphrasis* (Lanham, MD: Rowman and Littlefield Publishers, Inc, 1995), 23.

41 Ibid., 42–43.

42 Becker quotes Kenneth Burke as saying "Pick some particular nomenclature, some one terministic screen ... that you may proceed to track down the kinds of observation implicit in the terminology you have chosen ... [A] given terminology coaches us to look for certain kinds of things rather than others ... Some terminologies contain much richer modes of observation than others." Ibid., 43n.79.

43 Ibid., 42.

44 Ibid., 42.

45 Becker quotes Andrew Ford who, speaking of Homer, says: "The poetry of the past fulfilled its design as long as audiences forgot the performing poet, and

themselves, and everything but the vivid and painless presence of heroic action of old." Ibid., 42.

[46] James A. W. Heffernan, *Museum of Words : The Poetics of Ekphrasis From Homer to Ashbery*, 20.

[47] Andrew Sprague Becker, *The Shield of Achilles and the Poetics of Ekphrasis*, 43.

[48] Ibid., 43n.78.

[49] Thucydides and M. I. Finley, *History of the Peloponnesian War*, trans. Rex Warner (London: Penguin Books, 1972) p.402.

[50] This is similar to the three levels of knowledge in Plato's *Republic*.

[51] This self-generative effect is particularly clear in the case of the war in Iraq.

[52] This is the entire thrust of shield logic. This is also the thrust that ekphrasis as a critical tool is useful in parrying.

[53] Or in Becker's terms, this is the *opus ipsum* disguising itself as *res ipsae*.

[54] This was a question asked by a student of mine after the opening lecture in a course on the politics of fear. My response, then as now is a resounding "No!"

[55] Barack Obama, "Remarks By the President on a New Strategy for Afghanistan and Pakistan" (2009).

[56] The three levels of analysis—the individual, the state and the system—have already been touched upon in the introductory chapter of this book. Kenneth Waltz, *Theory of International Politics* (New York: Random House, 1979).

[57] This may appear to be a rather grand claim, but it is based on the conceit that the three levels of analysis can provide a complete picture of "the way things really are." If the threat posed by al Qaeda cuts across all three levels, and there are no other levels, then by this assumption it is indeed existential .

[58] I suspect that in this role, each of these should be capitalized; Reason, Nature, History, Science.

[59] Andrew Sprague Becker, *The Shield of Achilles and the Poetics of Ekphrasis* (Lanham: Rowman and Littlefield Publishers, Inc, 1995), 87.

[60] Emphasis added.

[61] Ibid.

[62] Ibid.

[63] Ibid.

[64] The overall picture is of a situation that is not only perilous, but precarious. It thereby lends rhetorical weight to the need to act both urgently and correctly. Only a clear goal and a "cause that could not be more just" can redeem "us." Or so the story goes.

[65] Emphasis added.

8

Conclusion

Globalization is a process through which the parameters of our existing frameworks, our current mythologies, are breaking down. In this moment there is no predominant metanarrative, no overriding framework, only a plethora of contenders for that mantle along with a living possibility that the mantle itself can be questioned. In this time of competing frameworks, it is to be expected that those that have held dominant positions will prove the loudest at proclaiming themselves still relevant. They have the most to lose, after all. Hence the rise of fundamentalisms of all kinds. They share a common structure: "I am right, everybody else is wrong"; the law of the excluded middle; this *or* that; one single way. They share an affinity for the logic of the shield. But the time for such things has come and gone. They are like soldiers on the battlefield whose war cry is loud, but terminal.[1]

What I have done in this book is to demonstrate one way that the politics of fear, or at least a particular if widespread expression of it, can be undone. It is not hard to identify examples of the logic of fear even in our own day-to-day lives. It is a political tool that is used because it is effective, and effective because it is so often used. You and I have been conditioned to accept it to the point where it simply becomes part of the background, part of a "commonsense" understanding of the way things work. I have shown how this logic can be called into question. I have shown how its paralyzing effects can be undone. But what of it?

I began with the metaphor of the Shield of Achilles, drawn from classical mythology. By demonstrating its usefulness in understanding a number of contemporary issues, I have suggested that these issues too can be understood as mythological. Myth itself is ubiquitous, pervasive and inescapable. This is not to deny the existence of the real, but it is to deny the possibility of any unfettered or "objective" access to it, as "objectivity" is itself mythical.

I have spoken about this in the terms of the "divine sanction" that is part of shield logic. For example, in the rise of the scientific method we do not witness the triumph of fact over fiction as such, nor do we witness the dispelling of the magical. What we do see is the casting of a new spell: the dispelling of one magical framework by another.

By reminding ourselves of the mythical nature of our intellectual frameworks, we remind ourselves of the magical nature of reality. In other words, by living mythologically and doing so self-consciously we are more prone to remembering the infinite richness of the real, and we are less prone to a dogmatic, and therefore exclusionary, adherence to one particular way of understanding it. To live mythologically is to consistently remind ourselves that we don't have it all right; that we could be wrong and should remain open to other possibilities.

Ekphrasis as a form of critique is yet another way to remind ourselves that things are never what they seem to be, no matter how unsettling that realization might be. It is a reminder of the uncertain grasp we have on the world, in spite of all our attempts to convince ourselves otherwise. Any speech that employs the logic of the shield can be understood in this way. They cannot be taken at face value but must remain open to question, challengeable, and debatable, even because of their insistence on their own status as unquestionable, unchallengeable, and non-debatable. Ekphrasis is also a reminder of a collective responsibility for shaping the world in which we live. Not only are shield-like claims perpetually open to question, challenge, and debate, they must be questioned, challenged and debated. The omission of this step is tantamount to an abdication of one's own role as a creator, a role that is always already there. It is to live dishonestly. Ekphrasis as critique is a call for political action buried within the very attempt to shut it down.

We should remain open to other possibilities, but does this include all of them? Does the critique offered by ekphrasis lead to the "anything goes" of radical relativism? For example, in President Obama's speech, I argued that both "their" world and "our" world are illusory. How is one to choose between them? If the choice is simply between illusion and illusion, the possibility arises that ethics as a whole might be impossible. This is the very criticism that Christopher Norris levies against Baudrillard.[2] Although a complete answer, if there is such a thing, would require volumes, the beginnings of one can be found in the argument presented thus far.

First, it is important to note that the term "illusory" is somewhat misleading. It tends to retain within it a notion of a "real" or "original" behind it. Ekphrasis disrupts this easy distinction. It is never a choice between the illusory and the real. The real may or may not be there, we just have no final way of knowing. Hence it must remain as a perpetually open question. To use ekphrasis as a means to disrupt the logic of the shield is to disrupt the very either/or logic that would insist on there being only two choices. What emerges is the option to choose "neither," whatever the particular content of that might be. One could always do something else.

Second, the entire purpose of using ekphrasis as a critical tool is to provide a means of escaping the paralyzing power of shield logic. This paralysis is the result of collapsing all potential options to a single one. If we are left with a choice between one "illusion" and another, then it is safer, or at least more prudent, to eliminate the one that is most prone to shutting down all further discourse. If ekphrasis serves as a reminder that there is always something relevant being left out, then any option that presents itself as absolutely certain becomes immediately suspect. It is not a case of "anything goes" at all. In an ironic twist, it is precisely those positions that insist on there being only one way that do not "go."

The real exists, but only as an open question. It cannot be either encapsulated or dismissed. It is dynamic and never what it was. If we are to follow the time-honored tradition of aligning our politics with our ontologies, then totalitarianism, absolutism, and fundamentalisms of all stripes must be ruled out as viable options. Only a democracy can accommodate this kind of incessant dynamism.[3] This leaves open the question of what exactly a democracy is, but then again, that is the point.[4]

There is some degree of tension between the dynamism that ekphrasis uncovers and the formulaic structure of it that has been presented here. Does its formality weaken it as a critical tool designed to counter such formality? While it can be argued that other critical approaches to a text such as Derrida's deconstructive techniques are better suited for the task, it is also the case that in a social and educational environment where the formula still rules, such free flowing techniques can be too easily marginalized. Ekphrasis serves as something like a bridge between the formulaic and the anti-formulaic. It is a step-by-step approach to critique with roots in the apparent free-for-all of deconstructive practice. Because of its clear structure, it appeals to those who are more structurally minded, who are more geared to the acceptance of formulas. At the same time it can and does serve to expose the "illusory" qualities of such formulas.

Ekphrasis does not in itself offer specific policy suggestions, but it does set limits on what such suggestions might look like. Whatever course of action is to be taken, ekphrasis as a critical tool reminds us that it cannot be backed with the force of absolute, unimpeachable certainty or by an *unqualified must.*

Notes

[1] This analogy itself is flawed as it carries forward the combative presumptions of those who would reassert themselves in a position of dominance.

[2] Christopher Norris, *What's Wrong With Postmodernism: Critical Theory and the Ends of Philosophy* (Baltimore, MD: Johns Hopkins University Press, 1990).

[3] This is the case even if the incessant dynamism itself can accommodate all of the various forms of governance and more.

[4] At this point, another curious and ironic twist comes to the fore. If one adheres to a Burkean notion of conservatism, traditions are not to be abandoned lightly, if at all. This position requires certainty as to what that tradition is. What I have done here is to offer not an abandonment of tradition, but rather a rereading of it. For example, I have shown how if Homer is associated with a tradition that claims "all is warfare," he can also be understood, through the character of Odysseus, to challenge that tradition. I have argued that Thucydides and Machiavelli are not only central figures in the "realist" tradition, but also critics of that tradition. I have demonstrated Plato's poetics in his attack on the poets. The persistence of the questions that each of these authors are concerned with need not be indicative of some fixed and permanent human nature in the Hobbesian sense. It can instead point to the persistence of the real issues they address *as questions.* Where orthodoxy has looked to the answers they provide as most important, perhaps it is the question itself that matters? Perhaps Thucydides' insistence that "the strong do what they can and the weak suffer what they must" is less important than the persistence of the question "what is the nature of power?"

APPENDIX A

President Bush's Address to a Joint Session of Congress

United States Capitol
Washington, D.C.
September 20, 2001
9:00 P.M. EDT

THE PRESIDENT: Mr. Speaker, Mr. President Pro Tempore, members of Congress, and fellow Americans:

In the normal course of events, Presidents come to this chamber to report on the state of the Union. Tonight, no such report is needed. It has already been delivered by the American people.

We have seen it in the courage of passengers, who rushed terrorists to save others on the ground—passengers like an exceptional man named Todd Beamer. And would you please help me to welcome his wife, Lisa Beamer, here tonight.(Applause.)

We have seen the state of our Union in the endurance of rescuers, working past exhaustion. We have seen the unfurling of flags, the lighting of candles, the giving of blood, the saying of prayers—in English, Hebrew, and Arabic. We have seen the decency of a loving and giving people who have made the grief of strangers their own.

My fellow citizens, for the last nine days, the entire world has seen for itself the state of our Union—and it is strong. (Applause.)

Tonight we are a country awakened to danger and called to defend freedom. Our grief has turned to anger, and anger to resolution. Whether we bring our enemies to justice, or bring justice to our enemies, justice will be done. (Applause.)

I thank the Congress for its leadership at such an important time. All of America was touched on the evening of the tragedy to see Republicans and Democrats joined together on the steps of this Capitol, singing "God Bless

America." And you did more than sing; you acted, by delivering $40 billion to rebuild our communities and meet the needs of our military.

Speaker Hastert, Minority Leader Gephardt, Majority Leader Daschle and Senator Lott, I thank you for your friendship, for your leadership and for your service to our country.(Applause.)

And on behalf of the American people, I thank the world for its outpouring of support. America will never forget the sounds of our National Anthem playing at Buckingham Palace, on the streets of Paris, and at Berlin's Brandenburg Gate.

We will not forget South Korean children gathering to pray outside our embassy in Seoul, or the prayers of sympathy offered at a mosque in Cairo. We will not forget moments of silence and days of mourning in Australia and Africa and Latin America.

Nor will we forget the citizens of 80 other nations who died with our own: dozens of Pakistanis; more than 130 Israelis; more than 250 citizens of India; men and women from El Salvador, Iran, Mexico and Japan; and hundreds of British citizens. America has no truer friend than Great Britain. (Applause.) Once again, we are joined together in a great cause— so honored the British Prime Minister has crossed an ocean to show his unity of purpose with America. Thank you for coming, friend. (Applause.)

On September the 11th, enemies of freedom committed an act of war against our country. Americans have known wars—but for the past 136 years, they have been wars on foreign soil, except for one Sunday in 1941. Americans have known the casualties of war—but not at the center of a great city on a peaceful morning. Americans have known surprise attacks—but never before on thousands of civilians. All of this was brought upon us in a single day—and night fell on a different world, a world where freedom itself is under attack.

Americans have many questions tonight. Americans are asking: Who attacked our country? The evidence we have gathered all points to a collection of loosely affiliated terrorist organizations known as al Qaeda. They are the same murderers indicted for bombing American embassies in Tanzania and Kenya, and responsible for bombing the USS Cole.

Al Qaeda is to terror what the mafia is to crime. But its goal is not making money; its goal is remaking the world—and imposing its radical beliefs on people everywhere.

The terrorists practice a fringe form of Islamic extremism that has been rejected by Muslim scholars and the vast majority of Muslim clerics— a fringe movement that perverts the peaceful teachings of Islam. The terrorists' directive commands them to kill Christians and Jews, to kill all

Americans, and make no distinction among military and civilians, including women and children.

This group and its leader—a person named Osama bin Laden—are linked to many other organizations in different countries, including the Egyptian Islamic Jihad and the Islamic Movement of Uzbekistan. There are thousands of these terrorists in more than 60 countries. They are recruited from their own nations and neighborhoods and brought to camps in places like Afghanistan, where they are trained in the tactics of terror. They are sent back to their homes or sent to hide in countries around the world to plot evil and destruction.

The leadership of al Qaeda has great influence in Afghanistan and supports the Taliban regime in controlling most of that country. In Afghanistan, we see al Qaeda's vision for the world.

Afghanistan's people have been brutalized—many are starving and many have fled. Women are not allowed to attend school. You can be jailed for owning a television. Religion can be practiced only as their leaders dictate. A man can be jailed in Afghanistan if his beard is not long enough.

The United States respects the people of Afghanistan—after all, we are currently its largest source of humanitarian aid—but we condemn the Taliban regime. (Applause.) It is not only repressing its own people, it is threatening people everywhere by sponsoring and sheltering and supplying terrorists. By aiding and abetting murder, the Taliban regime is committing murder.

And tonight, the United States of America makes the following demands on the Taliban: Deliver to United States authorities all the leaders of al Qaeda who hide in your land. (Applause.) Release all foreign nationals, including American citizens, you have unjustly imprisoned. Protect foreign journalists, diplomats and aid-workers in your country. Close immediately and permanently every terrorist training camp in Afghanistan, and hand over every terrorist, and every person in their support structure, to appropriate authorities. (Applause.) Give the United States full access to terrorist training camps, so we can make sure they are no longer operating.

These demands are not open to negotiation or discussion. (Applause.) The Taliban must act, and act immediately. They will hand over the terrorists, or they will share in their fate.

I also want to speak tonight directly to Muslims throughout the world. We respect your faith. It's practiced freely by many millions of Americans, and by millions more in countries that America counts as friends. Its teachings are good and peaceful, and those who commit evil in the name of Allah blaspheme the name of Allah. (Applause.) The terrorists are traitors to their own faith, trying, in effect, to hijack Islam itself. The enemy of America is not our many Muslim friends; it is not our many Arab friends. Our enemy is a radical network of terrorists, and every government that supports them. (Applause.)

Our war on terror begins with al Qaeda, but it does not end there. It will not end until every terrorist group of global reach has been found, stopped and defeated. (Applause.)

Americans are asking, why do they hate us? They hate what we see right here in this chamber—a democratically elected government. Their leaders are self-appointed. They hate our freedoms—our freedom of religion, our freedom of speech, our freedom to vote and assemble and disagree with each other.

They want to overthrow existing governments in many Muslim countries, such as Egypt, Saudi Arabia, and Jordan. They want to drive Israel out of the Middle East. They want to drive Christians and Jews out of vast regions of Asia and Africa.

These terrorists kill not merely to end lives, but to disrupt and end a way of life. With every atrocity, they hope that America grows fearful, retreating from the world and forsaking our friends. They stand against us, because we stand in their way.

We are not deceived by their pretenses to piety. We have seen their kind before. They are the heirs of all the murderous ideologies of the twentieth century. By sacrificing human life to serve their radical visions— by abandoning every value except the will to power—they follow in the path of fascism, and Nazism, and totalitarianism.And they will follow that path all the way, to where it ends: in history's unmarked grave of discarded lies. (Applause.)

Americans are asking: How will we fight and win this war? We will direct every resource at our command—every means of diplomacy, every tool of intelligence, every instrument of law enforcement, every financial influence, and every necessary weapon of war—to the disruption and to the defeat of the global terror network.

This war will not be like the war against Iraq a decade ago, with a decisive liberation of territory and a swift conclusion. It will not look like the air war above Kosovo two years ago, where no ground troops were used and not a single American was lost in combat.

Our response involves far more than instant retaliation and isolated strikes. Americans should not expect one battle, but a lengthy campaign, unlike any other we have ever seen. It may include dramatic strikes, visible on TV, and covert operations, secret even in success. We will starve terrorists of funding, turn them one against another, drive them from place to place, until there is no refuge or no rest. And we will pursue nations that provide aid or safe haven to terrorism. Every nation, in every region, now has a decision to make. Either you are with us, or you are with the terrorists. (Applause.) From this day forward, any nation that continues to harbor or support terrorism will be regarded by the United States as a hostile regime.

Our nation has been put on notice: We are not immune from attack. We will take defensive measures against terrorism to protect Americans. Today, dozens of federal departments and agencies, as well as state and local governments, have responsibilities affecting homeland security. These efforts must be coordinated at the highest level. So tonight I announce the creation of a Cabinet-level position reporting directly to me—the Office of Homeland Security.

And tonight I also announce a distinguished American to lead this effort, to strengthen American security: a military veteran, an effective governor, a true patriot, a trusted friend—Pennsylvania's Tom Ridge. (Applause.) He will lead, oversee and coordinate a comprehensive national strategy to safeguard our country against terrorism, and respond to any attacks that may come.

These measures are essential. But the only way to defeat terrorism as a threat to our way of life is to stop it, eliminate it, and destroy it where it grows. (Applause.)

Many will be involved in this effort, from FBI agents to intelligence operatives to the reservists we have called to active duty. All deserve our thanks, and all have our prayers. And tonight, a few miles from the damaged Pentagon, I have a message for our military: Be ready. I've called the Armed Forces to alert, and there is a reason. The hour is coming when America will act, and you will make us proud. (Applause.)

This is not, however, just America's fight. And what is at stake is not just America's freedom. This is the world's fight. This is civilization's fight. This is the fight of all who believe in progress and pluralism, tolerance and freedom.

We ask every nation to join us. We will ask, and we will need, the help of police forces, intelligence services, and banking systems around the world. The United States is grateful that many nations and many international organizations have already responded—with sympathy and with support. Nations from Latin America, to Asia, to Africa, to Europe, to the Islamic world. Perhaps the NATO Charter reflects best the attitude of the world: An attack on one is an attack on all.

The civilized world is rallying to America's side. They understand that if this terror goes unpunished, their own cities, their own citizens may be next. Terror, unanswered, can not only bring down buildings, it can threaten the stability of legitimate governments. And you know what—we're not going to allow it. (Applause.)

Americans are asking: What is expected of us? I ask you to live your lives, and hug your children. I know many citizens have fears tonight, and I ask you to be calm and resolute, even in the face of a continuing threat.

I ask you to uphold the values of America, and remember why so many have come here. We are in a fight for our principles, and our first responsibility is to live by them. No one should be singled out for unfair treatment or unkind words because of their ethnic background or religious faith. (Applause.)

I ask you to continue to support the victims of this tragedy with your contributions. Those who want to give can go to a central source of information, libertyunites.org, to find the names of groups providing direct help in New York, Pennsylvania, and Virginia.

The thousands of FBI agents who are now at work in this investigation may need your cooperation, and I ask you to give it.

I ask for your patience, with the delays and inconveniences that may accompany tighter security; and for your patience in what will be a long struggle.

I ask your continued participation and confidence in the American economy. Terrorists attacked a symbol of American prosperity. They did not touch its source. America is successful because of the hard work, and creativity, and enterprise of our people. These were the true strengths of our economy before September 11th, and they are our strengths today. (Applause.)

And, finally, please continue praying for the victims of terror and their families, for those in uniform, and for our great country. Prayer has comforted us in sorrow, and will help strengthen us for the journey ahead.

Tonight I thank my fellow Americans for what you have already done and for what you will do. And ladies and gentlemen of the Congress, I thank you, their representatives, for what you have already done and for what we will do together.

Tonight, we face new and sudden national challenges. We will come together to improve air safety, to dramatically expand the number of air marshals on domestic flights, and take new measures to prevent hijacking. We will come together to promote stability and keep our airlines flying, with direct assistance during this emergency. (Applause.)

We will come together to give law enforcement the additional tools it needs to track down terror here at home. (Applause.) We will come together to strengthen our intelligence capabilities to know the plans of terrorists before they act, and find them before they strike. (Applause.)

We will come together to take active steps that strengthen America's economy, and put our people back to work.

Tonight we welcome two leaders who embody the extraordinary spirit of all New Yorkers: Governor George Pataki, and Mayor Rudolph Giuliani. (Applause.) As a symbol of America's resolve, my administration will work with Congress, and these two leaders, to show the world that we will rebuild New York City. (Applause.)

After all that has just passed—all the lives taken, and all the possibilities and hopes that died with them—it is natural to wonder if America's future is one of fear. Some speak of an age of terror. I know there are struggles ahead, and dangers to face. But this country will define our times, not be defined by them. As long as the United States of America is determined and strong, this will not be an age of terror; this will be an age of liberty, here and across the world. (Applause.)

Great harm has been done to us. We have suffered great loss. And in our grief and anger we have found our mission and our moment. Freedom and fear are at war. The advance of human freedom—the great achievement of our time, and the great hope of every time—now depends on us. Our nation—this generation—will lift a dark threat of violence from our people and our future. We will rally the world to this cause by our efforts, by our courage. We will not tire, we will not falter, and we will not fail. (Applause.)

It is my hope that in the months and years ahead, life will return almost to normal. We'll go back to our lives and routines, and that is good. Even grief recedes with time and grace. But our resolve must not pass. Each of us will remember what happened that day, and to whom it happened. We'll remember the moment the news came—where we were and what we were doing. Some will remember an image of a fire, or a story of rescue. Some will carry memories of a face and a voice gone forever.

And I will carry this: It is the police shield of a man named George Howard, who died at the World Trade Center trying to save others. It was given to me by his mom, Arlene, as a proud memorial to her son. This is my reminder of lives that ended, and a task that does not end. (Applause.)

I will not forget this wound to our country or those who inflicted it. I will not yield; I will not rest; I will not relent in waging this struggle for freedom and security for the American people.

The course of this conflict is not known, yet its outcome is certain. Freedom and fear, justice and cruelty, have always been at war, and we know that God is not neutral between them. (Applause.)

Fellow citizens, we'll meet violence with patient justice—assured of the rightness of our cause, and confident of the victories to come. In all that lies before us, may God grant us wisdom, and may He watch over the United States of America.

Thank you. (Applause.)

END 9:41 P.M. EDT

APPENDIX B

Remarks by the President on a New Strategy for Afghanistan and Pakistan

Room 450 Dwight D. Eisenhower Executive Office Building
March 27, 2009
9:40 A.M. EDT

THE PRESIDENT: Good morning. Please be seated.

Before I begin today, let me acknowledge, first of all, Your Excellencies, all the ambassadors who are in attendance. I also want to acknowledge both the civilians and our military personnel that are about to be deployed to the region. And I am very grateful to all of you for your extraordinary work.

I want to acknowledge General David Petraeus, who's here, and has been doing an outstanding job at CENTCOM, and we appreciate him. I want to thank Bruce Reidel—Bruce is down at the end here—who has worked extensively on our strategic review. I want to acknowledge Karl Eikenberry, who's here, and is our Ambassador-designate to Afghanistan. And to my national security team, thanks for their outstanding work.

Today, I'm announcing a comprehensive, new strategy for Afghanistan and Pakistan. And this marks the conclusion of a careful policy review, led by Bruce, that I ordered as soon as I took office. My administration has heard from our military commanders, as well as our diplomats. We've consulted with the Afghan and Pakistani governments, with our partners and our NATO allies, and with other donors and international organizations. We've also worked closely with members of Congress here at home. And now I'd like to speak clearly and candidly to the American people.

The situation is increasingly perilous. It's been more than seven years since the Taliban was removed from power, yet war rages on, and insurgents control parts of Afghanistan and Pakistan. Attacks against our troops, our NATO allies, and the Afghan government have risen steadily. And most painfully, 2008 was the deadliest year of the war for American forces.

Many people in the United States—and many in partner countries that have sacrificed so much—have a simple question: What is our purpose in Afghanistan? After so many years, they ask, why do our men and women still fight and die there? And they deserve a straightforward answer.

So let me be clear: al Qaeda and its allies—the terrorists who planned and supported the 9/11 attacks—are in Pakistan and Afghanistan. Multiple intelligence estimates have warned that al Qaeda is actively planning attacks on the United States homeland from its safe haven in Pakistan. And if the Afghan government falls to the Taliban—or allows al Qaeda to go unchallenged—that country will again be a base for terrorists who want to kill as many of our people as they possibly can.

The future of Afghanistan is inextricably linked to the future of its neighbor, Pakistan. In the nearly eight years since 9/11, al Qaeda and its extremist allies have moved across the border to the remote areas of the Pakistani frontier. This almost certainly includes al Qaeda's leadership: Osama bin Laden and Ayman al-Zawahiri. They have used this mountainous terrain as a safe haven to hide, to train terrorists, to communicate with followers, to plot attacks, and to send fighters to support the insurgency in Afghanistan. For the American people, this border region has become the most dangerous place in the world.

But this is not simply an American problem—far from it. It is, instead, an international security challenge of the highest order. Terrorist attacks in London and Bali were tied to al Qaeda and its allies in Pakistan, as were attacks in North Africa and the Middle East, in Islamabad and in Kabul. If there is a major attack on an Asian, European, or African city, it, too, is likely to have ties to al Qaeda's leadership in Pakistan. The safety of people around the world is at stake.

For the Afghan people, a return to Taliban rule would condemn their country to brutal governance, international isolation, a paralyzed economy, and the denial of basic human rights to the Afghan people—especially women and girls. The return in force of al Qaeda terrorists who would accompany the core Taliban leadership would cast Afghanistan under the shadow of perpetual violence.

As President, my greatest responsibility is to protect the American people. We are not in Afghanistan to control that country or to dictate its future. We are in Afghanistan to confront a common enemy that threatens the United States, our friends and our allies, and the people of Afghanistan and Pakistan who have suffered the most at the hands of violent extremists.

So I want the American people to understand that we have a clear and focused goal: to disrupt, dismantle and defeat al Qaeda in Pakistan and

Afghanistan, and to prevent their return to either country in the future. That's the goal that must be achieved. That is a cause that could not be more just. And to the terrorists who oppose us, my message is the same: We will defeat you.

To achieve our goals, we need a stronger, smarter and comprehensive strategy. To focus on the greatest threat to our people, America must no longer deny resources to Afghanistan because of the war in Iraq. To enhance the military, governance and economic capacity of Afghanistan and Pakistan, we have to marshal international support. And to defeat an enemy that heeds no borders or laws of war, we must recognize the fundamental connection between the future of Afghanistan and Pakistan—which is why I've appointed Ambassador Richard Holbrooke, who is here, to serve as Special Representative for both countries, and to work closely with General Petraeus to integrate our civilian and military efforts.

Let me start by addressing the way forward in Pakistan.

The United States has great respect for the Pakistani people. They have a rich history and have struggled against long odds to sustain their democracy. The people of Pakistan want the same things that we want: an end to terror, access to basic services, the opportunity to live their dreams, and the security that can only come with the rule of law. The single greatest threat to that future comes from al Qaeda and their extremist allies, and that is why we must stand together.

The terrorists within Pakistan's borders are not simply enemies of America or Afghanistan—they are a grave and urgent danger to the people of Pakistan. Al Qaeda and other violent extremists have killed several thousand Pakistanis since 9/11. They've killed many Pakistani soldiers and police. They assassinated Benazir Bhutto. They've blown up buildings, derailed foreign investment, and threatened the stability of the state. So make no mistake: al Qaeda and its extremist allies are a cancer that risks killing Pakistan from within.

It's important for the American people to understand that Pakistan needs our help in going after al Qaeda. This is no simple task. The tribal regions are vast, they are rugged, and they are often ungoverned. And that's why we must focus our military assistance on the tools, training and support that Pakistan needs to root out the terrorists. And after years of mixed results, we will not, and cannot, provide a blank check.

Pakistan must demonstrate its commitment to rooting out al Qaeda and the violent extremists within its borders. And we will insist that action be taken—one way or another—when we have intelligence about high-level terrorist targets.

The government's ability to destroy these safe havens is tied to its own strength and security. To help Pakistan weather the economic crisis, we must continue to work with the IMF, the World Bank and other international partners. To lessen tensions between two nuclear-armed nations that too often teeter on the edge of escalation and confrontation, we must pursue constructive diplomacy with both India and Pakistan. To avoid the mistakes of the past, we must make clear that our relationship with Pakistan is grounded in support for Pakistan's democratic institutions and the Pakistani people. And to demonstrate through deeds as well as words a commitment that is enduring, we must stand for lasting opportunity.

A campaign against extremism will not succeed with bullets or bombs alone. Al Qaeda offers the people of Pakistan nothing but destruction. We stand for something different. So today, I am calling upon Congress to pass a bipartisan bill co-sponsored by John Kerry and Richard Lugar that authorizes $1.5 billion in direct support to the Pakistani people every year over the next five years—resources that will build schools and roads and hospitals, and strengthen Pakistan's democracy. I'm also calling on Congress to pass a bipartisan bill co-sponsored by Maria Cantwell, Chris Van Hollen and Peter Hoekstra that creates opportunity zones in the border regions to develop the economy and bring hope to places plagued with violence. And we will ask our friends and allies to do their part—including at the donors conference in Tokyo next month.

I don't ask for this support lightly. These are challenging times. Resources are stretched. But the American people must understand that this is a down payment on our own future—because the security of America and Pakistan is shared. Pakistan's government must be a stronger partner in destroying these safe havens, and we must isolate al Qaeda from the Pakistani people. And these steps in Pakistan are also indispensable to our efforts in Afghanistan, which will see no end to violence if insurgents move freely back and forth across the border.

Security demands a new sense of shared responsibility. And that's why we will launch a standing, trilateral dialogue among the United States, Afghanistan and Pakistan. Our nations will meet regularly, with Secretaries Clinton and Secretary Gates leading our effort. Together, we must enhance intelligence sharing and military cooperation along the border, while addressing issues of common concern like trade, energy, and economic development.

This is just one part of a comprehensive strategy to prevent Afghanistan from becoming the al Qaeda safe haven that it was before 9/11. To succeed, we and our friends and allies must reverse the Taliban's gains, and promote a more capable and accountable Afghan government.

Our troops have fought bravely against a ruthless enemy. Our civilians have made great sacrifices. Our allies have borne a heavy burden. Afghans have suffered and sacrificed for their future. But for six years, Afghanistan has been denied the resources that it demands because of the war in Iraq. Now, we must make a commitment that can accomplish our goals.

I've already ordered the deployment of 17,000 troops that had been requested by General McKiernan for many months. These soldiers and Marines will take the fight to the Taliban in the south and the east, and give us a greater capacity to partner with Afghan security forces and to go after insurgents along the border. This push will also help provide security in advance of the important presidential elections in Afghanistan in August.

At the same time, we will shift the emphasis of our mission to training and increasing the size of Afghan security forces, so that they can eventually take the lead in securing their country. That's how we will prepare Afghans to take responsibility for their security, and how we will ultimately be able to bring our own troops home.

For three years, our commanders have been clear about the resources they need for training. And those resources have been denied because of the war in Iraq. Now, that will change. The additional troops that we deployed have already increased our training capacity. And later this spring we will deploy approximately 4,000 U.S. troops to train Afghan security forces. For the first time, this will truly resource our effort to train and support the Afghan army and police. Every American unit in Afghanistan will be partnered with an Afghan unit, and we will seek additional trainers from our NATO allies to ensure that every Afghan unit has a coalition partner. We will accelerate our efforts to build an Afghan army of 134,000 and a police force of 82,000 so that we can meet these goals by 2011—and increases in Afghan forces may very well be needed as our plans to turn over security responsibility to the Afghans go forward.

This push must be joined by a dramatic increase in our civilian effort. Afghanistan has an elected government, but it is undermined by corruption and has difficulty delivering basic services to its people. The economy is undercut by a booming narcotics trade that encourages criminality and funds the insurgency. The people of Afghanistan seek the promise of a better future. Yet once again, we've seen the hope of a new day darkened by violence and uncertainty.

So to advance security, opportunity and justice—not just in Kabul, but from the bottom up in the provinces—we need agricultural specialists and educators, engineers and lawyers. That's how we can help the Afghan government serve its people and develop an economy that isn't dominated by illicit drugs. And that's why I'm ordering a substantial increase in our civilians on the ground. That's also why we must seek civilian support from our partners and allies, from the United Nations and international aid organizations—an effort that Secretary Clinton will carry forward next week in The Hague.

At a time of economic crisis, it's tempting to believe that we can short-change this civilian effort. But make no mistake: Our efforts will fail in Afghanistan and Pakistan if we don't invest in their future. And that's why my budget includes indispensable investments in our State Department and foreign assistance programs. These investments relieve the burden on our troops. They contribute directly to security. They make the American people safer. And they save us an enormous amount of money in the long run—because it's far cheaper to train a policeman to secure his or her own village than to help a farmer seed a crop—or to help a farmer seed a crop than it is to send our troops to fight tour after tour of duty with no transition to Afghan responsibility.

As we provide these resources, the days of unaccountable spending, no-bid contracts, and wasteful reconstruction must end. So my budget will increase funding for a strong Inspector General at both the State Department and USAID, and include robust funding for the special inspector generals for Afghan Reconstruction.

And I want to be clear: We cannot turn a blind eye to the corruption that causes Afghans to lose faith in their own leaders. Instead, we will seek a new compact with the Afghan government that cracks down on corrupt behavior, and sets clear benchmarks, clear metrics for international assistance so that it is used to provide for the needs of the Afghan people.

In a country with extreme poverty that's been at war for decades, there will also be no peace without reconciliation among former enemies. Now, I have no illusion that this will be easy. In Iraq, we had success in reaching out to former adversaries to isolate and target al Qaeda in Iraq. We must pursue a similar process in Afghanistan, while understanding that it is a very different country.

There is an uncompromising core of the Taliban. They must be met with force, and they must be defeated. But there are also those who've taken up arms because of coercion, or simply for a price. These Afghans must have the option to choose a different course. And that's why we will work with local leaders, the Afghan government, and international partners to have a reconciliation process in every province. As their ranks dwindle, an enemy that has nothing to offer the Afghan people but terror and repression must be further isolated. And we will continue to support the basic human rights of all Afghans—including women and girls.

Going forward, we will not blindly stay the course. Instead, we will set clear metrics to measure progress and hold ourselves accountable. We'll consistently assess our efforts to train Afghan security forces and our progress in combating insurgents. We will measure the growth of Afghanistan's economy, and its illicit narcotics production. And we will review whether we are using the right tools and tactics to make progress towards accomplishing our goals.

None of the steps that I've outlined will be easy; none should be taken by America alone. The world cannot afford the price that will come due if Afghanistan slides back into chaos or al Qaeda operates unchecked. We have a shared responsibility to act—not because we seek to project power for its own sake, but because our own peace and security depends on it. And what's at stake at this time is not just our own security—it's the very idea that free nations can come together on behalf of our common security. That was the founding cause of NATO six decades ago, and that must be our common purpose today.

My administration is committed to strengthening international organizations and collective action, and that will be my message next week in Europe. As America does more, we will ask others to join us in doing their part. From our partners and NATO allies, we will seek not simply troops, but rather clearly defined capabilities: supporting the Afghan elections, training Afghan security forces, a greater civilian commitment to the Afghan people. For the United Nations, we seek greater progress for its mandate to coordinate international action and assistance, and to strengthen Afghan institutions.

And finally, together with the United Nations, we will forge a new Contact Group for Afghanistan and Pakistan that brings together all who should have a stake in the security of the region—our NATO allies and other partners, but also the Central Asian states, the Gulf nations and Iran; Russia, India and China. None of these nations benefit from a base for al Qaeda terrorists, and a region that descends into chaos. All have a stake in the promise of lasting peace and security and development.

That is true, above all, for the coalition that has fought together in Afghanistan, side by side with Afghans. The sacrifices have been enormous. Nearly 700 Americans have lost their lives. Troops from over 20 countries have also paid the ultimate price. All Americans honor the service and cherish the friendship of those who have fought, and worked, and bled by our side. And all Americans are awed by the service of our own men and women in uniform, who've borne a burden as great as any other generation's. They and their families embody the example of selfless sacrifice.

I remind everybody, the United States of America did not choose to fight a war in Afghanistan. Nearly 3,000 of our people were killed on September 11, 2001, for doing nothing more than going about their daily lives. Al Qaeda and its allies have since killed thousands of people in many countries. Most of the blood on their hands is the blood of Muslims, who al Qaeda has killed and maimed in far greater number than any other people. That is the future that al Qaeda is offering to the people of Pakistan and Afghanistan—a future without hope or opportunity; a future without justice or peace.

So understand, the road ahead will be long and there will be difficult days ahead. But we will seek lasting partnerships with Afghanistan and Pakistan that promise a new day for their people. And we will use all elements of our national power to defeat al Qaeda, and to defend America, our allies, and all who seek a better future. Because the United States of America stands for peace and security, justice and opportunity. That is who we are, and that is what history calls on us to do once more.

Thank you. God bless you, and God bless the United States of America. (Applause.)

END 10:02 A.M. EDT

Bibliography

Adam, Barbara. "The Temporal Landscape of Global/Izing Culture and the Paradox of Postmodern Futures." In *Theorizing Culture*, edited by Barbara Adam, and Stuart Allan, 249–62. London: University College of London Press, 1995.

—. *Time*. Cambridge, UK; Malden, MA: Polity, 2004.

Adkins, Jenny, and Zehfuss, Maja. "Generalising the International." *Review of International Studies* 31, no. 3 (2005): 451–72.

Agathangelou, Anna M., and Ling, L. H. M. "Power and Play through Poisies: Reconstructing Self and the Other in the 9/11 Commission Report." *Millennium: Journal of International Studies* 33, no. 3 (2005): 827–54.

Alker, Hayward. "Emancipation in the Critical Security Studies Project." In *Critical Security Studies and World Politics*, edited by Ken Booth, 189–213. Boulder, CO: Lynne Rienner Publishers, 2005.

Alkire, Sabina. 2003. "A Conceptual Framework for Human Security." www.crise.ox.ac.uk/pubs/workingpaper2.pdf (accessed June 23, 2008).

Amin, Shahid. *Event, Metaphor, Memory: Chauri Chaura 1922–1992*. Berkeley, CA: University of California Press, 1995.

Anderson, Amanda. "The Divided Legacy of Modernity." In *Cosmopolotics: Thinking and Feeling Beyond the Nation*, edited by Pheng Cheah and Bruce Robbins, 265–89. Minneapolis, MN: University of Minnesota Press, 1998.

Anderson, Benedict. *Imagined Communities: Reflections on the Origin and Spread of Nationalism*. London: Verso, 1991.

Annas, Julia. *An Introduction to Plato's Republic*. Oxford: Clarendon Press, 1981.

Archibold, Randal C. "Cheney, Invoking the Specter of a Nuclear Attack, Questions Kerry's Strength." *New York Times* October 20 2004.

Arendt, Hannah. *The Human Condition*. Chicago, IL: University of Chicago Press, 1958.

—. *Imperialism*. New York: Harcourt Brace and Company, 1994.

Artz, Lee, Yahya R. Kamalipour, and Robert E. Jr. Denton, (eds) *Bring 'Em on: Media and Politics in the Iraq War. Communication, Media, and Politics*. Lanham, MD: Rowman & Littlefield Publishers, Inc, 2005.

Ashley, Richard. "Living on Borderlines: Man, Poststructuralism, and War." In *International/Intertextual Relations: Postmodern Readings of World Politics*, edited by James Der Derian, and Michael J. Shapiro, 259–321. New York: Lexington Books, 1989.

Atchity, Kenneth. *Homer's Iliad: The Shield of Memory*. Carbondale, IL: Southern Illinois University Press, 1978.

Auerbach, Erich. *Mimesis: The Representation of Reality in Western Literature*. Princeton, NJ: Princeton University Press, 2003.

Aydinli, Ersel, and James N. Rosenau, (eds) *Globalization, Security and the Nation State: Paradigms in Transition*. New York: State University of New York Press, 2005.

Barthes, Roland. *Elements of Semiology*. Translated by Annette Lavers, and Colin Smith. London: Johnathan Cape, 1967.

—. *S/Z*. Translated by Richard Miller. London: Johnathan Cape, 1975.

Baudrillard, Jean. *Simulations*. Translated by Paul Foss, Paul Patton, and Philip Beitchman. Edited by Jim Fleming, and Sylvere Lotringer. *Semiotext(E) Foreign Agents Series*. New York: Semiotext(e), 1983.

—. *Symbolic Exchange and Death*. Translated by Iain Hamilton Grant. Edited by Michael Featherstone. *Theory, Culture & Society*. London: Sage Publications, 1993.

—. *The Illusion of the End*. Translated by Chris Turner. Cambridge: Polity Press, 1994.

—. *The Spirit of Terrorism and Requiem for the Twin Towers*. Translated by Chris Turner. London: Verso, 2002.

Bauman, Zygmunt. *Modernity and the Holocaust*. Ithaca, NY: Cornell University Press, 1989.

Bauml, Franz H. "Writing the Emperor's Clothes On: Literacy and the Production of Facts." In *Written Voices, Spokensigns: Tradition, Performance and the Epic Text*, edited by Egbert Bakker, and Ahuvia Kahane, 37–55. Cambridge, MA: Harvard University Press, 1997.

Becker, Andrew Sprague. *The Shield of Achilles and the Poetics of Ekphrasis*. Lanham, MD: Rowman and Littlefield Publishers, Inc, 1995.

Beiner, Roland, (ed.) *Theorizing Nationalism*. Albany, NY: State University of New York Press, 1999.

Benjamin, Walter. "Doctrine of the Similar." *New German Critique* Spring 79, no. 17 (1933): 65–70.

—. "Theories of German Fascism: On the Collection of Essays War and Warrior." *New German Critique* Spring 79, no. 17 (1933): 120–9.

Blanchard, Marc. "Review: Mimesis Not Mimicry." *Comparative Literature* 49, no. 2 (1997): 176–90.

Bobbitt, Philip. *The Shield of Achilles War, Peace, and the Course of History*. New York: Anchor Books, 2002.

Bogue, Ronald, Guiseppe Mazzotta, and Mihai Spariosu, (eds) *Mimesis in Contemporary Theory: Mimesis, Semiosis and Power*. Vol. 2, *Cultra Ludens: Imitation and Play in Western Culture*. Philadelphia, PA: John Benjamins Publishing Company, 1984.

Booth, Ken, (ed.) *Critical Security Studies and World Politics*. Critical Security Studies. Boulder, CO: Lynne Rienner Publishers, 2005.

Booth, Ken, and Tim Dunne, (eds) *Worlds in Collision: Terror and the Future of Global Order*. New York: Palgrave Macmillan, 2002.

Boutros-Ghali, Boutros. "An Agenda for Peace: Preventative Diplomacy, Peacemaking and Peace-Keeping." *International Relations* 11, no. 3 (1992): 201–18.

Brann, Eva. "The Music of the Republic." *Agon* 1, no. 1 (1967): 1–117.

Bremmer, Jan N. "Erich Auerbach and His Mimesis." *Poetics Today* 20, no. 1 (1999): 3–10.

Brennan, Teresa. *Globalization and Its Terrors: Daily Life in the West*. London: Routledge, 2003.

Brown, Chris. "Reflections on the 'War on Terror', 2 Years on." *International Politics* 41, no. 1 (2004): 51–64.

Buffet, Cyril, and Beatrice Heuser, (eds) *Haunted By History: Myths in International Relations*. Providence, RI: Berghahn Books, 1998.

Bush, George W. "President Bush Speaks to United Nations." (2001): November 10, 2001. http://georgewbush-whitehouse.archives.gov/news/releases/2001/11/20011110-3.html (accessed December 15, 2006).

—. "State of the Union Address." (2002): January 29, 2002. http://georgewbush-whitehouse.archives.gov/news/releases/2002/01/20020129-11.html (accessed December 15, 2006).

—. "President Bush Addresses United Nations General Assembly, September 23, 2003." (2003): http://georgewbush-whitehouse.archives.

gov/news/releases/2002/01/20020129-11.html (accessed December 15, 2006).

—. "State of the Union Address." (2003): December 29, 2003. http://georgewbush-whitehouse.archives.gov/news/releases/2003/01/20030128-19.html (accessed December 15, 2006).

—. "Transcript From Bush Speech on American Strategy in Iraq." *New York Times* (2004): May 24, 2004. www.nytimes.com/2004/05/24/politics/25PTEX-FULL.html (accessed June 1, 2006).

—. "Innaugural Address." (2005) January 20, 2005. http://georgewbush-whitehouse.archives.gov/news/releases/2005/01/20050120-1.html (accessed December 15, 2006).

—. " Address to a Joint Session of Congress and the American People, 20 September, 2001." (2001): http://georgewbush-whitehouse.archives.gov/news/releases/2005/01/20050120-1.html (accessed December 15, 2006).

Butterfield, Bradley. "The Baudrillardian Symbolic, 9/11, and the War of Good and Evil." *Postmodern Culture* 13, no. 1 (2002): http://muse.jhu.edu/journals/pmc/v013/13.1butterfield.html (accessed May 5, 2005)

—. "A Response to Leonard Wicox's 'Baudrillard, September 11, and the Haunting Abyss of Reversal.'" *Postmodern Culture* 14, no. 1 (2003): http://muse.jhu.edu/journals/postmodern_culture/v014/14.1butterfield.html (accessed May 5, 2005).

Buzan, Barry. *People, States, and Fear: The National Security Problem in International Relations.* Brighton: Wheatsheaf Books, 1983.

Buzan, Barry, Ole Waever, and Jaap de Wilde. *Security: A New Framework for Analysis.* Boulder, CO: Lynne Rienner Publishers, 1998.

Byre, Calvin S. "Narration, Description and Theme in the Shield of Achilles." *The Classical Journal* 88, no. 1 (1992): 33–42.

Cairns, Douglas L., (ed.) *Oxford Readings in Homer's* Iliad. Oxford: Oxford University Press, 2001.

Call, Lewis. *Postmodern Anarchism.* Lanham, MD: Lexington Books, 2002.

Callaway, Rhonda, and Harrelson-Stephens, Julie. "Toward a Theory of Terrorism: Human Security as a Determinant of Terrorism." *Studies in Conflict and Terrorism* 29, no. 6 (2006): 773–96.

Campbell, Blair. "The Epic Hero as Politico." *History of Political Thought* 11, no. 2 (1990): 189–212.

Campbell, David. *National Deconstruction: Violence, Identity, and Justice in Bosnia.* Minneapolis, MN: University of Minnesota Press, 1998.

Carr, Edward Hallett. *The Twenty Years' Crisis, 1919–1939: An Introduction to the Study of International Relations*, 2nd ed. *Harper Torchbooks. Academy Library*. New York,: Harper & Row, 1964.

Casey, Gerard. "The Shield of Achilles." *Studies in Comparative Religion* 10, no. 2 (1976): 93–7.

Chan, Stephen. "A Story Beyond Telos: Redeeming the Shield of Achilles for a Realism of Rights in IR [International Relations]." *Millennium: Journal of International Studies* 28, no. 1 (1999): 101–15.

Cheah, Pheng, and Bruce Robbins, (eds) *Cosmopolitics: Thinking and Feeling Beyond the Nation. Cultural Politics*. Minneapolis, MN: University of Minnesota Press, 1998.

Cindi, Katz. "The Death Wish of Modernity and the Politics of Mimesis." *Public Culture* 20, no. 3 (2008): 551–60.

Clausewitz, Carl Von. On War. Translated by Michael Howard, and Peter Paret. New York: Knopf, 1993.

Clayton, Barbara. *A Penelopean Poetics: Reweaving the Feminine in Homer's Odyssey, Greek Studies: Interdisciplinary Studies*, edited by Gregory Nagy, Lanham, MD: Lexington Books, 2004.

Cocks, Joan. "A New Cosmopolitanism? V. S. Naipaul and Edward Said." *Constellations: An International Journal of Critical & Democratic Theory* 7, no. 1 (2000): 46–63.

Collins, Christopher. *Authority Figures: Metaphors of Mastery From the Iliad to the Apocalypse*. Lanham, MD: Rowman & Littlefield Publishers, 1996.

Colton, Michael. 1999. I'm Sorry, Tinky Winky. www.salon.com/news/1999/02/13newsb.html (accessed May 23, 2009).

Connolly, William E. *The Ethos of Pluralization*. Minneapolis, MN: University of Minnesota Press, 1995.

—. *Neuropolitics: Thinking, Culture, Speed*. Vol. 23, *Theory Out of Bounds*. Minneapolis, MN: University of Minnesota Press, 2002.

Cooper, Barry. "Why the Koran Matters in Understanding Jihadist Terrorists." *Terrorism, Democracy and Empire* (2005): Paper at a conference held in Ottawa in October of 2005.

Cooper, John M., (ed.) *Plato: Complete Works*. Indianapolis, IN: Hackett Publishing Company, Inc, 1997.

Cornford, Francis MacDonald. *Thucydides Mythistoricus*. London: E. Arnold, 1907.

Crawford, Neta. "Fear Itself: Why Retaliation Doesn't Work." (2001): www.brown.edu/Administration/News_Bureau//2001-02/01-032.html (accessed July 5, 2005).

—. "The Pernicious Effects of Fear: Why We Must Have Greater Deliberation." (2001): www.brown.edu/Administration/News_Bureau//2001-02/01-032.html (accessed July 5, 2005).

—. "Just War Theory and the Us Counterterror War." *Perspectives on Politics* 1, no. 1 (2003): 5–25.

Damrosch, David. "Auerbach in Exile." *Comparative Literature* 47, no. 2 (1995): 97–117.

Danziger, James. *Understanding the Political World: A Comparative Introduction to Political Science*, 9th ed. New York: Pearson Longman, 2009.

Darby, Tom. *The Feast: Meditations on Politics and Time.* Toronto, ON: University of Toronto Press, 1982.

Deleuze, Gilles, and Felix Guattari. *A Thousand Plateaus: Capitalism and Schizophrenia.* Translated by Brian Massumi. Minneapolis, MN: University of Minnesota Press, 1987.

Der Derian, James. "The Value of Security: Hobbes, Marx, Nietzsche, and Baudrillard." In *On Security*, edited by John Gerard Ruggie, 24–45. New York: Columbia University Press, 1995.

—. "The Value of Security: Hobbes, Marx, Nietzsche, and Baudrillard." In *On Security*, edited by Ronnie D. Lipshutz, 24–45. New York: Columbia University Press, 1995.

—. "A Virtual Theory of Global Politics, Mimetic War, and the Spectral State." *Angelaki: journal of the theoretical humanities* 4, no. 2 (1999): 53–67.

—. *Virtuous War: Mapping the Military-Industrial-Media-Entertainment Network.* Boulder, CO: Westview Press, 2001.

Der Derian, James, and Michael J. Shapiro, (eds) *International/Intertextual Relations: Postmodern Readings of World Politics. Issues in World Politics Series.* Lexington: Lexington Books, 1989.

Derrida, Jacques. *Spurs: Nietzsche's Styles/Eperons: Les Styles De Nietzsche.* Translated by Barbara Harlow. Chicago, IL: The University of Chicago Press, 1979.

—. *Dissemination.* Translated by Barbara Johnson. Chicago, IL: The University of Chicago Press, 1981.

—. *Spectres of Marx: The State of the Debt, the Work of Mourning, and the New International.* Translated by Peggy Kamuf. London: Routledge, 1994.

Dowden, Bradley. Liar Paradox. www.iep.utm.edu/p/par-liar.htm (accessed Feb 5, 2009).

Dunn, John. "Nationalism." In *Theorizing Nationalism*, edited by Roland Beiner, Albany, NY: SUNY Press, 1999.

Dunphy, Floyd B. "Post Deconstructive Humanism: The 'New International' as an-Arche." *Theory and Event* 7, no. 7 (2004): http://muse.jhu.edu/journals/theory_and_event/v007/7.2dunphy.html (accessed July 15, 2005).

Durix, Jean-Pierre. *Mimesis, Genres and Post Colonial Discourse,: Deconstructing Magic Realism*. New York: St. Martin's Press, Inc, 1998.

Edmunds, Lowell. "Myth in Homer." In *A New Companion to Homer*, edited by Ian Morris, and Barry Powell, 415–41. Leiden: Brill, 1997.

Edwards, Mark W, and G. S. Kirk, (eds) *The Illiad: A Commentary*. Vol. 5: Books 17–20, Cambridge: Cambridge University Press, 1991.

Eldredge, Richard, Salim Kemal, and Ivan Gaskel, (eds) *Beyond Representation: Philosophy and Poetic Imagination. Cambridge Studies in Philosophy and the Arts*. Cambridge: Cambridge University Press, 1996.

Erickson, Chris. "The Shield of Achilles and the War on Terror: Ekphrasis as Critique." University of Massachusetts, 2006. *Electronic Doctoral Dissertations for UMass Amherst*. Paper AAI3215770. http://scholarworks.umass.edu/dissertations/AAI3215770 (January 1, 2006).

Fanon, Frantz. *The Wretched of the Earth*. New York: Grove Press, 1963.

—. *Black Skin, White Masks*. New York: Grove, 1967.

Feith, Douglas J. "Strategy and the Idea of Freedom." (2003): www.dod.gov/speeches/2004/sp20040414-0261.html (accessed June1, 2004).

—. "Iraq: One Year Later." (2004): www.dod.gov/speeches/2004/sp20040504-0321.html (accessed May 10, 2004).

Ferry, Luc, and Alain Renaut. *Why We Are Not Nietzscheans*. Chicago, IL: The University of Chicago Press, 1997.

Flaumenhaft, Mera J. "Priam the Patriarch, His City, and His Sons." *Interpretation* 32, no. 1 (2004): 3–32.

Frerks, Georg. "Human Security as a Discourse and Counter-Discourse." *Security & Human Rights* 19, no. 1 (2008): 8–14.

Frum, David, and Richard Perle. *An End to Evil: How to Win the War on Terror*. New York: Random House, 2003.

Fuchs, Barbara. *Mimesis and Empire the New World, Islam, and European Identities. Cambridge Studies in Renaissance Literature and Culture*. Cambridge: Cambridge University Press, 2001.

Furedi, Frank. *Culture of Fear Revisited: Risk Taking and the Morality of Low Expectation.* New York: Continuum, 2006.

Gallie, W. B. "Essentially Contested Concepts." *Proceedings of the Aristotelian Society* 56 (1956): 167–98.

Game, Ann. "Belonging: Experience in Sacred Time and Space." In *Timespace: Geographies of Temporality*, edited by Jon May, and Nigel Thrift, 226–39. New York: Routledge, 2001.

1999. Gay Tinky Winky Bad for Children. http://news.bbc.co.uk/2/hi/entertainment/276677.stm (accessed June 9, 2009).

Gebauer, Gunter, and Christoph Wulf. *Mimesis: Culture, Art, Society.* Berkeley, CA: University of California Press, 1995.

Geertz, Clifford. "Description: Toward an Interpretive Theory of Culture." In *The Interpretation of Culture*, 3–32. New York: Basic Books, 1973.

Gellner, Ernest. *Nations and Nationalism.* Ithaca, NY: Cornell University Press, 1983.

—. "Nationalism and the Narcissism of Minor Differences." In *Theorizing Nationalism*, edited by Roland Beiner, 91–102. Albany, NY: SUNY Press, 1999.

Gerring, John. *Social Science Methodology: A Criterial Framework.* Cambridge: Cambridge University Press, 2001.

Gilbert, Paul. *New Terror New Wars.* Edited by Brenda Almond. *Contemporary Ethical Debates.* Edinburgh: Edinburg University Press, 2003.

Girard, René. *Violence and the Sacred.* Translated by Patrick Gregory. Baltimore, MD: Johns Hopkins University Press, 1977.

—. *To Double Business Bound:Essays on Literature, Mimesis, and Anthropology.* Baltimore, MD: Johns Hopkins University Press, 1978.

Glenn, Paul F. "The Politics of Truth: Power in Nietzsche's Epistemology." *Political Research Quarterly* 57, no. 4 (2004): 575–83.

Goldberg, Jonah. "State of Confusion." (2003): www.nationalreview.com/goldberg/goldberg051603.asp (accessed October 15, 2004).

—. "The End of Neoconservativsm." (2003): www.nationalreview.com/goldberg/goldberg051603.asp (accessed October 15, 2004).

—. "The Neoconservative Invention." (2003): www.nationalreview.com/goldberg/goldberg052003.asp (accessed October 15, 2004).

Graves, Robert. *The Greek Myths.* New York: George Brazillier, Inc, 1955.

Greene, David, Richard Lattimore, David Greene, and Richard Lattimore, (eds) *Sophocles 2/Four Tragedies. The Complete Greek Tragedies.* Chicago, IL: University of Chicago Press, 1957.

Griffin, Jasper. *Homer, Iliad Book Nine.* Oxford: Clarendon Press, 1995.

Grunberg, Isabelle. "Exploring the Myth of Hegemonic Stability." *International Organization* 44, no. 4 (1990): 431–78.

Gunnell, John. *Political Philosophy and Time.* Middletown: Wesleyan University Press, 1968.

Gusterson, Hugh. "Missing the End of the Cold War in International Security." In *Cultures of Insecurity*, edited by Jutta Weldes, Mark Laffey, Hugh Gusterson, and Raymond Duvall, 319–46. Minneapolis, MN: University of Minnesota Press, 1999.

Hammer, Dean. *The Iliad as Politics: The Performance of Political Thought.* Norman, OK: University of Oklahoma Press, 2002.

Hansen, Lene. *Security as Practice: Discourse Analysis and the Bosnian War.* Edited by Barry Buzan, and Richard Little. *The New International Relations.* London: Routledge, 2006.

Hanssen, Beatrice. "Language and Mimesis in Walter Benjamin's Work." In *The Cambridge Companion to Walter Benjamin*, edited by David S. Ferris, 54–72. Cambridge: Cambridge University Press, 2004.

Hartog, Francois. *The Mirror of Herodotus: The Representation of the Other in the Writing of History.* Translated by Janet Lloyd. Berkeley, CA: University of California Press, 1988.

Hawkes, Terrence. *Structuralism and Semiotics*, 2nd ed. London: Routledge, 2003.

Heffernan, James A. W. *Museum of Words: The Poetics of Ekphrasis From Homer to Ashbery.* Chicago, IL: University of Chicago Press, 1993.

Herodotus. *Histories.* Edited by Michael A. Flower, and John Marincola. *Cambridge Greek and Latin Classics.* Cambridge: Cambridge University Press, 2002.

Herron, James. "Popular Culture/Popular Violence: Postmodernism and the Malling of Semiotics." In *Mimesis in Contemporary Theory: An Interdisciplinary Approach*, edited by Ronald Bogue, 185–206. Philadelphia, PA: John Benjamins Publishing Company, 1991.

Hesiod. "The Shield of Herakles." In *The Poems and Fragments Done Into English Prose With Introduction and Appendices* edited by A. W. Mair, 69–85. Oxford: Clarendon, 1908.

Heymann, Philip B. *Terrorism, Freedom and Security: Winning Without War.* Cambridge: MIT Press, 2003.

Hobbes, Thomas. *Leviathan.* Edited by Richard Tuck. Cambridge: Cambridge University Press, 1996.

Homer. *The Iliad*. Translated by Robert Fagles. New York: Penguin Books, 1990.

—. *The Odyssey*. Translated by Robert Fagles. New York: Penguin Books, 1996.

Horkheimer, Max, and Theodor Adorno. *Dialectic of Enlightenment*. Edited by Mieke Bal, and Hent de Vries. *Cultural Memory in the Present*. Stanford, CA: Stanford University Press, 2002.

Hough, Peter. "Global Steps Towards Human Security." *Security & Human Rights* 19, no. 1 15–23.

Hume, Kathryn. *Fantasy and Mimesis: Responses to Reality in Western Literature*. New York: Methuen, 1984.

Hunter, Larry, Gingrich, Newt, Walker, Robert and Armey, Richard. 1994. "Republican Contract With America." www.house.gov/house/Contract/CONTRACT.html (accessed June 11, 2009).

Huntington, Samuel P. "The Clash of Civilizations." *Foreign Affairs* 72, no. 3 (1993): 22–8.

Johnson, James Turner. "Jihad and Just War." *First Things* (2002): 12–14.

Johnston, Ian C. *The Ironies of War: An Introduction to Homer's Iliad*. Lanham, MD: University Press of America, 1988.

Jung, Carl. *Man and His Symbols*. New York: Dell Publishing Company, Inc, 1964.

Kaldor, Mary. "Cosmopolitanism Versus Nationalism: The New Divide?" In *Europe's New Nationalism*, edited by R. Caplan and J. Feiffer, 42–58. New York: Oxford University Press, 1996.

—. *New and Old Wars: Organized Violence in a Global Era*. Stanford, CA: Stanford University Press, 1999.

Kaldor, Mary, Martin, Mary, and Selchow, Sabine. "Human Security: A New Strategic Narrative for Europe." *International Affairs* 83, no. 2 (2007): 273–88.

Kalyvas, Andreas. "Back to Adorno? Critical Social Theory between Past and Future." *Political Theory* 32, no. 2 (2004): 247–56.

Kay, Sean. *Global Security in the Twenty First Century: The Quest for Power and the Search for Peace*. Lanham, MD: Rowman & Littlefield Publishers, Inc, 2006.

King, Gary, Robert O. Keohane, and Sidney Verba. *Designing Social Inquiry: Scientific Inference in Qualitative Research*. Princeton, NJ: Princeton University Press, 1994.

Klonoski, Richard. "The Preservation of Homeric Tradition: Heroic Re-Performance in the Republic and the Odyssey." *Clio* 22, no. 3 (1993): 251–72.

Koepnick, Lutz. *Walter Benjamin and the Aesthetics of Power*. Lincoln, NE: University of Nebraska Press, 1999.

Krieger, Murray. *Ekphrasis: The Illusion of the Natural Sign*. Baltimore, MD: Johns Hopkins University Press, 1992.

Kristol, Irving. "The Neoconservative Persuasion." *The Weekly Standard* 8, no. 47 (2003): www.lexisnexis.com:80/us/lnacademic/search/homesubmitForm.do (accessed January 3, 2005).

Kullman, Wolfgang. "Past and Future in the Iliad." In *Oxford Readings in Homers Illiad*, edited by Douglas L. Cairns, 385–408. Oxford: Oxford University Press, 2002.

Kvale, Steinar. *Interviews: An Introduction to Qualitative Research Interviewing*. London: Sage Publications, 1996.

Kwiatkowski, Karen. "Of Mice and Men." (2003): www.lewrockwell.com/kwiatkowski/kwiatkowski46.html (accessed December 5, 2004).

Kwok Kui, Wong. "Nietzsche, Plato and Aristotle on Mimesis." *Dogma* www.dogma.lu/txt/KwokKuiNietzschePlatoAristotle.htm (accessed January 3, 2005).

Kymlicka, William. *Multicultural Citizenship: A Liberal Theory of Minority Rights*. Oxford: Clarendon Press, 1995.

Lakoff, George. *Moral Politics: What Conservatives Know That Liberals Don't*. Chicago, IL: University of Chicago Press, 1996.

—. *Moral Politics: How Liberals and Conservatives Think*, 2nd ed. Chicago, IL: University of Chicago Press, 2002.

—. "Simple Framing: An Introduction to Framing and Its Uses in Politics." 2004. www.rockridgeinstitute.org/projects/strategic/simple_framing/ (accessed January 13, 2008).

Lakoff, George, and Mark Johnson. *Metaphors We Live By*. Chicago, IL: University of Chicago Press, 1980.

Lampert, Laurence. "Socrates' Defence of Polytropic Odysseus: Lying and Wrong-Doing in Plato's *Lesser Hippias*." *Review of Politics* 64, no. 2 (2002): 231–60.

—. "Nietzsche and Plato." In *Nietzsche and Antiquity: His Reaction and Response to the Classical Tradition*, edited by Paul Bishop, 205–19. Rochester, MN: Camden House, 2004.

Landauer, Carl. "'Mimesis' and Erich Auerbach's Self-Mythologizing." *German Studies Review* 11, no. 1 (1988): 83–96.

Legros, Robert. "The Nietzschean Metaphysics of Life." In *Why We Are Not Nietzscheans*, edited by Luc Ferry and Alain Renaut, 110–40. Chicago, IL: University of Chicago Press, 1997.

Lessing, G.E. *Laocoon: An Essay on the Limits of Painting and Poetry.* Translated by Edward Allen McCormick. Baltimore, MD: Johns Hopkins University Press, 1984.

Levi-Strauss, Claude. *Structural Anthropology.* Translated by Claire Jacobsen and Brooke Grundfest Schoepf. New York: Basic Books, Inc, 1963.

Levine, George Lewis. *Realism and Representation: Essays on the Problem of Realism in Relation to Science, Literature, and Culture. Science and Literature.* Madison, WI: University of Wisconsin Press, 1993.

Lichtenberg, Judith. "How Liberal Can Nationalism be." In *Theorizing Nationalism,* edited by Roland Beiner, 167–88. Albany, NY: SUNY Press, 1999.

Linklater, Andrew. "Political Community and Human Society." In *Critical Security Studies and World Politics,* edited by Ken Booth, 113–132. Boulder, CO: Lynne Rienner Publishers, 2005.

Luther, Tim. "Deconstructing Democracy: Derrida and the Other." *ISA-NE* (2004): Paper at the Northeastern Political Science Association/ International Studies Association – North East (NPSA/ISA-NE) conference held in Boston in November of 2004.

Machiavelli, Niccolo. *The Prince.* Translated by Luigi Ricci. Signet Classic. New York: Oxford University Press, 1999.

Machiavelli, Niccolò. *Art of War.* Chicago, IL: University of Chicago Press, 2003.

Machiavelli, Niccolò, and Robert Martin Adams. *The Prince: A Revised Translation, Backgrounds, Interpretations, Marginalia,* 2nd ed. New York: Norton, 1992.

Madhu, R. Chandran. "Plato's Homer." *Ancient Philosophy* 19 (1999): 87–96.

Marks, Michael P. and Fischer, Zachary M. "The King's New Bodies: Simulating Consent in the Age of Celebrity." *New Political Science* 24, no. 3 (2002): 371–95.

Martel, Yann. *Life of Pi.* Orlando, FL: Harcourt Books, 2001.

McKirahan, Richard Jr. *Philosophy Before Socrates.* Indianapolis, IN: Hackett Publishing Company, Inc, 1994.

McRae, Rob and Don Hubert, (eds) *Human Security and the New Diplomacy: Protecting People, Promoting Peace*. Montreal, QC: McGill-Queen's University Press, 2001.

Melberg, Arne. *Theories of Mimesis, Literature, Culture, Theory*. Cambridge: Cambridge University Press, 1995.

Merleau-Ponty, Maurice. *The Visible and the Invisible*. Translated by Alphonso Lignis. Edited by Claude Lefort. Evanston, IL: Northwestern University Press, 1968.

Mgbeoji, Ikechi. "The Civilised Self and the Barbaric Other: Imperial Delusions of Order and the Challenges of Human Security." *Third World Quarterly* 27, no. 5 (2006): 855–69.

Mitchell, W. J. T. "Ekphrasis and the Other." (1994): www.rc.umd.edu/editions/shelley/medusa/mitchell.html#one (accessed May 10, 2005).

Mowitt, John. "In/Security and the Politics of Disciplinarity." In *Cultures of Insecurity*, edited by Jutta Weldes, Mark Laffey, Hugh Gusterson, and Raymond Duvall, 347–62. Minneapolis, MN: University of Minnesota Press, 1999a.

—. "In/Security and the Politics of Disciplinarity." In *Cultures of Insecurity*, edited by Jutta Weldes, Mark Laffey, Hugh Gusterson, and Raymond Duvall, 347–62. Minneapolis, MN: University of Minnesota Press, 1999b.

Munck, Gerardo L. "Canons of Research Design in Qualitative Analysis." *Comparative International Development* 33, no. 3 (1998): 18–45.

Naas, Michael. *Taking on the Tradition: Jacques Derrida and the Legacies of Deconstruction, Cultural Memory in the Present*. Stanford, CA: Stanford University Press, 2003.

Nagy, Gregory. *Homeric Questions*. Austin, TX: University of Texas Press, 1996.

Nietzsche, Friedrich Wilhelm. "Homer and Classical Philology." In *On the Future of Our Educational Institutions*, edited by Oscar Levy, 145–70. London: George Allen & Unwin, Ltd, 1924.

—. "Homer's Contest." In *Nietzsche: Early Greek Philosophy*, edited by Oscar Levy, 49–62. London: George Allen & Unwin, Ltd, 1924.

—. *Beyond Good and Evil; Prelude to a Philosophy of the Future*. Translated by Walter Arnold Kaufmann. New York: Vintage Books, 1966.

—. *Thus Spoke Zarathustra; a Book for All and None*. Translated by Walter Arnold Kaufmann. Vol. C196, *Compass Books*. New York: Viking Press, 1966.

—. *Twilight of the Idols and the Anti-Christ*. Translated by R. J. Hollingdale. *Penguin Classics*. Harmondsworth: Penguin, 1968.

—. *Beyond Good and Evil*. Translated by R. J. Hollingdale. *Penguin Classics*. London: Penguin Books, 1973.

—. *The Anti-Christ*. Translated by R. J. Hollingdale. London: Penguin Books, 1990.

—. *The Gay Science: With a Prelude in Rhymes and an Appendix of Songs*. Translated by Walter Arnold Kaufmann, 1st ed. New York: Random House, 1974.

Nietzsche, Friedrich Wilhelm, Keith Ansell-Pearson, and Carol Diethe. *On the Genealogy of Morality*. Rev. student ed. *Cambridge Texts in the History of Political Thought*. Cambridge; New York: Cambridge University Press, 2007.

Nietzsche, Friedrich Wilhelm, Raymond Geuss, and Ronald Speirs. *The Birth of Tragedy and Other Writings*. *Cambridge Texts in the History of Philosophy*. Cambridge, U.K.; New York: Cambridge University Press, 1999.

Nietzsche, Friedrich Wilhelm and R. J. Hollingdale. *Human, All Too Human*. *Cambridge Texts in the History of Philosophy*. Cambridge; New York: Cambridge University Press, 1996.

—. *Untimely Meditations*. *Cambridge Texts in the History of Philosophy*. Cambridge; New York: Cambridge University Press, 1997.

Nietzsche, Friedrich Wilhelm, Rolf-Peter Horstmann, and Judith Norman. *Beyond Good and Evil: Prelude to a Philosophy of the Future*. *Cambridge Texts in the History of Philosophy*. Cambridge; New York: Cambridge University Press, 2002.

Nietzsche, Friedrich Wilhelm and Douglas Smith. *The Birth of Tragedy*. Oxford: Oxford University Press, 2000.

Nimis, Stephen A. *Narrative Semiotics in the Epic Tradition: The Simile*. Bloomington, IN: Indiana University Press, 1987.

Norris, Christopher. *Deconstruction Theory and Practice*. Edited by Terrence Hawkes. *New Accents*. London: Methuen, 1982.

—. *What's Wrong With Postmodernism: Critical Theory and the Ends of Philosophy*. Baltimore, MD: Johns Hopkins University Press, 1990.

Novak, Michael. "Asymmetrical Warfare" & Just War: A Moral Obligation." *National Review* (2003): www.nationalreview.com/novak/novak021003.asp (accessed July 6, 2005).

Nuttall, A.D. "Auerbach's Mimesis." *Essays in Criticism* 54, no. 1 (2004): 60–74.

Obama, Barack. President Barack Obama's Inaugural Address. www.whitehouse.gov/the_press_office/President_Barack_Obamas_Inaugural_Address/ (accessed May 1, 2009).

—. "Obama's Speech on National Security." *New York Times*, May 21, 2009.

—. Address to Joint Session of Congress. 2009. www.whitehouse.gov/the_press_office/Remarks-of-President-Barack-Obama-Address-to-Joint-Session-of-Congress/ (accessed June 24, 2009).

—. Remarks By the President on a New Strategy for Afghanistan and Pakistan. 2009. www.whitehouse.gov/the_press_office/Remarks-by-the-President-on-a-New-Strategy-for-Afghanistan-and-Pakistan/ (accessed June 24, 2009).

Ong, Aihwa. "Flexible Citizenship." In *Cosmopolitics: Thinking and Feeling Beyond the Nation*, edited by Pheng Cheah, and Bruce Robbins, 134–62. Minneapolis, MN: University of Minnesota Press, 1998.

Otto, Walter F. *The Homeric Gods: The Spiritual Significance of Greek Religion*. Translated by Moses Hadas. Boston, MA: Beacon Press, 1954.

Ovid. *Ovid VI: Metamorphoses Books IX–XV*. Translated by Frank Justus Miller. Edited by G. P. Goold. Vol. 43, *The Loeb Classical Library*. Cambridge: Harvard University Press, 1984.

Owen, Taylor. "Human Security—Conflict, Critique and Consensus: Colloquium Remarks and a Proposal for a Threshold-Based Definition." *Security Dialogue* 35, no. 3 (2004): 373–87.

Parekh, Biku. "The Incoherence of Nationalism." In *Theorizing Nationalism*, edited by Roland Beiner, 295–326. Albany, NY: SUNY Press, 1999.

Payne, Thomas. "The Crito as a Mythological Mime." *Interpretation* 11, no. 1 (1983):1–23.

Peters, Michael. "'Antiglobalization' and Guattari's the Three Ecologies." In *Futures of Critical Theory: Dreams of Difference*, edited by Michael Peters, Mark Olssen, and Colin Lankshear, 275–88. Lanham, MD: Rowman and Littlefield Publishers, Inc, 2003.

—. "Nietzsche, Nihilism, and the Critique of Modernity." In *Futures of Critical Theory: Dreams of Difference*, edited by Michael Peters, Mark Olssen, and Colin Lankshear, 23–38. Lanham, MD: Rowman and Littlefield Publishers, Inc, 2003.

Peters, Michael, Mark Olssen, and Colin Lankshear, (eds) *Futures of Critical Theory: Dreams of Difference*. Lanham, MD: Rowman and Littlefield Publishers, Inc, 2003.

Peterson, M. J. "The Use of Analogies in Developing Outer Space Law." *International Organization* Spring (1997): 245–74.

Planinc, Zdravko. "Ascending With Socrates: Plato's Use of Homeric Imagery in the Symposium." *Interpretation: A Journal of Political Philosophy* 31, no. 3 (2004): 325–50.

Plato. *Republic*. Translated by G. M. A. Grube. Indianapolis, IN: Hackett Publishing Company, 1974.

—. *Apology*. In *Plato: Complete Works*, edited by John M. Cooper, 17–36. Indianapolis, IN: Hackett Publishing Company, 1997.

—. *Cratylus*. In *Plato: Complete Works*, edited by John M. Cooper, 101–56. Indianapolis, IN: Hackett Publishing Company, 1997.

—. *Euthyphro*. In *Plato: Complete Works*, edited by John M. Cooper, 1–16. Indianapolis, IN: Hackett Publishing Company, 1997.

—. *Laws*. In *Plato: Complete Works*, edited by John M. Cooper, 1318–1616. Indianapolis, IN: Hackett Publishing Company, 1997.

—. *Lesser Hippias*. In *Plato: Complete Works*, edited by John M. Cooper, 922–936. Indianapolis, IN: Hackett Publishing Company, 1997.

—. *Republic*. In *Plato: Complete Works*, edited by John M. Cooper, 971–1223. Indianapolis, IN: Hackett Publishing Company, 1997.

—. *Statesman*. In *Plato: Complete Works*, edited by John M. Cooper, 294–358. Indianapolis, IN: Hackett Publishing Company, 1997.

—. *Symposium*. In *Plato: Complete Works*, edited by John M. Cooper, 457–505. Indianapolis, IN: Hackett Publishing Company, 1997.

—. *Republic*. Translated by C. D. C. Reeve. Indianapolis, IN: Hackett Publishing Company, Inc, 2004.

Porter, James I. "Nietzsche, Homer, and the Classical Tradition." In *Nietzsche and Antiquity: His Reaction and Response to the Classical Tradition*, edited by Paul Bishop, 7–26. Rochester, MN: Camden House, 2004.

Poster, Mark, (ed.) *Jean Baudrillard: Selected Writings*. Stanford, CA: Stanford University Press, 1988.

Pressfield, Steven. *Gates of Fire*. New York: Doubleday, 1998.

Prince, Susan. "Ajax, Odysseus and the Act of Self-Representation." *Ancient Philosophy* 19 (1999): 55–64.

Pulkkinen, Tuija. "The Postmodern Moment in Political Thought." *Finnish Yearbook of Political Thought* 1 (1997): 87–94.

Putnam, Hilary. *Representation and Reality*. Cambridge: MIT Press, 1992.

Qureshi, Emran, and Martin A. Sells, (eds) *The New Crusades: Constructing the Muslim Enemy*. New York: Columbia University Press, 2003.

Reagan, Ronald. 1983. President Reagan's Speech to the National Association of Evangelicals. www.hbci.com/~tgort/empire.htm (accessed August 11, 2009).

Reid, Tim and Zahid Hussain. "Barack Obama Offers New Strategy to Tame Pakistan." *Times Online*, March 28, 2009.

Ripsman, Norrin. "False Dichotomy: When Low Politics is High Politics." Paper presented at the International Studies Association, Montreal, March 17, 2004.

Robbins, Bruce. "Introduction, Part I." In *Cosmopolitics: Thinking and Feeling Beyond the Nation*, edited by Pheng Cheah, and Bruce Robbins, 1–19. Minneapolis, MN: University of Minnesota Press, 1998.

Robert, Doran. "Literary History and the Sublime in Erich Auerbach's 'Mimesis' ('Mimesis, the Representation of Reality in Western Literature')." *New Literary History* 38, no. 2 (2007): 353–69.

Rorty, Richard. "A Comment on Robert Scholes's 'Tlon and Truth.'" In *Realism and Representation*, edited by George Lewis Levine, 186–92. Madison, WI: The University of Wisconsin Press, 1993.

Roth, Evan. Typographical Illustrations of Evan Roth. Evan Roth.Com. www.evan-roth.com (accessed February 5, 2009).

Ruggie, John Gerard, (ed.) *On Security. New Directions in World Politics*. New York: Columbia University Press, 1995.

Rumsfeld, Donald H. "A New Kind of War." (2001): www.defenselink.mil/speeches/2001/s20010927-secdef.html (accessed April 12, 2004).

—. "Beyond Nation Building." (2003): www.dod.gov/speeches/2003/sp20030214-secdef0024.html (accessed April 12, 2004).

—. "Remarks to the Heritage Foundation." (2004): www.dod.gov/speeches/2004/sp20040517-secdef0422.html (accessed June 7, 2004).

—. "Secretary Rumsfeld Remarks At the International Institute for Strategic Studies." (2004): www.defenselink.mil/transcripts/transcript.aspx?transcriptid=3335 (accessed December 15,. 2006).

Saddam's Capture May Bring Peace, Doesn't Excuse War, Cardinal Says. www.americancatholic.org/News/JustWar/Iraq/ (accessed July 6, 2005).

Saussure, Ferdinand de. *Course in General Linguistics*. Translated by Wade Baskin. Edited by Jonathan Culler. New York: Fontana/Collins, 1974.

Schein, Seth. "Verbal Adjectives in Sophocles: Necessity and Morality." *Classical Philology* 93 (1998): 293–307.

Scheuerman, William E. "Liberal Democracy and the Empire of Speed." *Polity* 34, no. 1 (2001): 41–68.

Scholes, Robert. "Tlon and Truth: Reflections on Literary Theory and Philosophy." In *Realism and Representation*, edited by George Lewis Levine, Madison, WI: The University of Wisconsin Press, 1993.

Scott, Grant F. "Shelly, Medusa, and the Perils of Ekphrasis." www.rc.umd. edu/editions/shelley/medusa/gscott.html (accessed June 6, 2005).

Seery, John. "Politics as Ironic Community: On the Themes of Descent and Return in Plato's Republic." *Political Theory* 16, no. 2 (1988): 229–56.

Shani, Giorgio, Makoto Sato, and Mustapha Kamal Pasha, (eds) *Protecting Human Security in a Post 9/11 World: Critical and Global Insights*. New York: Palgrave Macmillan, 2007.

Sharrett, Christopher. *Mythologies of Violence in Postmodern Media. Contemporary Film and Television Series*. Detroit, MI: Wayne State University Press, 1999.

Shaw, Jenny. "'Winning Territory': Changing Place to Change Pace." In *Timespace: Geographies of Temporality*, edited by Jon May and Nigel Thrift, 120–32. New York: Routledge, 2001.

Siplon, Patricia. "Scholar, Witness Or Activist? the Lessons and Dilemmas of an Aids Research Agenda." *PSOnline* (1999): 577–81.

Skocpol, Theda, and Somers, Margaret. "The Uses of Comparative History in Macrosocial Inquiry." *Comparative Studies in Society and History* 22, no. 2 (1980): 174–97.

Smilanski, Saul. "Terrorism, Justification, and Illusion." *Ethics* 114, no. 4 (2004): 790–805.

Smith, Steve. "The Contested Concept of Security." In *Critical Security Studies and World Politics*, edited by Ken Booth, 27–62. Boulder, CO: Lynne Rienner Publishers, 2005.

Solomon, Hussein, (ed.) *Challenges to Global Security: Geopolitics and Power in an Age of Transition*. London: I. B. Tauris & Co. Ltd, 2008.

Sophocles. "Ajax." In *Sophocles 2*, edited by David Greene, and Richard Lattimore, 1–62. Chicago, IL: University of Chicago Press, 1957.

—. "Philoctetes." In *Sophocles 2*, edited by David Greene, and Richard Lattimore, 655–60. Chicago, IL: University of Chicago Press, 1957.

—."Sophocles." www.sophocles.net/ 2009. (accessed January 21, 2009).

Spariosu, Mihai. "Mimesis and Contemporary French Theory." In *Mimesis in Contemporary Theory: An Interdisciplinary Approach*, edited by Mihai Spariosu, 65–108. Philadelphia, PA: John Benjamins Publishing Company, 1984.

—. "Plato's Ion: Mimesis, Poetry and Power." In *Mimesis in Contemporary Theory: An Interdisciplinary Approach*, edited by Ronald Bogue, 13–26. Philadelphia, PA: John Benjamins Publishing Company, 1991.

Spariosu, Mihai, Guiseppe Mazzotta and Mihai Spariosu, (eds) *Mimesis in Contemporary Theory: An Interdisciplinary Approach*. Vol. 1, *Cultura Ludens: Imitationand Play in Western Culture*. Philadelphia, PA: John Benjamins Publishing Company, 1984.

Spielberg, Stephen. Dir. *Saving Private Ryan*. (1998).

Srauss, Leo, and Joseph Cropsey, (eds) *History of Political Philosophy*. Chicago, IL: University of Chicago Press, 1987.

Stanford, W. B. *The Odyssey of Homer*. London: Macmillan, 1959.

Stevens, Jacqueline. *Reproducing the State*. Princeton, NJ: Princeton University Press, 1999.

Tagore, Saranindranath. "Tagore's Conception of Cosmopolitanism: A Reconstruction." *University of Toronto Quarterly* 77, no. 4 (2008): 1070–85.

Taplin, Oliver. "The Shield of Achilles Within the Illiad." In *Oxford Readings in Homers Illiad*, edited by Douglas L. Cairns, 342–64. Oxford: Oxford University Press, 2001.

Thucydides. *History of the Peloponnesian War*. Translated by Rex Warner. Edited by M. I. Finley. London: Penguin Books, 1972.

—. Robert B. Strassler (ed.) *The Landmark Thucydides: A Comprehensive Guide to the Peloponnesian War*. New York: The Free Press, 1996.

—. *The Peloponnesian War*. Edited by Steven Lattimore. Indianapolis, IN: Hackett Publishing Company, 1998.

Program, United Nations Development. 1994. Human Development Report 1994: New Dimensions of Human Security. http://hdr.undp.org/en/reports/global/hdr1994/ (accessed May 26, 2009).

Van Munster, Rens. "Security on a Shoestring: A Hitchhiker's Guide to Critical Schools of Security in Europe." *Cooperation and Conflict: Journal of the Nordic International Studies Association* 42 (2), no. 2 (2007): 235–43.

Varsava, Jerry A. *Contingent Meanings: Postmodern Fiction, Mimesis and the Reader*. Tallahassee, FL: The Florida State University Press, 1990.

Virilio, Paul. *Speed and Politics*. Translated by Mark Polizzotti. Edited by Jim Fleming, and Sylvere Lotringer. *Foreign Accents*. New York: Semiotext(e), 1986.

Waever, Ole. "Securitization and Desecuritization." In *On Security*, edited by John Gerard Ruggie, 46–86. New York: Columbia University Press, 1995.

—. "Identity, Integration and Security." *Journal of International Affairs* 48, no. 2 (1995): 389–432.

Walker, R. B. J. "The Prince and 'the Pauper': Tradition, Modernity, and Practice in the Theory of International Relations." In *International/ Intertextual Relations: Postmodern Readings of World Politics*, edited by James Der Derian, and Michael J. Shapiro, 25–48. New York: Lexington Books, 1989.

Waltz, Kenneth. *Theory of International Politics*. New York: Random House, 1979.

Weil, Simone. "The Iliad Or the Poem of Force." In *Critical Essays on Homer*, edited by Kenneth Atchity, Ron Hogart, and Doug Price, 152–9. Boston, MA: G. K. Hall & Co, 1987.

Weldes, Jutta. "The Cultural Production of Crises: U.S. Identity and Missiles in Cuba." In *Cultures of Insecurity: States, Communities, and the Production of Danger*, edited by Jutta Weldes, Mark Laffey, Hugh Gusterson, and Raymond Duvall, 35–62. Minneapolis, MN: University of Minnesota Press, 1999.

Weldes, Jutta, Mark Laffey, Hugh Gusterson, Raymond Duvall, David Campbell, and Michael J. Shapiro, (eds) *Cultures of Insecurity: States, Communities, and the Production of Danger*. *Borderlines*. Minneapolis, MN: University of Minnesota Press, 1999.

Whitby, Mary. "Telemachus Transformed? The Origins of Neoptolemus in Sophocles' 'Philoctetes.'" *Greece & Rome* 43, no. 1 (1996): 31–42.

White, Hayden V. *Figural Realism: Studies in the Mimesis Effect*. Baltimore, MD: Johns Hopkins University Press, 1999.

Wilcox, Leonard. "Baudrillard, September 11, and the Haunting Abyss of Reversal." *Postmodern Culture* 14, no. 1 (2003): http://muse.uq.edu.au/journals/postmodern_culture/v014/14.1wilcox.html (accessed March 15, 2005).

Williams, Dyfri. "Ajax, Odysseus and the Arms of Achilles." *Antike Kunst* 19 (1980): 137–45.

Williams, Michael C. "Words, Images, Enemies: Securitization and International Politics." *International Studies Quarterly* 47, no. 4 (2003): 511–31.

Wolf, F. A. *Prolegomena to Homer (1795)*. Edited by Anthony Grafton, Glenn W. Most, and James E. G. Zetzel. Princeton, NJ: Princeton University Press, 1985.

Wolfowitz, Paul. Bridging the Dangerous Gap between the West and the Muslim World. 2002. www.dod.gov/speeches/2002/s20020503-depsecdef.html (accessed February 15, 2006).

—. Building a Better World: One Path From Crisis to Opportunity. 2002. www.dod.gov/speeches/2002/s20020905-depsecdef.html (accessed February 14, 2006).

—. The Gathering Storm: the Threat of Global Terror and Asia/Pacific 2002. Security. www.dod.gov/speeches/2002/s20020601-depsecdef. html (accessed February 13, 2006).

—. Georgetown Iden Lecture: "Winning the Battle of Ideas: Another Front in the War on Terror". 2003. www.dod.gov/speeches/2003/sp20031030-depsecdef0642.html (accessed February 15, 2006).

—. A Strategic Approach to the Challenge of Terrorism. 2004. www.defenselink.mil/speeches/2004/sp20040908-depsecdef0721.html (accessed February 15, 2006).

—. America's New Allies in the War on Terrorism. 2004. www.defenselink.mil/speeches/2004/sp20040709-depsecdef0561.html (accessed February 15, 2006).

Wyn Jones, Richard. "On Emancipation: Necessity, Capacity, and Concrete Utopias." In *Critical Security Studies and World Politics*, edited by Ken Booth, 215–36. Boulder, CO: Lynne Rienner Publishers, 2005.

Yack, Bernard. "The Myth of the Civic Nation." In *Theorizing Nationalism*, edited by Roland Beiner, 103–16. Albany, NY: SUNY Press, 1999.

Zanker, Graham. *The Heart of Achilles: Characterization and Personal Ethics in the Iliad*. Ann Arbour, MI: The University of Michigan Press, 1997.

Zehfuss, Maja. "Writing War, Against Good Conscience." *Millennium: Journal of International Studies* 33, no. 1 (2004): 91–121.

Breinigsville, PA USA
19 December 2010
251724BV00002B/11/P